THE BIBLE'S

FOUR
GOSPELS

BRIDGE
LOGOS

Newberry, FL 32669

The Bible's Four Gospels
Commentary by Ray Comfort

Published by:
Bridge-Logos, Inc.
Newberry, FL 32669, USA
bridgelogos.com

Edited by Lynn Copeland

Cover, page design, and production by Genesis Group, Inc. (genesis-group.net)

Printed in India

ISBN 978-1-61036-260-3
Library of Congress Control Number: 2021931872

Reprinted October 2022

CONTENTS

APPENDICES

PREFACE

TO THE NEW KING JAMES VERSION®
NEW TESTAMENT

The purpose of this most recent revision of the King James Version New Testament is in harmony with the purpose of the original King James scholars: "Not to make a new translation . . . but to make a good one better." The New King James Version is a continuation of the labors of the King James translators, unlocking for today's readers the spiritual treasures found especially in that version.

While seeking to maintain the excellent *form* of the traditional English New Testament, special care has also been taken to preserve the work of *precision* which is the legacy of the King James translators.

Where new translation has been necessary, the most complete representation of the original has been rendered by considering the definition and usage of the Greek words in their contexts. This translation principle, known as *complete equivalence*, seeks to preserve accurately all of the information in the text while presenting it in good literary form.

In addition to accuracy, the translators have also sought to maintain those lyrical and devotional qualities that are so highly regarded in the King James Version. The thought flow and selection of phrases from the King James Version have been preserved wherever possible without sacrificing clarity.

The format of the New King James Version is designed to enhance the vividness, devotional quality, and usefulness of the Bible. Words or phrases in italics indicate expressions in the original language that require clarification by additional English words, as was done in the King James Version. Oblique type in the New Testament indicates a quotation from the Old Testament. Poetry is structured as verse to reflect the form and beauty of the passage in the original language. The covenant name of God was usually translated from the Hebrew as LORD or GOD, using capital letters as shown, as in the King James Version. This convention is also maintained in the New King James Version when the Old Testament is quoted in the New.

The Greek text used for the New Testament is the one that was followed by the King James translators: the traditional text of the Greek-speaking churches, called the Received Text or Textus Receptus, first published in 1516. Footnotes indicate significant variants from the Textus Receptus as found in two other editions of the Greek New Testament:

(1) NU-Text: These variations generally represent the Alexandrian or Egyptian text type as found in the critical text published in the twenty-sixth edition of the Nestle-Aland Greek New Testament (N) and in the United Bible Societies' third edition (U).

(2) M-Text: These variations represent readings found in the text of the first edition of *The Greek New Testament Ac-*

cording to the Majority Text, which follows the consensus of the majority of surviving New Testament manuscripts.

The textual notes in the New King James Version make no evaluation, but objectively present the facts about variant readings.

Introduction

When Arnold Schwarzenegger arrived in Hollywood in the late 1970s, he broke all the rules. In those days, actors needed a name that was easy to remember, a great speaking voice, and the ability to act. But his name could barely be pronounced let alone remembered. His accent was so thick he was hard to understand, and in those days he couldn't act. But that didn't matter, because he had a body that looked like an inverted doorknob. He had the goods.

Any good book should begin with a "hook"—an attention-getting opening. But the New Testament breaks the rules. It begins with a long list of genealogies—names that are hard to pronounce and remember—yet it can do that because it has the goods. It tells us how we can find everlasting life, and those who know that they will die don't need any other hook.

The Gospels of Matthew, Mark, Luke, and John are eyewitness accounts of Jesus of Nazareth, detailing His birth, life, ministry, death, and resurrection. As you study these four detailed accounts, you will find that (like most eyewitness accounts) they sometimes differ, depending on the perspective of the witness and the audience being addressed. For example, one Gospel says that two blind men called out to Jesus as He was leaving the city of Jericho (see Matthew 20:29,30), while another Gospel mentions only one, actually naming him (see Mark 10:46,47). This isn't a mistake in Scripture, but simply the Gospel of Mark highlighting one of the two men.

There are also differences in the four narratives because each of the Gospels was tailored to a different audience. Matthew was written to the Jews, Mark to the Romans, and Luke to the Greeks, while the Gospel of John was universal. His Gospel includes the Bible's most well-known verse telling of God's love for the whole world (John 3:16).

As you read about Jesus, make sure you take the time to consider the uniqueness of His words. Among many other amazing things, He said not to marvel that every person who has died is going to be raised from the dead by His voice (see John 5:28,29). He said that He was the only way to God (see John 14:6), and that He had power over death (John 11:1–44).

It is impossible for any honest soul not to be deeply impressed by the statements Jesus made, the questions He asked, and the answers He gave. Great philosophers are merely lost sinners—those who are formulating their own thoughts about the mysteries of life. But nothing was a mystery to Jesus. He spoke with great authority because His words were explanatory truth. The greatest men in history who studied the New Testament in any depth couldn't help but be impressed by His person:

> "I am a Jew, but I am enthralled by the luminous figure of the Nazarene . . . No man can read the Gospels without feeling the actual presence of Jesus. His personality pulsates in every word. No myth is filled with such life."
> **—Albert Einstein**

> "I know men and I tell you that Jesus Christ is no mere man. Between Him and every other person in the world there is no possible term of comparison. Alexander, Caesar, Charlemagne, and I have founded empires. But on what did we rest the creations of our genius? Upon force. Jesus Christ founded His empire upon love; and at this hour millions of men would die for Him." **—Napoleon Bonaparte**

"For thirty-five years of my life I was, in the proper acceptation of the word, a nihilist—a man who believed in nothing. Five years ago my faith came to me. I believed in the doctrine of Jesus, and my whole life underwent a sudden transformation . . . Life and death ceased to be evil; instead of despair, I tasted joy and happiness that death could not take away." —**Leo Tolstoy**

Our BC/AD calendar marks Jesus' birth as the dividing point of history. No other historical figure so impacted humanity that they split time in two. It would do each of us well to keep these thoughts in mind as we read—and seriously consider—the Bible's amazing four Gospels. May God bless you as you read these wonderful accounts of unarguably the greatest human being who ever lived.

What This Bible Contains

To understand why Christianity is unique among religions in a world of diversity, please be sure to read the following section called "Why Christianity?" It will explain why the gospel is indeed "good news."

Throughout the pages of this book you will find helpful answers to common questions about Christianity.

At the end of this publication you will also find a section called "Save Yourself Some Pain." If you have placed your trust in Jesus, these very important principles for Christian growth may save you a lot of pain in life.

Scripture says, "How beautiful . . . are the feet of him who brings good news" (Isaiah 52:7). The closing pages explain the biblical method of evangelism, to help Christians follow in the footsteps of the Master and share the gospel the way Jesus did.

Thank you for opening this publication. It is my earnest prayer that you will come to know the Author.

Sincerely,

Ray Comfort

P.S. I suggest that you begin with the Gospel of John (the fourth Gospel), then read Matthew, Mark, and Luke. I would also encourage you to read the entire New Testament—from Acts to Revelation—all of which exalts Jesus as Lord, the ultimate Judge of the living and the dead.

Why Christianity?

Solving life's most important question

Imagine the excitement you would have if I offered you a choice of these four interesting gifts:

- The original Mona Lisa
- The keys to a brand new Lamborghini
- A million dollars in cash
- A parachute

You can pick only one. Which gift would you choose? Before you decide, here's some information that will help you to make the wisest choice: *You have to jump 10,000 feet out of an airplane.*

Does that help you to connect the dots? It should, because you need the parachute. It's the only one of the four gifts that will help with your dilemma. The others may have some value, but they are useless when it comes to facing the law of gravity in a 10,000-foot fall. The knowledge that you will have to jump should produce a healthy fear in you—and that kind of fear is good because it can save your life. Remember that.

Now think of the four major religions:

- Hinduism
- Buddhism
- Islam
- Christianity

Which one should you choose? Before you decide, here's some information that will help you determine which one is the *wisest* choice: All of humanity stands on the edge of eternity. We are *all* going to die. We will all have to pass through the door of death. It could happen to us in twenty years, or in six months, . . . or today. For most of humanity, death is a huge and terrifying plummet into the unknown. So what should we do?

Do you remember how it was your knowledge of the jump that produced that healthy fear, and that fear helped you to make the right choice? You know what the law of gravity can do to you. In the same way, we are going to look at another law, and hopefully your knowledge of what it can do to you will help you to make the right choice, about life's greatest issue. So, stay with me—and remember to let fear work for you.

The Leap

After we die we have to face what is called "the law of sin and of death."[1] That Law is known as "The Ten Commandments."

So let's look at that Law and see how you will do when you face it on Judgment Day. Have you loved God above all else? Is He first in your life? He should be. He's given you your life and everything that is dear to you. Do you love Him with all of your heart, soul, mind, and strength? That's the requirement of the First Commandment. Or have you broken the Second Commandment by making a god in your mind that you're comfortable with—where you say, "My god is a loving and merciful god who would never send anyone to Hell"? That god does not exist; he's a figment of the imagination. To create a god in your mind (your own image of God) is something the Bible calls "idolatry." Idolaters will not enter Heaven.

Have you ever used God's name in vain, as a cuss word to express disgust? That's called "blasphemy," and it's very serious in God's sight. This is breaking the Third Commandment, and the Bible says God will not hold him guiltless who takes His name in vain.

---

1. See Romans 8:2.

Have you always honored your parents implicitly, and kept the Sabbath holy? If not, you have broken the Fourth and Fifth Commandments. Have you ever hated someone? The Bible says, "Everyone who hates his brother is a murderer."[2]

The Seventh is "Do not commit adultery," but Jesus said, "Everyone who looks at a woman to lust for her has already committed adultery with her in his heart"[3] (the Seventh Commandment includes sex before marriage). Have you ever looked with lust or had sex outside of marriage? If you have, you've violated that Commandment.

Have you ever lied? Ever stolen anything, regardless of value? If so, then you're a lying thief. The Bible tells us, "Lying lips are detestable to the LORD,"[4] because He is a God of truth and holiness. Have you coveted (jealously desired) other people's things? This is a violation of the Tenth Commandment.

Little Jessica

That is God's moral Law that we each will face. We will be without excuse when we stand before God because He gave us our conscience to know right from wrong. Each time we lie, steal, commit adultery, murder, etc., we know that it's wrong. So here is the crucial question. On Judgment Day, when God judges you, will you be found innocent or guilty of breaking this Law? *Think before you answer.* Will you go to Heaven or Hell? The Bible warns that all murderers, idolaters, liars, thieves, fornicators, and adulterers will end up in Hell.[5] So where does that leave you?

Perhaps the thought of going to Hell doesn't scare you, because you don't believe in it. That's like standing in the open door of a plane 10,000 feet off the ground and saying, "I don't believe there will be

---

2. 1 John 3:15.
3. Matthew 5:27,28.
4. Proverbs 12:22.
5. See Revelation 21:8; 1 Corinthians 6:9,10.

any consequences if I jump without a parachute."

To say that there will be no consequences for breaking God's Law is to say that God is unjust, that He is evil. This is why.

On February 24, 2005, a nine-year-old girl was reported missing from her home in Homosassa, Florida. Three weeks later, police discovered that she had been kidnapped, brutally raped, and then buried alive. Little Jessica Lunsford was found tied up, in a kneeling position, clutching a stuffed toy.

How Do You React?

How do you feel toward the man who murdered that helpless little girl in such an unspeakably cruel way? Are you angered? I hope so. I hope you are *outraged*. If you were completely indifferent to her fate, it would reveal something horrible about your character.

Do you think that God is indifferent to such acts of evil? You can bet your precious soul He is not. He is *outraged* by them.

The fury of Almighty God against evil is *evidence* of His goodness. If He wasn't angered, He wouldn't be good. We cannot separate God's goodness from His anger. Again, if God is good by nature, He *must* be unspeakably angry at wickedness.

But His goodness is so great that His anger isn't confined to the evils of rape and murder. Nothing is hidden from His pure and holy eyes. He is outraged by torture, terrorism, abortion, theft, lying, adultery, fornication, pedophilia, homosexuality, and blasphemy. He also sees our *thought life*, and He will judge us for the hidden sins of the heart: for lust, hatred, rebellion, greed, unclean imaginations, ingratitude, selfishness, jealousy, pride, envy, deceit, etc. Jesus warned, "I say to you that for *every idle word* men may speak, they will give account of it in the day of judgment."[6]

The Bible says that God's wrath remains on each

---

6. Matthew 12:36 (emphasis added).

of us,[7] and that every time we sin, we're "storing up wrath"[8] that will be revealed on Judgment Day. We are even told that we are "*by nature* children of wrath."[9] Sinning against God comes naturally to us—and we naturally earn His anger by our sins.

Instant Death

Many people believe that because God is good, He will forgive everyone, and let all sinners into Heaven. But they misunderstand His goodness. When Moses once asked to see God's glory, God told him that he couldn't see Him and live. Moses would instantly die if he looked upon God. Consider this:

> [God] said, "*I will make all My goodness pass before you*, and...while *My glory passes by*, that I will put you in the cleft of the rock, and will cover you with My hand while I pass by.[10]

Notice that all of God's glory was displayed in His "goodness." The *goodness* of God would have killed Moses instantly *because of his personal sinfulness*. The fire of God's goodness would have consumed him, like a cup of water dropped onto the surface of the sun. The only way any of us can stand in the presence of God is to be pure in heart. Jesus said, "Blessed are the pure in heart, for they shall see God."[11] But as we've seen by looking at the Law, not a single one of us is "pure in heart."

These are extremely fearful thoughts, because the God we are speaking about is nothing like the commonly accepted image. He is not a benevolent Father-figure, who is happily smiling upon sinful humanity.

In the midst of these frightening thoughts, remember to let fear work for you. The fear of God is

---

7. See John 3:36.
8. Romans 2:5.
9. Ephesians 2:3 (emphasis added).
10. Exodus 33:19,22 (emphasis added).
11. Matthew 5:8.

the healthiest fear you can have. The Bible calls it "the beginning of wisdom."[12]

Again, your knowledge of God's Law should help you to see that you have a life-threatening dilemma: a huge problem of God's wrath (His justifiable anger) against your personal sins. The just penalty for sin—breaking even one Law—is death, and eternity in Hell. But you haven't broken just one Law. Like the rest of us, you've no doubt broken all these laws, countless times each. What kind of anger do you think a judge is justified in having toward a criminal guilty of breaking the law *thousands of times?*

Let's See

Let's now look at those four major religions to see if they can help you with your predicament.

Hinduism. The religion of Hinduism says that if you have been bad, you may come back as a rat or other animal.[13] If you've been good, you might come back as a prince. But that's like someone saying, "When you jump out of the plane, you'll get sucked back in as another passenger. If you've been bad, you go down to the Economy Class; if you've been good, you go up to First Class." It's an interesting concept, but it doesn't deal with your real problem of having sinned against God and the reality of Hell.

Buddhism. Amazingly, the religion of Buddhism denies that God even exists. It teaches that life and death are sort of an illusion.[14] That's like standing at

---

12. Psalm 111:10.
13. "Is it possible for a man to be reborn as a lower animal?" Maharshi: "Yes. It is possible, as illustrated by Jada Bharata—the scriptural anecdote of a royal sage having been reborn as a deer." <www.hinduism.co.za/reincarn.htm>.
14. "When you transcend your thinking mind in the realization of your own pure, timeless, ever-present awareness, then the illusion of time completely collapses, and you become utterly free of the samsaric cycle of time, change, impermanence, and suffering." <www.buddhistinformation.com>.

the door of the plane and saying, "I'm not really here, and there's no such thing as the law of gravity, and no ground that I'm going to hit." That may temporarily help you deal with your fears, but it doesn't square with reality. And it doesn't deal with your real problem of having sinned against God and the reality of Hell.

Islam. Interestingly, Islam acknowledges the reality of sin and Hell, and the justice of God, but the hope it offers is that sinners can escape God's justice if they do religious works. Muslims believe that God will see their works *and because of them* will hopefully show them mercy—but they won't know for sure.[15] Each person's works will be weighed on the Day of Judgment and it will then be decided who is saved and who is not—depending on whether they followed Islam, were sincere in repentance, and performed enough righteous deeds to outweigh their bad ones.

So Islam teaches that you can *earn* God's mercy by your own efforts. That's like jumping out of the plane, and believing that flapping your arms is going to counter the law of gravity and save you from a 10,000-foot drop.

And there's something else to consider. The Law of God shows us that the best of us is nothing but a wicked criminal, standing guilty and condemned before the throne of a perfect and holy Judge. When *that* is understood, then our "righteous deeds" are actually seen as an attempt to bribe the Judge of the Universe. The Bible says that *because of our guilt*, anything we offer God for our justification (our acquittal from His courtroom) is detestable to Him,[16] and only adds to our crimes.

---

15. "Then those whose balance (of good deeds) is heavy, they will be successful. But those whose balance is light, will be those who have lost their souls; in hell will they abide" (Surah 23:102,103).

16. See Proverbs 15:8.

Islam, like the other religions, doesn't solve your problem of having sinned against God and the reality of Hell.

Christianity. So why is Christianity different? Aren't all religions the same? Let's see. In Christianity, God Himself provided a "parachute" for us, and His Word says regarding the Savior, "Put on the Lord Jesus Christ."[17] Just as a parachute solved your dilemma with the law of gravity and its consequences, so the Savior perfectly solves your dilemma with the Law of God and its consequences! It is the missing puzzle-piece that you need.

How did God solve our dilemma? He satisfied His wrath by becoming a human being and taking our punishment upon Himself. The Bible tells us that God was in Christ, reconciling the world to Himself. Christianity provides the only parachute to save us from the consequences of the Law we have transgressed.

Back to the Plane

To illustrate this more clearly, let's go back to that plane for a moment. You are standing on the edge of a 10,000-foot drop. You *have* to jump. Your heart is thumping in your chest. Why? Because of fear. You know the law of gravity will kill you when you jump.

Someone offers you the original Mona Lisa. You push it aside.

Another person passes you the keys to a brand new Lamborghini. You let them drop to the floor.

Someone else tries to put a million dollars into your hands. You push the person's hand away, and stand there in horror at your impending fate.

Suddenly, you hear a voice say, "Here's a parachute!"

Which one of those four people is going to hold the most credibility in your eyes? The one who held up the parachute! Again, it is your fear of the jump that

---

17. See Romans 13:14.

turns you toward the good news of the parachute.

In the same way, knowledge of what God's Law will do to you produces a fear that makes the news of a Savior unspeakably good news! It solves your predicament of God's wrath. God loves you so much that He became a sinless human being in the person of Jesus of Nazareth. The Savior died an excruciating death on the cross, taking your punishment (the death penalty) upon Himself. The demands of eternal justice were satisfied the moment He cried, "It is finished!"

The lightning of God's wrath was stopped and the thunder of His indignation was silenced at Calvary's bloodied cross: "Christ has redeemed us from the curse of the law, having become a curse for us."[18] We broke the Law, but He became a man to pay our penalty in His life's blood.

Then He rose from the dead, defeating death. That means that God can now forgive every sin you have ever committed and commute your death sentence. If you repent and place your trust in Jesus, then you will experience this wonderful promise:

> The law of the Spirit of life in Christ Jesus has made me free from the law of sin and death.[19]

You no longer need to be tormented by a fear of death, and you don't need to look any further for ways to deal with the dilemma of sin and God's wrath.[20] The Savior is God's gift to you. *The gospel is unspeakably good news for the entire, sinful human race!*

God Himself can "justify" you. He can cleanse you, and give you the "righteousness" of Christ. He can make you pure in heart by washing away your sins. He can shelter you from His fierce wrath, in the Rock of Ages that He has cleft for you.[21]

---

18. Galatians 3:13.
19. Romans 8:2.
20. Beware of cults such as Jehovah's Witnesses and Mormons. They masquerade as "Christian," but they are rooted in self-righteousness (trying to do good works to earn salvation).
21. See 1 Corinthians 10:4.

Only Jesus can save you from death and Hell, something that you could never earn or deserve.[22]

Do It Today

To receive the gift of eternal life, you must repent of your sins (turn from them), and put on the Lord Jesus Christ as you would put on a parachute—trusting in Him alone for your salvation. That means you forsake your own good works as a means of trying to please God (trying to bribe Him), and trust only in what Jesus has done for you. Simply throw yourself on the mercy of the Judge. The Bible says that He's rich in mercy to all who call upon Him,[23] so call upon Him right now. He *will* hear you if you approach Him with a humble and sorrowful heart.

Do it right now because you don't know when you will take that leap through the door of death. Confess your sins to God, put your trust in Jesus to save you, and you will pass from death to life. You have God's promise on it.[24]

Pray something like this:

> "Dear God, today I turn away from all of my sins [name them] and I put my trust in Jesus Christ alone as my Lord and Savior. Please forgive me, change my heart, and grant me Your gift of everlasting life. In Jesus' name I pray. Amen."

Now have faith in God. He is absolutely trustworthy. Never doubt His promises. He is not a man that He should lie.

The sincerity of your prayer will be evidenced by your obedience to God's will, so read His Word (the Bible) daily and obey what you read.

I encourage you to turn to the back of this publication and read "Save Yourself Some Pain." There you will find principles to help you grow in your faith.

---

22. See Ephesians 2:8,9.
23. See Romans 10:12,13.
24. See John 5:24.

THE GOSPELS

THE GOSPELS

Matthew

The Genealogy of Jesus Christ

1 The book of the genealogy of Jesus Christ, the Son of David, the Son of Abraham:

² Abraham begot Isaac, Isaac begot Jacob, and Jacob begot Judah and his brothers. ³ Judah begot Perez and Zerah by Tamar, Perez begot Hezron, and Hezron begot Ram. ⁴ Ram begot Amminadab, Amminadab begot Nahshon, and Nahshon begot Salmon. ⁵ Salmon begot Boaz by Rahab, Boaz begot Obed by Ruth, Obed begot Jesse, ⁶ and Jesse begot David the king.

David the king begot Solomon by her *who had been the wife*ᵃ of Uriah. ⁷ Solomon begot Rehoboam, Rehoboam begot Abijah, and Abijah begot Asa.ᵃ ⁸ Asa begot Jehoshaphat, Jehoshaphat begot Joram, and Joram begot Uzziah. ⁹ Uzziah begot Jotham, Jotham begot Ahaz, and Ahaz begot Hezekiah. ¹⁰ Hezekiah begot Manasseh, Manasseh begot Amon,ᵃ and Amon begot Josiah. ¹¹ Josiah begot Jeconiah and his brothers about the time they were carried away to Babylon.

¹² And after they were brought to Babylon, Jeconiah begot Shealtiel, and Shealtiel begot Zerubbabel. ¹³ Zerubbabel begot Abiud, Abiud begot Eliakim, and Eliakim begot Azor. ¹⁴ Azor begot Zadok, Zadok begot Achim, and Achim begot Eliud. ¹⁵ Eliud begot Eleazar, Eleazar begot Matthan, and Matthan begot Jacob. ¹⁶ And Jacob begot Joseph the husband of Mary, of whom was

---

1:6 ᵃWords in italic type have been added for clarity. They are not found in the original Greek.   **1:7** ᵃNU-Text reads *Asaph*.
1:10 ᵃNU-Text reads *Amos*.

3

born Jesus who is called Christ.

¹⁷So all the generations from Abraham to David *are* fourteen generations, from David until the captivity in Babylon *are* fourteen generations, and from the captivity in Babylon until the Christ *are* fourteen generations.

Christ Born of Mary

¹⁸Now the birth of Jesus Christ was as follows: After His mother Mary was betrothed to Joseph, before they came together, she was found with child of the Holy Spirit. ¹⁹Then Joseph her husband, being a just *man*, and not wanting to make her a public example, was minded to put her away secretly. ²⁰But while he thought about these things, behold, an angel of the Lord appeared to him in a dream, saying, "Joseph, son of David, do not be afraid to take to you Mary your wife, for that which is conceived in her is of the Holy Spirit. ²¹And she will bring forth a Son, and you shall call His name Jesus, for He will save His people from their sins."

²²So all this was done that it might be fulfilled which was spoken by the Lord through the prophet, saying: ²³*"Behold, the virgin shall be with child, and bear a Son, and they shall call His name Immanuel,"*[a] which is translated, "God with us."

²⁴Then Joseph, being aroused from sleep, did as the angel of the Lord commanded him and took to him his wife, ²⁵and did not know her till she had brought forth her firstborn Son.[a] And he called His name Jesus.

1:23 [a]Isaiah 7:14. Words in oblique type in the New Testament are quoted from the Old Testament.   **1:25** [a]NU-Text reads *a Son.*

Wise Men from the East

2 Now after Jesus was born in Bethlehem of Judea in the days of Herod the king, behold, wise men from the East came to Jerusalem, [2]saying, "Where is He who has been born King of the Jews? For we have seen His star in the East and have come to worship Him."

[3]When Herod the king heard *this*, he was troubled, and all Jerusalem with him. [4]And when he had gathered all the chief priests and scribes of the people together, he inquired of them where the Christ was to be born.

[5]So they said to him, "In Bethlehem of Judea, for thus it is written by the prophet:

> [6]*'But you, Bethlehem, in the land of Judah,*
> *Are not the least among the rulers of Judah;*
> *For out of you shall come a Ruler*
> *Who will shepherd My people Israel.'"*[a]

[7]Then Herod, when he had secretly called the wise men, determined from them what time the star appeared. [8]And he sent them to Bethlehem and said, "Go and search carefully for the young Child, and when you have found *Him*, bring back word to me, that I may come and worship Him also."

[9]When they heard the king, they departed; and behold, the star which they had seen in the East went before them, till it came and stood over where the young Child was. [10]When they saw the star, they rejoiced with exceedingly great joy. [11]And when they had come into the house, they saw the young Child with Mary His mother,

---

2:6 [a]Micah 5:2

and fell down and worshiped Him. And when they had opened their treasures, they presented gifts to Him: gold, frankincense, and myrrh.

¹²Then, being divinely warned in a dream that they should not return to Herod, they departed for their own country another way.

The Flight into Egypt

¹³Now when they had departed, behold, an angel of the Lord appeared to Joseph in a dream, saying, "Arise, take the young Child and His mother, flee to Egypt, and stay there until I bring you word; for Herod will seek the young Child to destroy Him."

¹⁴When he arose, he took the young Child and His mother by night and departed for Egypt, ¹⁵and was there until the death of Herod, that it might be fulfilled which was spoken by the Lord through the prophet, saying, *"Out of Egypt I called My Son."*ᵃ

Massacre of the Innocents

¹⁶Then Herod, when he saw that he was deceived by the wise men, was exceedingly angry; and he sent forth and put to death all the male children who were in Bethlehem and in all its districts, from two years old and under, according to the time which he had determined from the wise men. ¹⁷Then was fulfilled what was spoken by Jeremiah the prophet, saying:

¹⁸*"A voice was heard in Ramah,*
Lamentation, weeping, and great mourning,
Rachel weeping for her children,
Refusing to be comforted,

2:15 ᵃHosea 11:1

Because they are no more." [a]

The Home in Nazareth

[19]Now when Herod was dead, behold, an angel of the Lord appeared in a dream to Joseph in Egypt, [20]saying, "Arise, take the young Child and His mother, and go to the land of Israel, for those who sought the young Child's life are dead." [21]Then he arose, took the young Child and His mother, and came into the land of Israel.

[22]But when he heard that Archelaus was reigning over Judea instead of his father Herod, he was afraid to go there. And being warned by God in a dream, he turned aside into the region of Galilee. [23]And he came and dwelt in a city called Nazareth, that it might be fulfilled which was spoken by the prophets, "He shall be called a Nazarene."

John the Baptist Prepares the Way

3 In those days John the Baptist came preaching in the wilderness of Judea, [2]and saying, "Repent, for the kingdom of heaven is at hand!" [3]For this is he who was spoken of by the prophet Isaiah, saying:

"The voice of one crying in the wilderness:
'Prepare the way of the Lord;
Make His paths straight.'" [a]

[4]Now John himself was clothed in camel's hair, with a leather belt around his waist; and his food was locusts and wild honey. [5]Then Jerusalem, all Judea, and all the region around the

---

2:18 [a]Jeremiah 31:15   3:3 [a]Isaiah 40:3

Jordan went out to him [6]and were baptized by him in the Jordan, confessing their sins.

[7]But when he saw many of the Pharisees and Sadducees coming to his baptism, he said to them, "Brood of vipers! Who warned you to flee from the wrath to come? [8]Therefore bear fruits worthy of repentance, [9]and do not think to say to yourselves, 'We have Abraham as *our* father.' For I say to you that God is able to raise up children to Abraham from these stones. [10]And even now the ax is laid to the root of the trees. Therefore every tree which does not bear good fruit is cut down and thrown into the fire. [11]I indeed baptize you with water unto repentance, but He who is coming after me is mightier than I, whose sandals I am not worthy to carry. He will baptize you with the Holy Spirit and fire.[a] [12]His winnowing fan *is* in His hand, and He will thoroughly clean out His threshing floor, and gather His wheat into the barn; but He will burn up the chaff with unquenchable fire."

John Baptizes Jesus

[13]Then Jesus came from Galilee to John at the Jordan to be baptized by him. [14]And John *tried to* prevent Him, saying, "I need to be baptized by You, and are You coming to me?"

[15]But Jesus answered and said to him, "Permit *it to be so* now, for thus it is fitting for us to fulfill all righteousness." Then he allowed Him.

[16]When He had been baptized, Jesus came up immediately from the water; and behold, the heavens were opened to Him, and He[a] saw the Spirit of God descending like a dove and alight-

---

3:11 [a]M-Text omits *and fire*.   3:16 [a]Or *he*

ing upon Him. [17]And suddenly a voice *came* from heaven, saying, "This is My beloved Son, in whom I am well pleased."

Satan Tempts Jesus

4 Then Jesus was led up by the Spirit into the wilderness to be tempted by the devil. [2]And when He had fasted forty days and forty nights, afterward He was hungry. [3]Now when the tempter came to Him, he said, "If You are the Son of God, command that these stones become bread."

[4]But He answered and said, "It is written, *'Man shall not live by bread alone, but by every word that proceeds from the mouth of God.' "*[a]

[5]Then the devil took Him up into the holy city, set Him on the pinnacle of the temple, [6]and said to Him, "If You are the Son of God, throw Yourself down. For it is written:

'He shall give His angels charge over you,'

and,

*'In their hands they shall bear you up,
Lest you dash your foot against a stone.' "*[a]

[7]Jesus said to him, "It is written again, *'You shall not tempt the Lord your God.'"*[a]

[8]Again, the devil took Him up on an exceedingly high mountain, and showed Him all the kingdoms of the world and their glory. [9]And he said to Him, "All these things I will give You if You will fall down and worship me."

[10]Then Jesus said to him, "Away with you,[a]

4:4 [a]Deuteronomy 8:3   4:6 [a]Psalm 91:11, 12   4:7 [a]Deuteronomy 6:16   4:10 [a]M-Text reads *Get behind Me.*

Satan! For it is written, *'You shall worship the
LORD your God, and Him only you shall serve.'*[b]

[11]Then the devil left Him, and behold, angels
came and ministered to Him.

Jesus Begins His Galilean Ministry

[12]Now when Jesus heard that John had been
put in prison, He departed to Galilee. [13]And
leaving Nazareth, He came and dwelt in Capernaum, which is by the sea, in the regions of Zebulun and Naphtali, [14]that it might be fulfilled
which was spoken by Isaiah the prophet, saying:

[15]*"The land of Zebulun and the land of Naphtali,
    By the way of the sea, beyond the Jordan,
    Galilee of the Gentiles:*
[16]*The people who sat in darkness have seen a
        great light,
    And upon those who sat in the region and
        shadow of death
    Light has dawned."*[a]

[17]From that time Jesus began to preach and
to say, "Repent, for the kingdom of heaven is at
hand."

Four Fishermen Called as Disciples

[18]And Jesus, walking by the Sea of Galilee,
saw two brothers, Simon called Peter, and Andrew his brother, casting a net into the sea; for
they were fishermen. [19]Then He said to them,
"Follow Me, and I will make you fishers of men."
[20]They immediately left *their* nets and followed
Him.

[21]Going on from there, He saw two other

4:10 [b]Deuteronomy 6:13   4:16 [a]Isaiah 9:1, 2

brothers, James *the son* of Zebedee, and John his brother, in the boat with Zebedee their father, mending their nets. He called them, ²²and immediately they left the boat and their father, and followed Him.

Jesus Heals a Great Multitude

²³And Jesus went about all Galilee, teaching in their synagogues, preaching the gospel of the kingdom, and healing all kinds of sickness and all kinds of disease among the people. ²⁴Then His fame went throughout all Syria; and they brought to Him all sick people who were afflicted with various diseases and torments, and those who were demon-possessed, epileptics, and paralytics; and He healed them. ²⁵Great multitudes followed Him—from Galilee, and *from* Decapolis, Jerusalem, Judea, and beyond the Jordan.

The Beatitudes

5 And seeing the multitudes, He went up on a mountain, and when He was seated His disciples came to Him. ²Then He opened His mouth and taught them, saying:

³"Blessed *are* the poor in spirit,
　　For theirs is the kingdom of heaven.
⁴Blessed *are* those who mourn,
　　For they shall be comforted.
⁵Blessed *are* the meek,
　　For they shall inherit the earth.
⁶Blessed *are* those who hunger and thirst for
　　　righteousness,
　　For they shall be filled.
⁷Blessed *are* the merciful,
　　For they shall obtain mercy.

    [8]Blessed *are* the pure in heart,
      For they shall see God.
    [9]Blessed *are* the peacemakers,
      For they shall be called sons of God.
    [10]Blessed *are* those who are persecuted for
      righteousness' sake,
      For theirs is the kingdom of heaven.

[11]"Blessed are you when they revile and persecute you, and say all kinds of evil against you falsely for My sake. [12]Rejoice and be exceedingly glad, for great *is* your reward in heaven, for so they persecuted the prophets who were before you.

Believers Are Salt and Light

[13]"You are the salt of the earth; but if the salt loses its flavor, how shall it be seasoned? It is then good for nothing but to be thrown out and trampled underfoot by men.

[14]"You are the light of the world. A city that is set on a hill cannot be hidden. [15]Nor do they light a lamp and put it under a basket, but on a lampstand, and it gives light to all *who are* in the house. [16]Let your light so shine before men, that they may see your good works and glorify your Father in heaven.

Christ Fulfills the Law

[17]"Do not think that I came to destroy the Law or the Prophets. I did not come to destroy but to fulfill. [18]For assuredly, I say to you, till heaven and earth pass away, one jot or one tittle will by no means pass from the law till all is fulfilled. [19]Whoever therefore breaks one of the least of these commandments, and teaches men so, shall be called least in the kingdom of heaven; but who-

ever does and teaches *them,* he shall be called great in the kingdom of heaven. ²⁰For I say to you, that unless your righteousness exceeds *the righteousness* of the scribes and Pharisees, you will by no means enter the kingdom of heaven.

Murder Begins in the Heart

²¹"You have heard that it was said to those of old, *'You shall not murder,*[a] and whoever murders will be in danger of the judgment.' ²²But I say to you that whoever is angry with his brother without a cause[a] shall be in danger of the judgment. And whoever says to his brother, 'Raca!' shall be in danger of the council. But whoever says, 'You fool!' shall be in danger of hell fire. ²³Therefore if you bring your gift to the altar, and there remember that your brother has something against you, ²⁴leave your gift there before the altar, and go your way. First be reconciled to your brother, and then come and offer your gift. ²⁵Agree with your adversary quickly, while you are on the way with him, lest your adversary deliver you to the judge, the judge hand you over to the officer, and you be thrown into prison. ²⁶Assuredly, I say to you, you will by no means get out of there till you have paid the last penny.

Adultery in the Heart

²⁷"You have heard that it was said to those of old,[a] *'You shall not commit adultery.'*[b] ²⁸But I say to you that whoever looks at a woman to lust for her has already committed adultery with her in his heart. ²⁹If your right eye causes you to sin,

---

5:21 [a]Exodus 20:13; Deuteronomy 5:17   **5:22** [a]NU-Text omits *without a cause.*   **5:27** [a]NU-Text and M-Text omit *to those of old.* [b]Exodus 20:14; Deuteronomy 5:18

pluck it out and cast *it* from you; for it is more profitable for you that one of your members perish, than for your whole body to be cast into hell. [30]And if your right hand causes you to sin, cut it off and cast *it* from you; for it is more profitable for you that one of your members perish, than for your whole body to be cast into hell.

Marriage Is Sacred and Binding

[31]"Furthermore it has been said, 'Whoever divorces his wife, let him give her a certificate of divorce.' [32]But I say to you that whoever divorces his wife for any reason except sexual immorality[a] causes her to commit adultery; and whoever marries a woman who is divorced commits adultery.

Jesus Forbids Oaths

[33]"Again you have heard that it was said to those of old, 'You shall not swear falsely, but shall perform your oaths to the Lord.' [34]But I say to you, do not swear at all: neither by heaven, for it is God's throne; [35]nor by the earth, for it is His footstool; nor by Jerusalem, for it is the city of the great King. [36]Nor shall you swear by your head, because you cannot make one hair white or black. [37]But let your 'Yes' be 'Yes,' and your 'No,' 'No.' For whatever is more than these is from the evil one.

Go the Second Mile

[38]"You have heard that it was said, *'An eye for an eye and a tooth for a tooth.'*[a] [39]But I tell you not to resist an evil person. But whoever slaps you on your right cheek, turn the other to him

---

5:32 [a]Or *fornication*   **5:38** [a]Exodus 21:24; Leviticus 24:20; Deuteronomy 19:21

also. ⁴⁰If anyone wants to sue you and take away your tunic, let him have *your* cloak also. ⁴¹And whoever compels you to go one mile, go with him two. ⁴²Give to him who asks you, and from him who wants to borrow from you do not turn away.

Love Your Enemies

⁴³"You have heard that it was said, '*You shall love your neighbor*ᵃ and hate your enemy.' ⁴⁴But I say to you, love your enemies, bless those who curse you, do good to those who hate you, and pray for those who spitefully use you and persecute you,ᵃ ⁴⁵that you may be sons of your Father in heaven; for He makes His sun rise on the evil and on the good, and sends rain on the just and on the unjust. ⁴⁶For if you love those who love you, what reward have you? Do not even the tax collectors do the same? ⁴⁷And if you greet your brethrenᵃ only, what do you do more *than others*? Do not even the tax collectorsᵇ do so? ⁴⁸Therefore you shall be perfect, just as your Father in heaven is perfect.

Do Good to Please God

6 "Take heed that you do not do your charitable deeds before men, to be seen by them. Otherwise you have no reward from your Father in heaven. ²Therefore, when you do a charitable deed, do not sound a trumpet before you as the hypocrites do in the synagogues and in the streets, that they may have glory from men.

5:43 ᵃCompare Leviticus 19:18   5:44 ᵃNU-Text omits three clauses from this verse, leaving, "*But I say to you, love your enemies and pray for those who persecute you.*"   5:47 ᵃM-Text reads *friends.* ᵇNU-Text reads *Gentiles.*

Assuredly, I say to you, they have their reward. [3]But when you do a charitable deed, do not let your left hand know what your right hand is doing, [4]that your charitable deed may be in secret; and your Father who sees in secret will Himself reward you openly.[a]

The Model Prayer

[5]"And when you pray, you shall not be like the hypocrites. For they love to pray standing in the synagogues and on the corners of the streets, that they may be seen by men. Assuredly, I say to you, they have their reward. [6]But you, when you pray, go into your room, and when you have shut your door, pray to your Father who is in the secret *place;* and your Father who sees in secret will reward you openly.[a] [7]And when you pray, do not use vain repetitions as the heathen *do.* For they think that they will be heard for their many words.

[8]"Therefore do not be like them. For your Father knows the things you have need of before you ask Him. [9]In this manner, therefore, pray:

Our Father in heaven,
Hallowed be Your name.
[10]Your kingdom come.
Your will be done
On earth as *it is* in heaven.
[11]Give us this day our daily bread.
[12]And forgive us our debts,
As we forgive our debtors.
[13]And do not lead us into temptation,
But deliver us from the evil one.
For Yours is the kingdom and the power and
the glory forever. Amen.[a]

6:4 [a]NU-Text omits *openly.*   6:6 [a]NU-Text omits *openly.*   6:13
[a]NU-Text omits *For Yours* through *Amen.*

¹⁴"For if you forgive men their trespasses, your heavenly Father will also forgive you. ¹⁵But if you do not forgive men their trespasses, neither will your Father forgive your trespasses.

Fasting to Be Seen Only by God

¹⁶"Moreover, when you fast, do not be like the hypocrites, with a sad countenance. For they disfigure their faces that they may appear to men to be fasting. Assuredly, I say to you, they have their reward. ¹⁷But you, when you fast, anoint your head and wash your face, ¹⁸so that you do not appear to men to be fasting, but to your Father who *is* in the secret *place;* and your Father who sees in secret will reward you openly.^a

Lay Up Treasures in Heaven

¹⁹"Do not lay up for yourselves treasures on earth, where moth and rust destroy and where thieves break in and steal; ²⁰but lay up for yourselves treasures in heaven, where neither moth nor rust destroys and where thieves do not break in and steal. ²¹For where your treasure is, there your heart will be also.

The Lamp of the Body

²²"The lamp of the body is the eye. If therefore your eye is good, your whole body will be full of light. ²³But if your eye is bad, your whole body will be full of darkness. If therefore the light that is in you is darkness, how great is that darkness!

6:18 ^aNU-Text and M-Text omit *openly.*

You Cannot Serve God and Riches

24"No one can serve two masters; for either he will hate the one and love the other, or else he will be loyal to the one and despise the other. You cannot serve God and mammon.

Do Not Worry

25"Therefore I say to you, do not worry about your life, what you will eat or what you will drink; nor about your body, what you will put on. Is not life more than food and the body more than clothing? 26Look at the birds of the air, for they neither sow nor reap nor gather into barns; yet your heavenly Father feeds them. Are you not of more value than they? 27Which of you by worrying can add one cubit to his stature?

28"So why do you worry about clothing? Consider the lilies of the field, how they grow: they neither toil nor spin; 29and yet I say to you that even Solomon in all his glory was not arrayed like one of these. 30Now if God so clothes the grass of the field, which today is, and tomorrow is thrown into the oven, *will He* not much more *clothe* you, O you of little faith?

31"Therefore do not worry, saying, 'What shall we eat?' or 'What shall we drink?' or 'What shall we wear?' 32For after all these things the Gentiles seek. For your heavenly Father knows that you need all these things. 33But seek first the kingdom of God and His righteousness, and all these things shall be added to you. 34Therefore do not worry about tomorrow, for tomorrow will worry about its own things. Sufficient for the day *is* its own trouble.

Do Not Judge

7 "Judge not, that you be not judged. [2]For with what judgment you judge, you will be judged; and with the measure you use, it will be measured back to you. [3]And why do you look at the speck in your brother's eye, but do not consider the plank in your own eye? [4]Or how can you say to your brother, 'Let me remove the speck from your eye'; and look, a plank is in your own eye? [5]Hypocrite! First remove the plank from your own eye, and then you will see clearly to remove the speck from your brother's eye.

[6]"Do not give what is holy to the dogs; nor cast your pearls before swine, lest they trample them under their feet, and turn and tear you in pieces.

Keep Asking, Seeking, Knocking

[7]"Ask, and it will be given to you; seek, and you will find; knock, and it will be opened to you. [8]For everyone who asks receives, and he who seeks finds, and to him who knocks it will be opened. [9]Or what man is there among you who, if his son asks for bread, will give him a stone? [10]Or if he asks for a fish, will he give him a serpent? [11]If you then, being evil, know how to give good gifts to your children, how much more will your Father who is in heaven give good things to those who ask Him! [12]Therefore, whatever you want men to do to you, do also to them, for this is the Law and the Prophets.

The Narrow Way

[13]"Enter by the narrow gate; for wide is the gate and broad is the way that leads to destruction, and there are many who go in by it. [14]Be-

cause[a] narrow is the gate and difficult is the way which leads to life, and there are few who find it.

You Will Know Them by Their Fruits

[15]Beware of false prophets, who come to you in sheep's clothing, but inwardly they are ravenous wolves. [16]You will know them by their fruits. Do men gather grapes from thornbushes or figs from thistles? [17]Even so, every good tree bears good fruit, but a bad tree bears bad fruit. [18]A good tree cannot bear bad fruit, nor *can* a bad tree bear good fruit. [19]Every tree that does not bear good fruit is cut down and thrown into the fire. [20]Therefore by their fruits you will know them.

I Never Knew You

[21]"Not everyone who says to Me, 'Lord, Lord,' shall enter the kingdom of heaven, but he who does the will of My Father in heaven. [22]Many will say to Me in that day, 'Lord, Lord, have we not prophesied in Your name, cast out demons in Your name, and done many wonders in Your name?' [23]And then I will declare to them, 'I never knew you; depart from Me, you who practice lawlessness!'

Build on the Rock

[24]"Therefore whoever hears these sayings of Mine, and does them, I will liken him to a wise man who built his house on the rock: [25]and the rain descended, the floods came, and the winds blew and beat on that house; and it did not fall, for it was founded on the rock.

[26]"But everyone who hears these sayings of

7:14 [a]NU-Text and M-Text read *How . . . !*

Mine, and does not do them, will be like a foolish man who built his house on the sand: ²⁷and the rain descended, the floods came, and the winds blew and beat on that house; and it fell. And great was its fall."

²⁸And so it was, when Jesus had ended these sayings, that the people were astonished at His teaching, ²⁹for He taught them as one having authority, and not as the scribes.

Jesus Cleanses a Leper

8 When He had come down from the mountain, great multitudes followed Him. ²And behold, a leper came and worshiped Him, saying, "Lord, if You are willing, You can make me clean."

³Then Jesus put out *His* hand and touched him, saying, "I am willing; be cleansed." Immediately his leprosy was cleansed.

⁴And Jesus said to him, "See that you tell no one; but go your way, show yourself to the priest, and offer the gift that Moses commanded, as a testimony to them."

Jesus Heals a Centurion's Servant

⁵Now when Jesus had entered Capernaum, a centurion came to Him, pleading with Him, ⁶saying, "Lord, my servant is lying at home paralyzed, dreadfully tormented."

⁷And Jesus said to him, "I will come and heal him."

⁸The centurion answered and said, "Lord, I am not worthy that You should come under my roof. But only speak a word, and my servant will be healed. ⁹For I also am a man under authority, having soldiers under me. And I say to this *one,*

How do you know God exists?

One evidence for the reality of God is the fact that a belief in Him seems to be universal. According to anthropologists, belief in God is found in virtually every culture on earth. Of 6.5 billion people worldwide, less than 3 percent are atheists. That's not surprising. Since God created us to be in relationship with Him, He would naturally have designed us so that we could believe in Him. We have internal evidence of Him through our innate sense that He exists.

He also gives us external evidence through the order and design of our marvelous creation—so much evidence, in fact, that the Bible says we are without excuse (Romans 1:20). When you look at a Coke can, you would never in a million years believe that its components came from out of nowhere and simply evolved over millions of years. You know that if the soda can has been made, there must be a maker. If it was designed, there must be a designer. To believe it happened by sheer chance—created out of nothing—is to move into an intellectual-free zone.

Yet this is exactly what atheists claim: something can bring itself into being from nothing, and with enough time, complex systems can be assembled by chance through random, unguided processes. We intuitively know when something is designed, and we know that things don't design and create themselves. For some reason, we understand this logic for every subject except our incredible creation—with its amazing design, complexity, beauty, and order. That just doesn't make sense.

If man, with all his genius, can't create a grain of sand from nothing, obviously something infinitely more intelligent than man created this incredible creation. To believe it happened by sheer random chance is lunacy. That's why the Bible says, "The fool has said in his heart, 'There is no God'" (Psalm 14:1).

Who made God?

Many people refuse to believe in God because they can't fathom how something could be eternal. Yet when scientists thought the universe itself was eternal—it just always was—atheists believed that. So if you believe it is possible for *something* to be eternal (such as the universe), to be logically consistent you would also have to admit it's possible that there is an infinite, omnipotent Being who is eternal.

Scientists now know the universe had a beginning, so when Christians claim it was begun by God, atheists naturally ask, "Then who made God?" It's a logical question. According to the Law of Cause and Effect, every effect must have a cause; everything that came into being has something that caused it.

The question of who made God can be answered by simply asking, "Does space have an end?" Obviously, it doesn't. If there is a brick wall with "The End" written on it, the question arises, "What is behind the brick wall?" Strain the mind though it may, we have to believe (have faith) that space has no beginning and no end.

The same applies with God. He has no beginning and no end. He is eternal, and has always existed. The Bible also informs us that time is a dimension that God created, into which man was subjected. It even tells us that one day time will no longer exist. That will be "eternity." God Himself dwells outside of the dimension He created (Titus 1:2; Isaiah 57:15).

God moves through time as a man flips through a history book. Because we live in the dimension of time, logic and reason demand that everything must have a beginning and an end. But we can understand the concept of God's eternal nature the same way we understand the concept of space having no beginning and end—by faith. We simply *have* to believe they are so, even though such thoughts strain our distinctly insufficient cerebrum.

'Go,' and he goes; and to another, 'Come,' and he comes; and to my servant, 'Do this,' and he does it."

¹⁰When Jesus heard *it,* He marveled, and said to those who followed, "Assuredly, I to you, I have not found such great faith, not even in Israel! ¹¹And I say to you that many will come from east and west, and sit down with Abraham, Isaac, and Jacob in the kingdom of heaven. ¹²But the sons of the kingdom will be cast out into outer darkness. There will be weeping and gnashing of teeth." ¹³Then Jesus said to the centurion, "Go your way; and as you have believed, *so* let it be done for you." And his servant was healed that same hour.

Peter's Mother-in-Law Healed

¹⁴Now when Jesus had come into Peter's house, He saw his wife's mother lying sick with a fever. ¹⁵So He touched her hand, and the fever left her. And she arose and served them.ᵃ

Many Healed in the Evening

¹⁶When evening had come, they brought to Him many who were demon-possessed. And He cast out the spirits with a word, and healed all who were sick, ¹⁷that it might be fulfilled which was spoken by Isaiah the prophet, saying:

"He Himself took our infirmities
  *And bore our sicknesses."*ᵃ

The Cost of Discipleship

¹⁸And when Jesus saw great multitudes about Him, He gave a command to depart to the other

---

8:15 ᵃNU-Text and M-Text read *Him.*   8:17 ᵃIsaiah 53:4

side. ¹⁹Then a certain scribe came and said to
Him, "Teacher, I will follow You wherever You go."

²⁰And Jesus said to him, "Foxes have holes
and birds of the air *have* nests, but the Son of
Man has nowhere to lay *His* head."

²¹Then another of His disciples said to Him,
"Lord, let me first go and bury my father."

²²But Jesus said to him, "Follow Me, and let
the dead bury their own dead."

Wind and Wave Obey Jesus

²³Now when He got into a boat, His disciples
followed Him. ²⁴And suddenly a great tempest
arose on the sea, so that the boat was covered
with the waves. But He was asleep. ²⁵Then His
disciples came to *Him* and awoke Him, saying,
"Lord, save us! We are perishing!"

²⁶But He said to them, "Why are you fearful,
O you of little faith?" Then He arose and rebuked
the winds and the sea, and there was a great calm.
²⁷So the men marveled, saying, "Who can this
be, that even the winds and the sea obey Him?"

Two Demon-Possessed Men Healed

²⁸When He had come to the other side, to the
country of the Gergesenes,^a there met Him two
demon-possessed *men*, coming out of the tombs,
exceedingly fierce, so that no one could pass that
way. ²⁹And suddenly they cried out, saying,
"What have we to do with You, Jesus, You Son of
God? Have You come here to torment us before
the time?"

³⁰Now a good way off from them there was a
herd of many swine feeding. ³¹So the demons

8:28 ^aNU-Text reads *Gadarenes*.

begged Him, saying, "If You cast us out, permit us to go away[a] into the herd of swine."

³²And He said to them, "Go." So when they had come out, they went into the herd of swine. And suddenly the whole herd of swine ran violently down the steep place into the sea, and perished in the water.

³³Then those who kept *them* fled; and they went away into the city and told everything, including what *had happened* to the demon-possessed *men.* ³⁴And behold, the whole city came out to meet Jesus. And when they saw Him, they begged *Him* to depart from their region.

Jesus Forgives and Heals a Paralytic

9 So He got into a boat, crossed over, and came to His own city. ²Then behold, they brought to Him a paralytic lying on a bed. When Jesus saw their faith, He said to the paralytic, "Son, be of good cheer; your sins are forgiven you."

³And at once some of the scribes said within themselves, "This Man blasphemes!"

⁴But Jesus, knowing their thoughts, said, "Why do you think evil in your hearts? ⁵For which is easier, to say, '*Your* sins are forgiven you,' or to say, 'Arise and walk'? ⁶But that you may know that the Son of Man has power on earth to forgive sins"—then He said to the paralytic, "Arise, take up your bed, and go to your house." ⁷And he arose and departed to his house.

⁸Now when the multitudes saw *it,* they marveled[a] and glorified God, who had given such power to men.

8:31 [a]NU-Text reads *send us.*   9:8 [a]NU-Text reads *were afraid.*

Matthew the Tax Collector

⁹As Jesus passed on from there, He saw a man named Matthew sitting at the tax office. And He said to him, "Follow Me." So he arose and followed Him.

¹⁰Now it happened, as Jesus sat at the table in the house, *that* behold, many tax collectors and sinners came and sat down with Him and His disciples. ¹¹And when the Pharisees saw *it,* they said to His disciples, "Why does your Teacher eat with tax collectors and sinners?"

¹²When Jesus heard *that,* He said to them, "Those who are well have no need of a physician, but those who are sick. ¹³But go and learn what *this* means: *'I desire mercy and not sacrifice.'*ᵃ For I did not come to call the righteous, but sinners, to repentance."ᵇ

Jesus Is Questioned About Fasting

¹⁴Then the disciples of John came to Him, saying, "Why do we and the Pharisees fast often,ᵃ but Your disciples do not fast?"

¹⁵And Jesus said to them, "Can the friends of the bridegroom mourn as long as the bridegroom is with them? But the days will come when the bridegroom will be taken away from them, and then they will fast. ¹⁶No one puts a piece of unshrunk cloth on an old garment; for the patch pulls away from the garment, and the tear is made worse. ¹⁷Nor do they put new wine into old wineskins, or else the wineskins break, the wine is spilled, and the wineskins are ruined. But they put new wine into new wineskins, and both are preserved."

9:13 ᵃHosea 6:6 ᵇNU-Text omits *to repentance.* 9:14 ᵃNU-Text brackets *often* as disputed.

A Girl Restored to Life
and a Woman Healed

[18]While He spoke these things to them, behold, a ruler came and worshiped Him, saying, "My daughter has just died, but come and lay Your hand on her and she will live." [19]So Jesus arose and followed him, and so *did* His disciples.

[20]And suddenly, a woman who had a flow of blood for twelve years came from behind and touched the hem of His garment. [21]For she said to herself, "If only I may touch His garment, I shall be made well." [22]But Jesus turned around, and when He saw her He said, "Be of good cheer, daughter; your faith has made you well." And the woman was made well from that hour.

[23]When Jesus came into the ruler's house, and saw the flute players and the noisy crowd wailing, [24]He said to them, "Make room, for the girl is not dead, but sleeping." And they ridiculed Him. [25]But when the crowd was put outside, He went in and took her by the hand, and the girl arose. [26]And the report of this went out into all that land.

Two Blind Men Healed

[27]When Jesus departed from there, two blind men followed Him, crying out and saying, "Son of David, have mercy on us!"

[28]And when He had come into the house, the blind men came to Him. And Jesus said to them, "Do you believe that I am able to do this?"

They said to Him, "Yes, Lord."

[29]Then He touched their eyes, saying, "According to your faith let it be to you." [30]And their eyes were opened. And Jesus sternly warned them, saying, "See *that* no one knows *it*." [31]But when

they had departed, they spread the news about Him in all that country.

A Mute Man Speaks

³²As they went out, behold, they brought to Him a man, mute and demon-possessed. ³³And when the demon was cast out, the mute spoke. And the multitudes marveled, saying, "It was never seen like this in Israel!"

³⁴But the Pharisees said, "He casts out demons by the ruler of the demons."

The Compassion of Jesus

³⁵Then Jesus went about all the cities and villages, teaching in their synagogues, preaching the gospel of the kingdom, and healing every sickness and every disease among the people.ᵃ ³⁶But when He saw the multitudes, He was moved with compassion for them, because they were wearyᵃ and scattered, like sheep having no shepherd. ³⁷Then He said to His disciples, "The harvest truly *is* plentiful, but the laborers *are* few. ³⁸Therefore pray the Lord of the harvest to send out laborers into His harvest."

The Twelve Apostles

10And when He had called His twelve disciples to *Him,* He gave them power *over* unclean spirits, to cast them out, and to heal all kinds of sickness and all kinds of disease. ²Now the names of the twelve apostles are these: first, Simon, who is called Peter, and Andrew his brother; James the *son* of Zebedee, and John his brother; ³Philip and Bartholomew; Thomas and

9:35 ᵃNU-Text omits *among the people.*   9:36 ᵃNU-Text and M-Text read *harassed.*

Matthew the tax collector; James the *son* of Alphaeus, and Lebbaeus, whose surname was[a] Thaddaeus; [4]Simon the Cananite,[a] and Judas Iscariot, who also betrayed Him.

Sending Out the Twelve

[5]These twelve Jesus sent out and commanded them, saying: "Do not go into the way of the Gentiles, and do not enter a city of the Samaritans. [6]But go rather to the lost sheep of the house of Israel. [7]And as you go, preach, saying, 'The kingdom of heaven is at hand.' [8]Heal the sick, cleanse the lepers, raise the dead,[a] cast out demons. Freely you have received, freely give. [9]Provide neither gold nor silver nor copper in your money belts, [10]nor bag for *your* journey, nor two tunics, nor sandals, nor staffs; for a worker is worthy of his food.

[11]"Now whatever city or town you enter, inquire who in it is worthy, and stay there till you go out. [12]And when you go into a household, greet it. [13]If the household is worthy, let your peace come upon it. But if it is not worthy, let your peace return to you. [14]And whoever will not receive you nor hear your words, when you depart from that house or city, shake off the dust from your feet. [15]Assuredly, I say to you, it will be more tolerable for the land of Sodom and Gomorrah in the day of judgment than for that city!

Persecutions Are Coming

[16]"Behold, I send you out as sheep in the midst of wolves. Therefore be wise as serpents

10:3 [a]NU-Text omits *Lebbaeus, whose surname was.*   10:4 [a]NU-Text reads *Cananaean.*   10:8 [a]NU-Text reads *raise the dead, cleanse the lepers;* M-Text omits *raise the dead.*

and harmless as doves. ¹⁷But beware of men, for they will deliver you up to councils and scourge you in their synagogues. ¹⁸You will be brought before governors and kings for My sake, as a testimony to them and to the Gentiles. ¹⁹But when they deliver you up, do not worry about how or what you should speak. For it will be given to you in that hour what you should speak; ²⁰for it is not you who speak, but the Spirit of your Father who speaks in you.

²¹"Now brother will deliver up brother to death, and a father *his* child; and children will rise up against parents and cause them to be put to death. ²²And you will be hated by all for My name's sake. But he who endures to the end will be saved. ²³When they persecute you in this city, flee to another. For assuredly, I say to you, you will not have gone through the cities of Israel before the Son of Man comes.

²⁴"A disciple is not above *his* teacher, nor a servant above his master. ²⁵It is enough for a disciple that he be like his teacher, and a servant like his master. If they have called the master of the house Beelzebub,^a how much more *will they call* those of his household! ²⁶Therefore do not fear them. For there is nothing covered that will not be revealed, and hidden that will not be known.

Jesus Teaches the Fear of God

²⁷"Whatever I tell you in the dark, speak in the light; and what you hear in the ear, preach on the housetops. ²⁸And do not fear those who kill the body but cannot kill the soul. But rather fear Him who is able to destroy both soul and body in hell.

10:25 ^aNU-Text and M-Text read *Beelzebul*.

²⁹Are not two sparrows sold for a copper coin? And not one of them falls to the ground apart from your Father's will. ³⁰But the very hairs of your head are all numbered. ³¹Do not fear therefore; you are of more value than many sparrows.

Confess Christ Before Men

³²"Therefore whoever confesses Me before men, him I will also confess before My Father who is in heaven. ³³But whoever denies Me before men, him I will also deny before My Father who is in heaven.

Christ Brings Division

³⁴"Do not think that I came to bring peace on earth. I did not come to bring peace but a sword. ³⁵For I have come to *'set a man against his father, a daughter against her mother, and a daughter-in-law against her mother-in-law',* ³⁶and *'a man's enemies will be those of his own household.'*ᵃ ³⁷He who loves father or mother more than Me is not worthy of Me. And he who loves son or daughter more than Me is not worthy of Me. ³⁸And he who does not take his cross and follow after Me is not worthy of Me. ³⁹He who finds his life will lose it, and he who loses his life for My sake will find it.

A Cup of Cold Water

⁴⁰"He who receives you receives Me, and he who receives Me receives Him who sent Me. ⁴¹He who receives a prophet in the name of a prophet shall receive a prophet's reward. And he who receives a righteous man in the name of a righteous man shall receive a righteous man's reward.

10:36 ᵃMicah 7:6

⁴²And whoever gives one of these little ones only a cup of cold *water* in the name of a disciple, assuredly, I say to you, he shall by no means lose his reward."

John the Baptist Sends Messengers to Jesus

11 Now it came to pass, when Jesus finished commanding His twelve disciples, that He departed from there to teach and to preach in their cities.

²And when John had heard in prison about the works of Christ, he sent two of[a] his disciples ³and said to Him, "Are You the Coming One, or do we look for another?"

⁴Jesus answered and said to them, "Go and tell John the things which you hear and see: ⁵*The* blind see and *the* lame walk; *the* lepers are cleansed and *the* deaf hear; *the* dead are raised up and *the* poor have the gospel preached to them. ⁶And blessed is he who is not offended because of Me."

⁷As they departed, Jesus began to say to the multitudes concerning John: "What did you go out into the wilderness to see? A reed shaken by the wind? ⁸But what did you go out to see? A man clothed in soft garments? Indeed, those who wear soft *clothing* are in kings' houses. ⁹But what did you go out to see? A prophet? Yes, I say to you, and more than a prophet. ¹⁰For this is *he* of whom it is written:

'Behold, I send My messenger before Your face,
Who will prepare Your way before You.'[a]

11:2 [a]NU-Text reads *by* for *two of.*   11:10 [a]Malachi 3:1

¹¹"Assuredly, I say to you, among those born of women there has not risen one greater than John the Baptist; but he who is least in the kingdom of heaven is greater than he. ¹²And from the days of John the Baptist until now the kingdom of heaven suffers violence, and the violent take it by force. ¹³For all the prophets and the law prophesied until John. ¹⁴And if you are willing to receive *it*, he is Elijah who is to come. ¹⁵He who has ears to hear, let him hear!

¹⁶"But to what shall I liken this generation? It is like children sitting in the marketplaces and calling to their companions, ¹⁷and saying:

'We played the flute for you,
   And you did not dance;
We mourned to you,
   And you did not lament.'

¹⁸For John came neither eating nor drinking, and they say, 'He has a demon.' ¹⁹The Son of Man came eating and drinking, and they say, 'Look, a glutton and a winebibber, a friend of tax collectors and sinners!' But wisdom is justified by her children."ᵃ

Woe to the Impenitent Cities

²⁰Then He began to rebuke the cities in which most of His mighty works had been done, because they did not repent: ²¹"Woe to you, Chorazin! Woe to you, Bethsaida! For if the mighty works which were done in you had been done in Tyre and Sidon, they would have repented long ago in sackcloth and ashes. ²²But I say to you, it will be more tolerable for Tyre and

---

11:19 ᵃNU-Text reads *works*.

Sidon in the day of judgment than for you. [23]And you, Capernaum, who are exalted to heaven, will be[a] brought down to Hades; for if the mighty works which were done in you had been done in Sodom, it would have remained until this day. [24]But I say to you that it shall be more tolerable for the land of Sodom in the day of judgment than for you."

Jesus Gives True Rest

[25]At that time Jesus answered and said, "I thank You, Father, Lord of heaven and earth, that You have hidden these things from *the* wise and prudent and have revealed them to babes. [26]Even so, Father, for so it seemed good in Your sight. [27]All things have been delivered to Me by My Father, and no one knows the Son except the Father. Nor does anyone know the Father except the Son, and *the one* to whom the Son wills to reveal *Him.* [28]Come to Me, all *you* who labor and are heavy laden, and I will give you rest. [29]Take My yoke upon you and learn from Me, for I am gentle and lowly in heart, and you will find rest for your souls. [30]For My yoke *is* easy and My burden is light."

Jesus Is Lord of the Sabbath

12 At that time Jesus went through the grain-fields on the Sabbath. And His disciples were hungry, and began to pluck heads of grain and to eat. [2]And when the Pharisees saw *it,* they said to Him, "Look, Your disciples are doing what is not lawful to do on the Sabbath!"

[3]But He said to them, "Have you not read

11:23 [a]NU-Text reads *will you be exalted to heaven? No, you will be.*

what David did when he was hungry, he and those who were with him: [4]how he entered the house of God and ate the showbread which was not lawful for him to eat, nor for those who were with him, but only for the priests? [5]Or have you not read in the law that on the Sabbath the priests in the temple profane the Sabbath, and are blameless? [6]Yet I say to you that in this place there is *One* greater than the temple. [7]But if you had known what *this* means, '*I desire mercy and not sacrifice,*'[a] you would not have condemned the guiltless. [8]For the Son of Man is Lord even[a] of the Sabbath."

Healing on the Sabbath

[9]Now when He had departed from there, He went into their synagogue. [10]And behold, there was a man who had a withered hand. And they asked Him, saying, "Is it lawful to heal on the Sabbath?"—that they might accuse Him.

[11]Then He said to them, "What man is there among you who has one sheep, and if it falls into a pit on the Sabbath, will not lay hold of it and lift *it* out? [12]Of how much more value then is a man than a sheep? Therefore it is lawful to do good on the Sabbath." [13]Then He said to the man, "Stretch out your hand." And he stretched *it* out, and it was restored as whole as the other. [14]Then the Pharisees went out and plotted against Him, how they might destroy Him.

Behold, My Servant

[15]But when Jesus knew *it*, He withdrew from there. And great multitudes[a] followed Him, and

---

12:7 [a]Hosea 6:6   12:8 [a]NU-Text and M-Text omit *even.*   12:15 [a]NU-Text brackets *multitudes* as disputed.

He healed them all. [16]Yet He warned them not to make Him known, [17]that it might be fulfilled which was spoken by Isaiah the prophet, saying:

[18]*"Behold! My Servant whom I have chosen,*
   My Beloved in whom My soul is well pleased!
   I will put My Spirit upon Him,
   And He will declare justice to the Gentiles.
[19]*He will not quarrel nor cry out,*
   Nor will anyone hear His voice in the streets.
[20]*A bruised reed He will not break,*
   And smoking flax He will not quench,
   Till He sends forth justice to victory;
[21]*And in His name Gentiles will trust."*[a]

A House Divided Cannot Stand

[22]Then one was brought to Him who was demon-possessed, blind and mute; and He healed him, so that the blind and[a] mute man both spoke and saw. [23]And all the multitudes were amazed and said, "Could this be the Son of David?"

[24]Now when the Pharisees heard *it* they said, "This *fellow* does not cast out demons except by Beelzebub,[a] the ruler of the demons."

[25]But Jesus knew their thoughts, and said to them: "Every kingdom divided against itself is brought to desolation, and every city or house divided against itself will not stand. [26]If Satan casts out Satan, he is divided against himself. How then will his kingdom stand? [27]And if I cast out demons by Beelzebub, by whom do your sons cast *them* out? Therefore they shall be your judges. [28]But if I cast out demons by the Spirit of

---

12:21 [a]Isaiah 42:1–4   **12:22** [a]NU-Text omits *blind and.*   **12:24** [a]NU-Text and M-Text read *Beelzebul.*

God, surely the kingdom of God has come upon you. [29]Or how can one enter a strong man's house and plunder his goods, unless he first binds the strong man? And then he will plunder his house. [30]He who is not with Me is against Me, and he who does not gather with Me scatters abroad.

The Unpardonable Sin

[31]"Therefore I say to you, every sin and blasphemy will be forgiven men, but the blasphemy *against* the Spirit will not be forgiven men. [32]Anyone who speaks a word against the Son of Man, it will be forgiven him; but whoever speaks against the Holy Spirit, it will not be forgiven him, either in this age or in the *age* to come.

A Tree Known by Its Fruit

[33]"Either make the tree good and its fruit good, or else make the tree bad and its fruit bad; for a tree is known by *its* fruit. [34]Brood of vipers! How can you, being evil, speak good things? For out of the abundance of the heart the mouth speaks. [35]A good man out of the good treasure of his heart[a] brings forth good things, and an evil man out of the evil treasure brings forth evil things. [36]But I say to you that for every idle word men may speak, they will give account of it in the day of judgment. [37]For by your words you will be justified, and by your words you will be condemned."

The Scribes and Pharisees Ask for a Sign

[38]Then some of the scribes and Pharisees an-

12:35 [a]NU-Text and M-Text omit *of his heart.*

swered, saying, "Teacher, we want to see a sign from You."

³⁹But He answered and said to them, "An evil and adulterous generation seeks after a sign, and no sign will be given to it except the sign of the prophet Jonah. ⁴⁰For as Jonah was three days and three nights in the belly of the great fish, so will the Son of Man be three days and three nights in the heart of the earth. ⁴¹The men of Nineveh will rise up in the judgment with this generation and condemn it, because they repented at the preaching of Jonah; and indeed a greater than Jonah *is* here. ⁴²The queen of the South will rise up in the judgment with this generation and condemn it, for she came from the ends of the earth to hear the wisdom of Solomon; and indeed a greater than Solomon *is* here.

An Unclean Spirit Returns

⁴³"When an unclean spirit goes out of a man, he goes through dry places, seeking rest, and finds none. ⁴⁴Then he says, 'I will return to my house from which I came.' And when he comes, he finds *it* empty, swept, and put in order. ⁴⁵Then he goes and takes with him seven other spirits more wicked than himself, and they enter and dwell there; and the last *state* of that man is worse than the first. So shall it also be with this wicked generation."

Jesus' Mother and Brothers Send for Him

⁴⁶While He was still talking to the multitudes, behold, His mother and brothers stood outside, seeking to speak with Him. ⁴⁷Then one said to Him, "Look, Your mother and Your broth-

ers are standing outside, seeking to speak with You."

⁴⁸But He answered and said to the one who told Him, "Who is My mother and who are My brothers?" ⁴⁹And He stretched out His hand toward His disciples and said, "Here are My mother and My brothers! ⁵⁰For whoever does the will of My Father in heaven is My brother and sister and mother."

The Parable of the Sower

13 On the same day Jesus went out of the house and sat by the sea. ²And great multitudes were gathered together to Him, so that He got into a boat and sat; and the whole multitude stood on the shore.

³Then He spoke many things to them in parables, saying: "Behold, a sower went out to sow. ⁴And as he sowed, some *seed* fell by the wayside; and the birds came and devoured them. ⁵Some fell on stony places, where they did not have much earth; and they immediately sprang up because they had no depth of earth. ⁶But when the sun was up they were scorched, and because they had no root they withered away. ⁷And some fell among thorns, and the thorns sprang up and choked them. ⁸But others fell on good ground and yielded a crop: some a hundredfold, some sixty, some thirty. ⁹He who has ears to hear, let him hear!"

The Purpose of Parables

¹⁰And the disciples came and said to Him, "Why do You speak to them in parables?"

¹¹He answered and said to them, "Because it has been given to you to know the mysteries of

the kingdom of heaven, but to them it has not been given. ¹²For whoever has, to him more will be given, and he will have abundance; but whoever does not have, even what he has will be taken away from him. ¹³Therefore I speak to them in parables, because seeing they do not see, and hearing they do not hear, nor do they understand. ¹⁴And in them the prophecy of Isaiah is fulfilled, which says:

> '*Hearing you will hear and shall not*
> *understand,*
> *And seeing you will see and not perceive;*
> ¹⁵*For the hearts of this people have grown dull.*
> *Their ears are hard of hearing,*
> *And their eyes they have closed,*
> *Lest they should see with their eyes and hear*
> *with their ears,*
> *Lest they should understand with their hearts*
> *and turn,*
> *So that I should*ᵃ *heal them.*'ᵇ

¹⁶But blessed *are* your eyes for they see, and your ears for they hear; ¹⁷for assuredly, I say to you that many prophets and righteous *men* desired to see what you see, and did not see *it*, and to hear what you hear, and did not hear *it*.

The Parable of the Sower Explained

¹⁸"Therefore hear the parable of the sower: ¹⁹When anyone hears the word of the kingdom, and does not understand *it*, then the wicked *one* comes and snatches away what was sown in his heart. This is he who received seed by the way-

---

13:15 ᵃNU-Text and M-Text read *would*. ᵇIsaiah 6:9,10

side. ²⁰But he who received the seed on stony places, this is he who hears the word and immediately receives it with joy; ²¹yet he has no root in himself, but endures only for a while. For when tribulation or persecution arises because of the word, immediately he stumbles. ²²Now he who received seed among the thorns is he who hears the word, and the cares of this world and the deceitfulness of riches choke the word, and he becomes unfruitful. ²³But he who received seed on the good ground is he who hears the word and understands it, who indeed bears fruit and produces: some a hundredfold, some sixty, some thirty."

The Parable of the Wheat and the Tares

²⁴Another parable He put forth to them, saying: "The kingdom of heaven is like a man who sowed good seed in his field; ²⁵but while men slept, his enemy came and sowed tares among the wheat and went his way. ²⁶But when the grain had sprouted and produced a crop, then the tares also appeared. ²⁷So the servants of the owner came and said to him, 'Sir, did you not sow good seed in your field? How then does it have tares?' ²⁸He said to them, 'An enemy has done this.' The servants said to him, 'Do you want us then to go and gather them up?' ²⁹But he said, 'No, lest while you gather up the tares you also uproot the wheat with them. ³⁰Let both grow together until the harvest, and at the time of harvest I will say to the reapers, "First gather together the tares and bind them in bundles to burn them, but gather the wheat into my barn." ' "

The Parable of the Mustard Seed

³¹Another parable He put forth to them, saying: "The kingdom of heaven is like a mustard seed, which a man took and sowed in his field, ³²which indeed is the least of all the seeds; but when it is grown it is greater than the herbs and becomes a tree, so that the birds of the air come and nest in its branches."

The Parable of the Leaven

³³Another parable He spoke to them: "The kingdom of heaven is like leaven, which a woman took and hid in three measures[a] of meal till it was all leavened."

Prophecy and the Parables

³⁴All these things Jesus spoke to the multitude in parables; and without a parable He did not speak to them, ³⁵that it might be fulfilled which was spoken by the prophet, saying:

"I will open My mouth in parables;
I will utter things kept secret from the
    foundation of the world."[a]

The Parable of the Tares Explained

³⁶Then Jesus sent the multitude away and went into the house. And His disciples came to Him, saying, "Explain to us the parable of the tares of the field."

³⁷He answered and said to them: "He who sows the good seed is the Son of Man. ³⁸The field is the world, the good seeds are the sons of the kingdom, but the tares are the sons of the wicked

13:33 ªGreek *sata*, approximately two pecks in all   13:35 ªPsalm 78:2

one. [39]The enemy who sowed them is the devil, the harvest is the end of the age, and the reapers are the angels. [40]Therefore as the tares are gathered and burned in the fire, so it will be at the end of this age. [41]The Son of Man will send out His angels, and they will gather out of His kingdom all things that offend, and those who practice lawlessness, [42]and will cast them into the furnace of fire. There will be wailing and gnashing of teeth. [43]Then the righteous will shine forth as the sun in the kingdom of their Father. He who has ears to hear, let him hear!

The Parable of the Hidden Treasure

[44]"Again, the kingdom of heaven is like treasure hidden in a field, which a man found and hid; and for joy over it he goes and sells all that he has and buys that field.

The Parable of the Pearl of Great Price

[45]"Again, the kingdom of heaven is like a merchant seeking beautiful pearls, [46]who, when he had found one pearl of great price, went and sold all that he had and bought it.

The Parable of the Dragnet

[47]"Again, the kingdom of heaven is like a dragnet that was cast into the sea and gathered some of every kind, [48]which, when it was full, they drew to shore; and they sat down and gathered the good into vessels, but threw the bad away. [49]So it will be at the end of the age. The angels will come forth, separate the wicked from among the just, [50]and cast them into the furnace of fire. There will be wailing and gnashing of teeth."

⁵¹Jesus said to them,ᵃ "Have you understood all these things?"

They said to Him, "Yes, Lord."ᵇ

⁵²Then He said to them, "Therefore every scribe instructed concerningᵃ the kingdom of heaven is like a householder who brings out of his treasure *things* new and old."

Jesus Rejected at Nazareth

⁵³Now it came to pass, when Jesus had finished these parables, that He departed from there. ⁵⁴When He had come to His own country, He taught them in their synagogue, so that they were astonished and said, "Where did this *Man* get this wisdom and *these* mighty works? ⁵⁵Is this not the carpenter's son? Is not His mother called Mary? And His brothers James, Joses,ᵃ Simon, and Judas? ⁵⁶And His sisters, are they not all with us? Where then did this *Man* get all these things?" ⁵⁷So they were offended at Him.

But Jesus said to them, "A prophet is not without honor except in his own country and in his own house." ⁵⁸Now He did not do many mighty works there because of their unbelief.

John the Baptist Beheaded

14 At that time Herod the tetrarch heard the report about Jesus ²and said to his servants, "This is John the Baptist; he is risen from the dead, and therefore these powers are at work in him." ³For Herod had laid hold of John and bound him, and put *him* in prison for the sake of Herodias, his brother Philip's wife. ⁴Because John had said to him, "It is not lawful for you to have

---

13:51 ᵃNU-Text omits *Jesus said to them*. ᵇNU-Text omits *Lord*.
13:52 ᵃOr *for*   13:55 ᵃNU-Text reads *Joseph*.

her." ⁵And although he wanted to put him to death, he feared the multitude, because they counted him as a prophet.

⁶But when Herod's birthday was celebrated, the daughter of Herodias danced before them and pleased Herod. ⁷Therefore he promised with an oath to give her whatever she might ask.

⁸So she, having been prompted by her mother, said, "Give me John the Baptist's head here on a platter."

⁹And the king was sorry; nevertheless, because of the oaths and because of those who sat with him, he commanded *it* to be given to *her*. ¹⁰So he sent and had John beheaded in prison. ¹¹And his head was brought on a platter and given to the girl, and she brought *it* to her mother. ¹²Then his disciples came and took away the body and buried it, and went and told Jesus.

Feeding the Five Thousand

¹³When Jesus heard *it,* He departed from there by boat to a deserted place by Himself. But when the multitudes heard it, they followed Him on foot from the cities. ¹⁴And when Jesus went out He saw a great multitude; and He was moved with compassion for them, and healed their sick. ¹⁵When it was evening, His disciples came to Him, saying, "This is a deserted place, and the hour is already late. Send the multitudes away, that they may go into the villages and buy themselves food."

¹⁶But Jesus said to them, "They do not need to go away. You give them something to eat."

¹⁷And they said to Him, "We have here only five loaves and two fish."

¹⁸He said, "Bring them here to Me." ¹⁹Then

He commanded the multitudes to sit down on the grass. And He took the five loaves and the two fish, and looking up to heaven, He blessed and broke and gave the loaves to the disciples; and the disciples gave to the multitudes. [20]So they all ate and were filled, and they took up twelve baskets full of the fragments that remained. [21]Now those who had eaten were about five thousand men, besides women and children.

Jesus Walks on the Sea

[22]Immediately Jesus made His disciples get into the boat and go before Him to the other side, while He sent the multitudes away. [23]And when He had sent the multitudes away, He went up on the mountain by Himself to pray. Now when evening came, He was alone there. [24]But the boat was now in the middle of the sea,[a] tossed by the waves, for the wind was contrary.

[25]Now in the fourth watch of the night Jesus went to them, walking on the sea. [26]And when the disciples saw Him walking on the sea, they were troubled, saying, "It is a ghost!" And they cried out for fear.

[27]But immediately Jesus spoke to them, saying, "Be of good cheer! It is I; do not be afraid."

[28]And Peter answered Him and said, "Lord, if it is You, command me to come to You on the water."

[29]So He said, "Come." And when Peter had come down out of the boat, he walked on the water to go to Jesus. [30]But when he saw that the wind *was* boisterous,[a] he was afraid; and beginning to sink he cried out, saying, "Lord, save me!"

14:24 [a]NU-Text reads *many furlongs away from the land.*   **14:30** [a]NU-Text brackets *that* and *boisterous* as disputed.

³¹And immediately Jesus stretched out *His* hand and caught him, and said to him, "O you of little faith, why did you doubt?" ³²And when they got into the boat, the wind ceased.

³³Then those who were in the boat came and[a] worshiped Him, saying, "Truly You are the Son of God."

Many Touch Him and Are Made Well

³⁴When they had crossed over, they came to the land of[a] Gennesaret. ³⁵And when the men of that place recognized Him, they sent out into all that surrounding region, brought to Him all who were sick, ³⁶and begged Him that they might only touch the hem of His garment. And as many as touched *it* were made perfectly well.

Defilement Comes from Within

15 Then the scribes and Pharisees who were from Jerusalem came to Jesus, saying, ²"Why do Your disciples transgress the tradition of the elders? For they do not wash their hands when they eat bread."

³He answered and said to them, "Why do you also transgress the commandment of God because of your tradition? ⁴For God commanded, saying, *'Honor your father and your mother';*[a] and, *'He who curses father or mother, let him be put to death.'*[b] ⁵But you say, 'Whoever says to his father or mother, "Whatever profit you might have received from me *is* a gift *to God*"— ⁶then he need not honor his father or mother.'[a] Thus you have made the commandment[b] of God of no

---

14:33 [a]NU-Text omits *came and.*   14:34 [a]NU-Text reads *came to land at.*   15:4 [a]Exodus 20:12; Deuteronomy 5:16   [b]Exodus 21:17
15:6 [a]NU-Text omits *or mother.*   [b]NU-Text reads *word.*

effect by your tradition. [7]Hypocrites! Well did Isaiah prophesy about you, saying:

> [8]*'These people draw near to Me with their mouth,*
> *And*[a] *honor Me with their lips,*
> *But their heart is far from Me.*
> [9]*And in vain they worship Me,*
> *Teaching as doctrines the commandments of men.'* "[a]

[10]When He had called the multitude to *Himself*, He said to them, "Hear and understand: [11]Not what goes into the mouth defiles a man; but what comes out of the mouth, this defiles a man."

[12]Then His disciples came and said to Him, "Do You know that the Pharisees were offended when they heard this saying?"

[13]But He answered and said, "Every plant which My heavenly Father has not planted will be uprooted. [14]Let them alone. They are blind leaders of the blind. And if the blind leads the blind, both will fall into a ditch."

[15]Then Peter answered and said to Him, "Explain this parable to us."

[16]So Jesus said, "Are you also still without understanding? [17]Do you not yet understand that whatever enters the mouth goes into the stomach and is eliminated? [18]But those things which proceed out of the mouth come from the heart, and they defile a man. [19]For out of the heart proceed evil thoughts, murders, adulteries, fornications, thefts, false witness, blasphemies. [20]These are *the*

15:8 [a]NU-Text omits *draw near to Me with their mouth, And.*
15:9 [a]Isaiah 29:13

things which defile a man, but to eat with unwashed hands does not defile a man."

A Gentile Shows Her Faith

[21]Then Jesus went out from there and departed to the region of Tyre and Sidon. [22]And behold, a woman of Canaan came from that region
and cried out to Him, saying, "Have mercy on
me, O Lord, Son of David! My daughter is severely demon-possessed."

[23]But He answered her not a word.

And His disciples came and urged Him, saying, "Send her away, for she cries out after us."

[24]But He answered and said, "I was not sent
except to the lost sheep of the house of Israel."

[25]Then she came and worshiped Him, saying,
"Lord, help me!"

[26]But He answered and said, "It is not good to
take the children's bread and throw *it* to the little
dogs."

[27]And she said, "Yes, Lord, yet even the little
dogs eat the crumbs which fall from their masters' table."

[28]Then Jesus answered and said to her, "O
woman, great *is* your faith! Let it be to you as you
desire." And her daughter was healed from that
very hour.

Jesus Heals Great Multitudes

[29]Jesus departed from there, skirted the Sea of
Galilee, and went up on the mountain and sat
down there. [30]Then great multitudes came to
Him, having with them *the* lame, blind, mute,
maimed, and many others; and they laid them
down at Jesus' feet, and He healed them. [31]So the
multitude marveled when they saw *the* mute

speaking, *the* maimed made whole, *the* lame walking, and *the* blind seeing; and they glorified the God of Israel.

Feeding the Four Thousand

[32]Now Jesus called His disciples to *Himself* and said, "I have compassion on the multitude, because they have now continued with Me three days and have nothing to eat. And I do not want to send them away hungry, lest they faint on the way."

[33]Then His disciples said to Him, "Where could we get enough bread in the wilderness to fill such a great multitude?"

[34]Jesus said to them, "How many loaves do you have?"

And they said, "Seven, and a few little fish."

[35]So He commanded the multitude to sit down on the ground. [36]And He took the seven loaves and the fish and gave thanks, broke *them* and gave *them* to His disciples; and the disciples *gave* to the multitude. [37]So they all ate and were filled, and they took up seven large baskets full of the fragments that were left. [38]Now those who ate were four thousand men, besides women and children. [39]And He sent away the multitude, got into the boat, and came to the region of Magdala.[a]

The Pharisees and Sadducees
Seek a Sign

16 Then the Pharisees and Sadducees came, and testing Him asked that He would show them a sign from heaven. [2]He answered and said to them, "When it is evening you say, 'It

---

15:39 [a]NU-Text reads *Magadan*.

will be fair weather, for the sky is red'; [3]and in the morning, '*It will be* foul weather today, for the sky is red and threatening.' Hypocrites![a] You know how to discern the face of the sky, but you cannot *discern* the signs of the times. [4]A wicked and adulterous generation seeks after a sign, and no sign shall be given to it except the sign of the prophet[a] Jonah." And He left them and departed.

The Leaven of the Pharisees and Sadducees

[5]Now when His disciples had come to the other side, they had forgotten to take bread. [6]Then Jesus said to them, "Take heed and beware of the leaven of the Pharisees and the Sadducees."

[7]And they reasoned among themselves, saying, "*It is* because we have taken no bread."

[8]But Jesus, being aware of *it,* said to them, "O you of little faith, why do you reason among yourselves because you have brought no bread?[a] [9]Do you not yet understand, or remember the five loaves of the five thousand and how many baskets you took up? [10]Nor the seven loaves of the four thousand and how many large baskets you took up? [11]How is it you do not understand that I did not speak to you concerning bread?— *but* to beware of the leaven of the Pharisees and Sadducees." [12]Then they understood that He did not tell *them* to beware of the leaven of bread, but of the doctrine of the Pharisees and Sadducees.

Peter Confesses Jesus as the Christ

[13]When Jesus came into the region of Caesarea Philippi, He asked His disciples, saying,

---

16:3 [a]NU-Text omits *Hypocrites.*   16:4 [a]NU-Text omits *the prophet.*   16:8 [a]NU-Text reads *you have no bread.*

"Who do men say that I, the Son of Man, am?"

¹⁴So they said, "Some *say* John the Baptist, some Elijah, and others Jeremiah or one of the prophets."

¹⁵He said to them, "But who do you say that I am?"

¹⁶Simon Peter answered and said, "You are the Christ, the Son of the living God."

¹⁷Jesus answered and said to him, "Blessed are you, Simon Bar-Jonah, for flesh and blood has not revealed *this* to you, but My Father who is in heaven. ¹⁸And I also say to you that you are Peter, and on this rock I will build My church, and the gates of Hades shall not prevail against it. ¹⁹And I will give you the keys of the kingdom of heaven, and whatever you bind on earth will be bound in heaven, and whatever you loose on earth will be loosed[a] in heaven."

²⁰Then He commanded His disciples that they should tell no one that He was Jesus the Christ.

Jesus Predicts His Death and Resurrection

²¹From that time Jesus began to show to His disciples that He must go to Jerusalem, and suffer many things from the elders and chief priests and scribes, and be killed, and be raised the third day.

²²Then Peter took Him aside and began to rebuke Him, saying, "Far be it from You, Lord; this shall not happen to You!"

²³But He turned and said to Peter, "Get behind Me, Satan! You are an offense to Me, for you are not mindful of the things of God, but the things of men."

16:19 [a]Or *will have been bound . . . will have been loosed*

Why do bad things happen?

You are probably aware that all of humanity is going to die. I'm sure you're also aware that many people are plagued with cancer, Alzheimer's, multiple sclerosis, heart disease, emphysema, Parkinson's, and a number of other debilitating illnesses. Think of all the children with leukemia, or people born with crippling diseases or without the mental capability to even feed themselves. The earth's inhabitants are afflicted with disease, pain, suffering, and death.

In addition, the earth is constantly assaulted with massive earthquakes, hurricanes, tornadoes, floods, and terrible drought. All these things should convince thinking minds that something is radically wrong.

Did God blow it when He created humanity? What sort of tyrant must our Creator be if this was His master plan?

Sadly, many use the issue of suffering as an excuse to reject any thought of God, when its existence is the *very reason* we should accept Him. The Bible tells us that God cursed the earth because of Adam's sin. Diseases and disasters are a curse. We live in a *fallen* creation.

In the beginning, God created man perfect, and he lived in a perfect world without suffering. *It was heaven on earth.* When man brought sin into the world, death and misery came with it. Sin and suffering cannot be separated. So the blame belongs not at God's feet, but at man's.

Those who understand the message of Holy Scripture and who trust in the Savior eagerly await a new heaven and a new earth "where righteousness dwells" (2 Peter 3:13). In that coming Kingdom there will be no more pain, suffering, disease, or death. We are told that no eye has ever seen, no ear has heard, and no man has ever imagined the wonderful things that God has in store for those who love Him (see 1 Corinthians 2:9).

How could a loving God create Hell?

If a judge turns a blind eye to the unlawful dealings of the Mafia—if he sees their murderous acts and deliberately looks the other way—is he a good or bad judge? He's obviously corrupt, and should be brought to justice himself. If he is a good judge, he must do everything within his power to bring those murderers to justice. He should make sure that they are justly punished for their crimes.

If Almighty God sees a man rape and strangle to death your sister or mother, do you think He should look the other way, or bring that murderer to justice? If He looks the other way, He's corrupt and should be brought to justice Himself. It makes sense then, that if God is good, He will do everything in His power to ensure that justice is done.

In the U.S. during the 1990s, there were 200,000 murders. But according to statistics, only 50% of U.S. homicides are solved. So in one decade, 100,000 people got away with murder. They killed another human being and were never brought to justice.

The Bible, however, tells us that God *will* punish murderers, and the place of punishment—the prison He will send them to—is a place called Hell.

So, the existence of Hell makes sense, if God is good (something we know intuitively). He *should* punish murderers and rapists. However, God is so perfect, just, holy, and good that the Bible warns He will also punish thieves, liars, adulterers, fornicators, and blasphemers. He will even punish those who desired to murder and rape, but never found the opportunity. He warns that if we hate someone, we commit murder in our hearts. If we lust, we commit adultery in the heart, etc.

So once we understand that God is perfect, holy, just, and good, we come to the conclusion, how can there *not* be such a place as Hell?

Take Up the Cross and Follow Him

[24]Then Jesus said to His disciples, "If anyone desires to come after Me, let him deny himself, and take up his cross, and follow Me. [25]For whoever desires to save his life will lose it, but whoever loses his life for My sake will find it. [26]For what profit is it to a man if he gains the whole world, and loses his own soul? Or what will a man give in exchange for his soul? [27]For the Son of Man will come in the glory of His Father with His angels, and then He will reward each according to his works.

Jesus Transfigured on the Mount

[28]Assuredly, I say to you, there are some standing here who shall not taste death till they see the Son of Man coming in His kingdom."

17 Now after six days Jesus took Peter, James, and John his brother, led them up on a high mountain by themselves; [2]and He was transfigured before them. His face shone like the sun, and His clothes became as white as the light. [3]And behold, Moses and Elijah appeared to them, talking with Him. [4]Then Peter answered and said to Jesus, "Lord, it is good for us to be here; if You wish, let us[a] make here three tabernacles: one for You, one for Moses, and one for Elijah."

[5]While he was still speaking, behold, a bright cloud overshadowed them; and suddenly a voice came out of the cloud, saying, "This is My beloved Son, in whom I am well pleased. Hear Him!" [6]And when the disciples heard *it,* they fell on their faces and were greatly afraid. [7]But Jesus

---

17:4 [a]NU-Text reads *I will.*

came and touched them and said, "Arise, and do not be afraid." [8]When they had lifted up their eyes, they saw no one but Jesus only.

[9]Now as they came down from the mountain, Jesus commanded them, saying, "Tell the vision to no one until the Son of Man is risen from the dead."

[10]And His disciples asked Him, saying, "Why then do the scribes say that Elijah must come first?"

[11]Jesus answered and said to them, "Indeed, Elijah is coming first[a] and will restore all things. [12]But I say to you that Elijah has come already, and they did not know him but did to him whatever they wished. Likewise the Son of Man is also about to suffer at their hands." [13]Then the disciples understood that He spoke to them of John the Baptist.

A Boy Is Healed

[14]And when they had come to the multitude, a man came to Him, kneeling down to Him and saying, [15]"Lord, have mercy on my son, for he is an epileptic[a] and suffers severely; for he often falls into the fire and often into the water. [16]So I brought him to Your disciples, but they could not cure him."

[17]Then Jesus answered and said, "O faithless and perverse generation, how long shall I be with you? How long shall I bear with you? Bring him here to Me." [18]And Jesus rebuked the demon, and it came out of him; and the child was cured from that very hour.

[19]Then the disciples came to Jesus privately and said, "Why could we not cast it out?"

17:11 [a]NU-Text omits *first*.   17:15 [a]Literally *moonstruck*

²⁰So Jesus said to them, "Because of your unbelief;[a] for assuredly, I say to you, if you have faith as a mustard seed, you will say to this mountain, 'Move from here to there,' and it will move; and nothing will be impossible for you. ²¹However, this kind does not go out except by prayer and fasting."[a]

Jesus Again Predicts His Death and Resurrection

²²Now while they were staying[a] in Galilee, Jesus said to them, "The Son of Man is about to be betrayed into the hands of men, ²³and they will kill Him, and the third day He will be raised up." And they were exceedingly sorrowful.

Peter and His Master Pay Their Taxes

²⁴When they had come to Capernaum,[a] those who received the *temple* tax came to Peter and said, "Does your Teacher not pay the *temple* tax?"

²⁵He said, "Yes."

And when he had come into the house, Jesus anticipated him, saying, "What do you think, Simon? From whom do the kings of the earth take customs or taxes, from their sons or from strangers?"

²⁶Peter said to Him, "From strangers."

Jesus said to him, "Then the sons are free. ²⁷Nevertheless, lest we offend them, go to the sea, cast in a hook, and take the fish that comes up first. And when you have opened its mouth, you will find a piece of money;[a] take that and

---

17:20 [a]NU-Text reads *little faith.*   17:21 [a]NU-Text omits this verse.   17:22 [a]NU-Text reads *gathering together.*   17:24 [a]NU-Text reads *Capharnaum* (here and elsewhere).   17:27 [a]Greek *stater,* the exact amount to pay the temple tax (didrachma) for two

give it to them for Me and you."

Who Is the Greatest?

18 At that time the disciples came to Jesus, saying, "Who then is greatest in the kingdom of heaven?"

²Then Jesus called a little child to Him, set him in the midst of them, ³and said, "Assuredly, I say to you, unless you are converted and become as little children, you will by no means enter the kingdom of heaven. ⁴Therefore whoever humbles himself as this little child is the greatest in the kingdom of heaven. ⁵Whoever receives one little child like this in My name receives Me.

Jesus Warns of Offenses

⁶"Whoever causes one of these little ones who believe in Me to sin, it would be better for him if a millstone were hung around his neck, and he were drowned in the depth of the sea. ⁷Woe to the world because of offenses! For offenses must come, but woe to that man by whom the offense comes!

⁸"If your hand or foot causes you to sin, cut it off and cast it from you. It is better for you to enter into life lame or maimed, rather than having two hands or two feet, to be cast into the everlasting fire. ⁹And if your eye causes you to sin, pluck it out and cast it from you. It is better for you to enter into life with one eye, rather than having two eyes, to be cast into hell fire.

The Parable of the Lost Sheep

¹⁰"Take heed that you do not despise one of these little ones, for I say to you that in heaven their angels always see the face of My Father who

is in heaven. ¹¹For the Son of Man has come to save that which was lost.ᵃ

¹²"What do you think? If a man has a hundred sheep, and one of them goes astray, does he not leave the ninety-nine and go to the mountains to seek the one that is straying? ¹³And if he should find it, assuredly, I say to you, he rejoices more over that *sheep* than over the ninety-nine that did not go astray. ¹⁴Even so it is not the will of your Father who is in heaven that one of these little ones should perish.

Dealing with a Sinning Brother

¹⁵"Moreover if your brother sins against you, go and tell him his fault between you and him alone. If he hears you, you have gained your brother. ¹⁶But if he will not hear, take with you one or two more, that *'by the mouth of two or three witnesses every word may be established.'*ᵃ ¹⁷And if he refuses to hear them, tell *it* to the church. But if he refuses even to hear the church, let him be to you like a heathen and a tax collector.

¹⁸"Assuredly, I say to you, whatever you bind on earth will be bound in heaven, and whatever you loose on earth will be loosed in heaven.

¹⁹"Again I sayᵃ to you that if two of you agree on earth concerning anything that they ask, it will be done for them by My Father in heaven. ²⁰For where two or three are gathered together in My name, I am there in the midst of them."

The Parable of the Unforgiving Servant

²¹Then Peter came to Him and said, "Lord, how often shall my brother sin against me, and I for-

18:11 ᵃNU-Text omits this verse.   18:16 ᵃDeuteronomy 19:15
18:19 ᵃNU-Text and M-Text read *Again, assuredly, I say.*

give him? Up to seven times?"

²²Jesus said to him, "I do not say to you, up to seven times, but up to seventy times seven. ²³Therefore the kingdom of heaven is like a certain king who wanted to settle accounts with his servants. ²⁴And when he had begun to settle accounts, one was brought to him who owed him ten thousand talents. ²⁵But as he was not able to pay, his master commanded that he be sold, with his wife and children and all that he had, and that payment be made. ²⁶The servant therefore fell down before him, saying, 'Master, have patience with me, and I will pay you all.' ²⁷Then the master of that servant was moved with compassion, released him, and forgave him the debt.

²⁸"But that servant went out and found one of his fellow servants who owed him a hundred denarii; and he laid hands on him and took *him* by the throat, saying, 'Pay me what you owe!' ²⁹So his fellow servant fell down at his feet[a] and begged him, saying, 'Have patience with me, and I will pay you all.'[b] ³⁰And he would not, but went and threw him into prison till he should pay the debt. ³¹So when his fellow servants saw what had been done, they were very grieved, and came and told their master all that had been done. ³²Then his master, after he had called him, said to him, 'You wicked servant! I forgave you all that debt because you begged me. ³³Should you not also have had compassion on your fellow servant, just as I had pity on you?' ³⁴And his master was angry, and delivered him to the torturers until he should pay all that was due to him.

³⁵"So My heavenly Father also will do to you if each of you, from his heart, does not forgive his

18:29 ªNU-Text omits *at his feet.* ᵇNU-Text and M-Text omit *all.*

brother his trespasses."ᵃ

Marriage and Divorce

19 Now it came to pass, when Jesus had finished these sayings, *that* He departed from Galilee and came to the region of Judea beyond the Jordan. ²And great multitudes followed Him, and He healed them there.

³The Pharisees also came to Him, testing Him, and saying to Him, "Is it lawful for a man to divorce his wife for *just* any reason?"

⁴And He answered and said to them, "Have you not read that He who madeᵃ them at the beginning *'made them male and female,'*ᵇ ⁵and said, *'For this reason a man shall leave his father and mother and be joined to his wife, and the two shall become one flesh'?*ᵃ ⁶So then, they are no longer two but one flesh. Therefore what God has joined together, let not man separate."

⁷They said to Him, "Why then did Moses command to give a certificate of divorce, and to put her away?"

⁸He said to them, "Moses, because of the hardness of your hearts, permitted you to divorce your wives, but from the beginning it was not so. ⁹And I say to you, whoever divorces his wife, except for sexual immorality,ᵃ and marries another, commits adultery; and whoever marries her who is divorced commits adultery."

¹⁰His disciples said to Him, "If such is the case of the man with *his* wife, it is better not to marry."

Jesus Teaches on Celibacy

¹¹But He said to them, "All cannot accept this

18:35 ᵃNU-Text omits *his trespasses.* 19:4 ᵃNU-Text reads *created.* ᵇGenesis 1:27; 5:2 19:5 ᵃGenesis 2:24 19:9 ᵃOr *fornication*

saying, but only *those* to whom it has been given: [12]For there are eunuchs who were born thus from *their* mother's womb, and there are eunuchs who were made eunuchs by men, and there are eunuchs who have made themselves eunuchs for the kingdom of heaven's sake. He who is able to accept *it,* let him accept *it.*"

Jesus Blesses Little Children

[13]Then little children were brought to Him that He might put *His* hands on them and pray, but the disciples rebuked them. [14]But Jesus said, "Let the little children come to Me, and do not forbid them; for such is the kingdom of heaven." [15]And He laid *His* hands on them and departed from there.

Jesus Counsels the Rich Young Ruler

[16]Now behold, one came and said to Him, "Good[a] Teacher, what good thing shall I do that I may have eternal life?"

[17]So He said to him, "Why do you call Me good?[a] No one *is* good but One, *that is,* God.[b] But if you want to enter into life, keep the commandments."

[18]He said to Him, "Which ones?"

Jesus said, " 'You shall not murder,' 'You shall not commit adultery,' 'You shall not steal,' 'You shall not bear false witness,' [19]'Honor your father and your mother,'[a] and, 'You shall love your neighbor as yourself.' "[b]

[20]The young man said to Him, "All these things I have kept from my youth.[a] What do I

19:16 [a]NU-Text omits *Good.*   19:17 [a]NU-Text reads *Why do you ask Me about what is good?* [b]NU-Text reads *There is One who is good.*   19:19 [a]Exodus 20:12–16; Deuteronomy 5:16–20 [b]Leviticus 19:18   19:20 [a]NU-Text omits *from my youth.*

still lack?"

²¹Jesus said to him, "If you want to be perfect, go, sell what you have and give to the poor, and you will have treasure in heaven; and come, follow Me."

²²But when the young man heard that saying, he went away sorrowful, for he had great possessions.

With God All Things Are Possible

²³Then Jesus said to His disciples, "Assuredly, I say to you that it is hard for a rich man to enter the kingdom of heaven. ²⁴And again I say to you, it is easier for a camel to go through the eye of a needle than for a rich man to enter the kingdom of God."

²⁵When His disciples heard *it,* they were greatly astonished, saying, "Who then can be saved?"

²⁶But Jesus looked at *them* and said to them, "With men this is impossible, but with God all things are possible."

²⁷Then Peter answered and said to Him, "See, we have left all and followed You. Therefore what shall we have?"

²⁸So Jesus said to them, "Assuredly I say to you, that in the regeneration, when the Son of Man sits on the throne of His glory, you who have followed Me will also sit on twelve thrones, judging the twelve tribes of Israel. ²⁹And everyone who has left houses or brothers or sisters or father or mother or wifeᵃ or children or lands, for My name's sake, shall receive a hundredfold, and inherit eternal life. ³⁰But many *who are* first will be last, and the last first.

19:29 ᵃNU-Text omits *or wife.*

The Parable of the Workers in the Vineyard

20 "For the kingdom of heaven is like a landowner who went out early in the morning to hire laborers for his vineyard. ²Now when he had agreed with the laborers for a denarius a day, he sent them into his vineyard. ³And he went out about the third hour and saw others standing idle in the marketplace, ⁴and said to them, 'You also go into the vineyard, and whatever is right I will give you.' So they went. ⁵Again he went out about the sixth and the ninth hour, and did likewise. ⁶And about the eleventh hour he went out and found others standing idle,ᵃ and said to them, 'Why have you been standing here idle all day?' ⁷They said to him, 'Because no one hired us.' He said to them, 'You also go into the vineyard, and whatever is right you will receive.'ᵃ

⁸"So when evening had come, the owner of the vineyard said to his steward, 'Call the laborers and give them *their* wages, beginning with the last to the first.' ⁹And when those came who *were hired* about the eleventh hour, they each received a denarius. ¹⁰But when the first came, they supposed that they would receive more; and they likewise received each a denarius. ¹¹And when they had received *it,* they complained against the landowner, ¹²saying, 'These last *men* have worked *only* one hour, and you made them equal to us who have borne the burden and the heat of the day.' ¹³But he answered one of them and said, 'Friend, I am doing you no wrong. Did you not agree with me for a denarius? ¹⁴Take

---

20:6 ᵃNU-Text omits *idle*.   **20:7** ᵃNU-Text omits the last clause of this verse.

what is yours and go your way. I wish to give to this last man *the same* as to you. [15]Is it not lawful for me to do what I wish with my own things? Or is your eye evil because I am good?' [16]So the last will be first, and the first last. For many are called, but few chosen."[a]

Jesus a Third Time Predicts His Death and Resurrection

[17]Now Jesus, going up to Jerusalem, took the twelve disciples aside on the road and said to them, [18]"Behold, we are going up to Jerusalem, and the Son of Man will be betrayed to the chief priests and to the scribes; and they will condemn Him to death, [19]and deliver Him to the Gentiles to mock and to scourge and to crucify. And the third day He will rise again."

Greatness Is Serving

[20]Then the mother of Zebedee's sons came to Him with her sons, kneeling down and asking something from Him.

[21]And He said to her, "What do you wish?"

She said to Him, "Grant that these two sons of mine may sit, one on Your right hand and the other on the left, in Your kingdom."

[22]But Jesus answered and said, "You do not know what you ask. Are you able to drink the cup that I am about to drink, and be baptized with the baptism that I am baptized with?"[a]

They said to Him, "We are able."

[23]So He said to them, "You will indeed drink My cup, and be baptized with the baptism that I

20:16 [a]NU-Text omits the last sentence of this verse.   20:22 [a]NU-Text omits *and be baptized with the baptism that I am baptized with.*

am baptized with;^a but to sit on My right hand and on My left is not Mine to give, but *it is for those* for whom it is prepared by My Father."

²⁴And when the ten heard *it,* they were greatly displeased with the two brothers. ²⁵But Jesus called them to *Himself* and said, "You know that the rulers of the Gentiles lord it over them, and those who are great exercise authority over them. ²⁶Yet it shall not be so among you; but whoever desires to become great among you, let him be your servant. ²⁷And whoever desires to be first among you, let him be your slave— ²⁸just as the Son of Man did not come to be served, but to serve, and to give His life a ransom for many."

Two Blind Men Receive Their Sight

²⁹Now as they went out of Jericho, a great multitude followed Him. ³⁰And behold, two blind men sitting by the road, when they heard that Jesus was passing by, cried out, saying, "Have mercy on us, O Lord, Son of David!"

³¹Then the multitude warned them that they should be quiet; but they cried out all the more, saying, "Have mercy on us, O Lord, Son of David!"

³²So Jesus stood still and called them, and said, "What do you want Me to do for you?"

³³They said to Him, "Lord, that our eyes may be opened." ³⁴So Jesus had compassion and touched their eyes. And immediately their eyes received sight, and they followed Him.

The Triumphal Entry

21 Now when they drew near Jerusalem, and came to Bethphage,^a at the Mount of

---

20:23 ^aNU-Text omits *and be baptized with the baptism that I am baptized with.*   21:1 ^aM-Text reads *Bethsphage.*

Olives, then Jesus sent two disciples, [2]saying to them, "Go into the village opposite you, and immediately you will find a donkey tied, and a colt with her. Loose *them* and bring *them* to Me. [3]And if anyone says anything to you, you shall say, 'The Lord has need of them,' and immediately he will send them."

[4]All[a] this was done that it might be fulfilled which was spoken by the prophet, saying:

[5]"Tell the daughter of Zion,
   'Behold, your King is coming to you,
   Lowly, and sitting on a donkey,
   A colt, the foal of a donkey.' "[a]

[6]So the disciples went and did as Jesus commanded them. [7]They brought the donkey and the colt, laid their clothes on them, and set Him[a] on them. [8]And a very great multitude spread their clothes on the road; others cut down branches from the trees and spread *them* on the road. [9]Then the multitudes who went before and those who followed cried out, saying:

"Hosanna to the Son of David!
   'Blessed is He who comes in the name of the LORD!'[a]
   Hosanna in the highest!"

[10]And when He had come into Jerusalem, all the city was moved, saying, "Who is this?"

[11]So the multitudes said, "This is Jesus, the prophet from Nazareth of Galilee."

21:4 [a]NU-Text omits *All.*   21:5 [a]Zechariah 9:9   21:7 [a]NU-Text reads *and He sat.*   21:9 [a]Psalm 118:26

Jesus Cleanses the Temple

[12]Then Jesus went into the temple of God[a] and drove out all those who bought and sold in the temple, and overturned the tables of the money changers and the seats of those who sold doves. [13]And He said to them, "It is written, *'My house shall be called a house of prayer,'*[a] but you have made it a *'den of thieves.'*"[b]

[14]Then *the* blind and *the* lame came to Him in the temple, and He healed them. [15]But when the chief priests and scribes saw the wonderful things that He did, and the children crying out in the temple and saying, "Hosanna to the Son of David!" they were indignant [16]and said to Him, "Do You hear what these are saying?"

And Jesus said to them, "Yes. Have you never read,

*'Out of the mouth of babes and nursing infants
    You have perfected praise'?"*[a]

[17]Then He left them and went out of the city to Bethany, and He lodged there.

The Fig Tree Withered

[18]Now in the morning, as He returned to the city, He was hungry. [19]And seeing a fig tree by the road, He came to it and found nothing on it but leaves, and said to it, "Let no fruit grow on you ever again." Immediately the fig tree withered away.

The Lesson of the Withered Fig Tree

[20]And when the disciples saw *it,* they mar-

21:12 [a]NU-Text omits *of God.*   21:13 [a]Isaiah 56:7   [b]Jeremiah 7:11   21:16 [a]Psalm 8:2

veled, saying, "How did the fig tree wither away so soon?"

[21]So Jesus answered and said to them, "Assuredly, I say to you, if you have faith and do not doubt, you will not only do what was done to the fig tree, but also if you say to this mountain, 'Be removed and be cast into the sea,' it will be done. [22]And whatever things you ask in prayer, believing, you will receive."

Jesus' Authority Questioned

[23]Now when He came into the temple, the chief priests and the elders of the people confronted Him as He was teaching, and said, "By what authority are You doing these things? And who gave You this authority?"

[24]But Jesus answered and said to them, "I also will ask you one thing, which if you tell Me, I likewise will tell you by what authority I do these things: [25]The baptism of John—where was it from? From heaven or from men?"

And they reasoned among themselves, saying, "If we say, 'From heaven,' He will say to us, 'Why then did you not believe him?' [26]But if we say, 'From men,' we fear the multitude, for all count John as a prophet." [27]So they answered Jesus and said, "We do not know."

And He said to them, "Neither will I tell you by what authority I do these things.

The Parable of the Two Sons

[28]"But what do you think? A man had two sons, and he came to the first and said, 'Son, go, work today in my vineyard.' [29]He answered and said, 'I will not,' but afterward he regretted it and went. [30]Then he came to the second and said

likewise. And he answered and said, 'I *go*, sir,' but he did not go. [31]Which of the two did the will of *his* father?"

They said to Him, "The first."

Jesus said to them, "Assuredly, I say to you that tax collectors and harlots enter the kingdom of God before you. [32]For John came to you in the way of righteousness, and you did not believe him; but tax collectors and harlots believed him; and when you saw *it*, you did not afterward relent and believe him.

The Parable of the Wicked Vinedressers

[33]"Hear another parable: There was a certain landowner who planted a vineyard and set a hedge around it, dug a winepress in it and built a tower. And he leased it to vinedressers and went into a far country. [34]Now when vintage-time drew near, he sent his servants to the vinedressers, that they might receive its fruit. [35]And the vinedressers took his servants, beat one, killed one, and stoned another. [36]Again he sent other servants, more than the first, and they did likewise to them. [37]Then last of all he sent his son to them, saying, 'They will respect my son.' [38]But when the vinedressers saw the son, they said among themselves, 'This is the heir. Come, let us kill him and seize his inheritance.' [39]So they took him and cast *him* out of the vineyard and killed *him*.

[40]"Therefore, when the owner of the vineyard comes, what will he do to those vinedressers?"

[41]They said to Him, "He will destroy those wicked men miserably, and lease *his* vineyard to other vinedressers who will render to him the fruits in their seasons."

⁴²Jesus said to them, "Have you never read in the Scriptures:

> 'The stone which the builders rejected
> Has become the chief cornerstone.
> This was the LORD's doing,
> And it is marvelous in our eyes'?ª

⁴³"Therefore I say to you, the kingdom of God will be taken from you and given to a nation bearing the fruits of it. ⁴⁴And whoever falls on this stone will be broken; but on whomever it falls, it will grind him to powder."

⁴⁵Now when the chief priests and Pharisees heard His parables, they perceived that He was speaking of them. ⁴⁶But when they sought to lay hands on Him, they feared the multitudes, because they took Him for a prophet.

The Parable of the Wedding Feast

22 And Jesus answered and spoke to them again by parables and said: ²"The kingdom of heaven is like a certain king who arranged a marriage for his son, ³and sent out his servants to call those who were invited to the wedding; and they were not willing to come. ⁴Again, he sent out other servants, saying, 'Tell those who are invited, "See, I have prepared my dinner; my oxen and fatted cattle *are* killed, and all things *are* ready. Come to the wedding." ' ⁵But they made light of it and went their ways, one to his own farm, another to his business. ⁶And the rest seized his servants, treated *them* spitefully, and killed *them*. ⁷But when the king heard *about*

21:42 ªPsalm 118:22, 23

it, he was furious. And he sent out his armies, destroyed those murderers, and burned up their city. [8]Then he said to his servants, 'The wedding is ready, but those who were invited were not worthy. [9]Therefore go into the highways, and as many as you find, invite to the wedding.' [10]So those servants went out into the highways and gathered together all whom they found, both bad and good. And the wedding *hall* was filled with guests.

[11]"But when the king came in to see the guests, he saw a man there who did not have on a wedding garment. [12]So he said to him, 'Friend, how did you come in here without a wedding garment?' And he was speechless. [13]Then the king said to the servants, 'Bind him hand and foot, take him away, and[a] cast *him* into outer darkness; there will be weeping and gnashing of teeth.'

[14]"For many are called, but few *are* chosen."

The Pharisees: Is It Lawful to Pay Taxes to Caesar?

[15]Then the Pharisees went and plotted how they might entangle Him in *His* talk. [16]And they sent to Him their disciples with the Herodians, saying, "Teacher, we know that You are true, and teach the way of God in truth; nor do You care about anyone, for You do not regard the person of men. [17]Tell us, therefore, what do You think? Is it lawful to pay taxes to Caesar, or not?"

[18]But Jesus perceived their wickedness, and said, "Why do you test Me, *you* hypocrites? [19]Show Me the tax money."

So they brought Him a denarius.

22:13 [a]NU-Text omits *take him away, and.*

²⁰And He said to them, "Whose image and inscription *is* this?"

²¹They said to Him, "Caesar's."

And He said to them, "Render therefore to Caesar the things that are Caesar's, and to God the things that are God's." ²²When they had heard *these words,* they marveled, and left Him and went their way.

The Sadducees: What About the Resurrection?

²³The same day the Sadducees, who say there is no resurrection, came to Him and asked Him, ²⁴saying: "Teacher, Moses said that if a man dies, having no children, his brother shall marry his wife and raise up offspring for his brother. ²⁵Now there were with us seven brothers. The first died after he had married, and having no offspring, left his wife to his brother. ²⁶Likewise the second also, and the third, even to the seventh. ²⁷Last of all the woman died also. ²⁸Therefore, in the resurrection, whose wife of the seven will she be? For they all had her."

²⁹Jesus answered and said to them, "You are mistaken, not knowing the Scriptures nor the power of God. ³⁰For in the resurrection they neither marry nor are given in marriage, but are like angels of God[a] in heaven. ³¹But concerning the resurrection of the dead, have you not read what was spoken to you by God, saying, ³²'*I am the God of Abraham, the God of Isaac, and the God of Jacob'?*[a] God is not the God of the dead, but of the living." ³³And when the multitudes heard *this,* they were astonished at His teaching.

22:30 [a]NU-Text omits *of God.*   **22:32** [a]Exodus 3:6, 15

The Scribes: Which Is the First Commandment of All?

³⁴But when the Pharisees heard that He had silenced the Sadducees, they gathered together. ³⁵Then one of them, a lawyer, asked *Him a question*, testing Him, and saying, ³⁶"Teacher, which is the great commandment in the law?"

³⁷Jesus said to him, " 'You shall love the LORD your God with all your heart, with all your soul, and with all your mind.'ᵃ ³⁸This is *the* first and great commandment. ³⁹And *the* second is like it: 'You shall love your neighbor as yourself.'ᵃ ⁴⁰On these two commandments hang all the Law and the Prophets."

Jesus: How Can David Call His Descendant Lord?

⁴¹While the Pharisees were gathered together, Jesus asked them, ⁴²saying, "What do you think about the Christ? Whose Son is He?"

They said to Him, "*The Son* of David."

⁴³He said to them, "How then does David in the Spirit call Him 'Lord,' saying:

⁴⁴'The LORD said to my Lord,
"Sit at My right hand,
Till I make Your enemies Your footstool" '?ᵃ

⁴⁵If David then calls Him 'Lord,' how is He his Son?" ⁴⁶And no one was able to answer Him a word, nor from that day on did anyone dare question Him anymore.

22:37 ᵃDeuteronomy 6:5   22:39 ᵃLeviticus 19:18   22:44 ᵃPsalm 110:1

Woe to the Scribes and Pharisees

23 Then Jesus spoke to the multitudes and to His disciples, ²saying: "The scribes and the Pharisees sit in Moses' seat. ³Therefore whatever they tell you to observe,ᵃ *that* observe and do, but do not do according to their works; for they say, and do not do. ⁴For they bind heavy burdens, hard to bear, and lay *them* on men's shoulders; but they *themselves* will not move them with one of their fingers. ⁵But all their works they do to be seen by men. They make their phylacteries broad and enlarge the borders of their garments. ⁶They love the best places at feasts, the best seats in the synagogues, ⁷greetings in the marketplaces, and to be called by men, 'Rabbi, Rabbi.' ⁸But you, do not be called 'Rabbi'; for One is your Teacher, the Christ,ᵃ and you are all brethren. ⁹Do not call anyone on earth your father; for One is your Father, He who is in heaven. ¹⁰And do not be called teachers; for One is your Teacher, the Christ. ¹¹But he who is greatest among you shall be your servant. ¹²And whoever exalts himself will be humbled, and he who humbles himself will be exalted.

¹³"But woe to you, scribes and Pharisees, hypocrites! For you shut up the kingdom of heaven against men; for you neither go in *yourselves,* nor do you allow those who are entering to go in. ¹⁴Woe to you, scribes and Pharisees, hypocrites! For you devour widows' houses, and for a pretense make long prayers. Therefore you will receive greater condemnation.ᵃ

¹⁵"Woe to you, scribes and Pharisees, hypocrites! For you travel land and sea to win one

---

23:3 ᵃNU-Text omits *to observe.*   23:8 ᵃNU-Text omits *the Christ.*
23:14 ᵃNU-Text omits this verse.

proselyte, and when he is won, you make him twice as much a son of hell as yourselves.

¹⁶"Woe to you, blind guides, who say, 'Whoever swears by the temple, it is nothing; but whoever swears by the gold of the temple, he is obliged *to perform it.*' ¹⁷Fools and blind! For which is greater, the gold or the temple that sanctifiesᵃ the gold? ¹⁸And, 'Whoever swears by the altar, it is nothing; but whoever swears by the gift that is on it, he is obliged *to perform it.*' ¹⁹Fools and blind! For which is greater, the gift or the altar that sanctifies the gift? ²⁰Therefore he who swears by the altar, swears by it and by all things on it. ²¹He who swears by the temple, swears by it and by Him who dwellsᵃ in it. ²²And he who swears by heaven, swears by the throne of God and by Him who sits on it.

²³"Woe to you, scribes and Pharisees, hypocrites! For you pay tithe of mint and anise and cummin, and have neglected the weightier *matters* of the law: justice and mercy and faith. These you ought to have done, without leaving the others undone. ²⁴Blind guides, who strain out a gnat and swallow a camel!

²⁵"Woe to you, scribes and Pharisees, hypocrites! For you cleanse the outside of the cup and dish, but inside they are full of extortion and self-indulgence.ᵃ ²⁶Blind Pharisee, first cleanse the inside of the cup and dish, that the outside of them may be clean also.

²⁷"Woe to you, scribes and Pharisees, hypocrites! For you are like whitewashed tombs which indeed appear beautiful outwardly, but inside are full of dead *men's* bones and all unclean-

---

23:17 ᵃNU-Text reads *sanctified.*   23:21 ᵃM-Text reads *dwelt.*
23:25 ᵃM-Text reads *unrighteousness.*

ness. [28]Even so you also outwardly appear righteous to men, but inside you are full of hypocrisy and lawlessness.

[29]"Woe to you, scribes and Pharisees, hypocrites! Because you build the tombs of the prophets and adorn the monuments of the righteous, [30]and say, 'If we had lived in the days of our fathers, we would not have been partakers with them in the blood of the prophets.'

[31]"Therefore you are witnesses against yourselves that you are sons of those who murdered the prophets. [32]Fill up, then, the measure of your fathers' *guilt*. [33]Serpents, brood of vipers! How can you escape the condemnation of hell? [34]Therefore, indeed, I send you prophets, wise men, and scribes: *some* of them you will kill and crucify, and *some* of them you will scourge in your synagogues and persecute from city to city, [35]that on you may come all the righteous blood shed on the earth, from the blood of righteous Abel to the blood of Zechariah, son of Berechiah, whom you murdered between the temple and the altar. [36]Assuredly, I say to you, all these things will come upon this generation.

Jesus Laments over Jerusalem

[37]"O Jerusalem, Jerusalem, the one who kills the prophets and stones those who are sent to her! How often I wanted to gather your children together, as a hen gathers her chicks under *her* wings, but you were not willing! [38]See! Your house is left to you desolate; [39]for I say to you, you shall see Me no more till you say, *'Blessed is He who comes in the name of the LORD!'* "[a]

23:39 [a]Psalm 118:26

Jesus Predicts the Destruction of the Temple

24 Then Jesus went out and departed from the temple, and His disciples came up to show Him the buildings of the temple. ²And Jesus said to them, "Do you not see all these things? Assuredly, I say to you, not *one* stone shall be left here upon another, that shall not be thrown down."

The Signs of the Times and the End of the Age

³Now as He sat on the Mount of Olives, the disciples came to Him privately, saying, "Tell us, when will these things be? And what *will be* the sign of Your coming, and of the end of the age?"

⁴And Jesus answered and said to them: "Take heed that no one deceives you. ⁵For many will come in My name, saying, 'I am the Christ,' and will deceive many. ⁶And you will hear of wars and rumors of wars. See that you are not troubled; for all^a *these things* must come to pass, but the end is not yet. ⁷For nation will rise against nation, and kingdom against kingdom. And there will be famines, pestilences,^a and earthquakes in various places. ⁸All these *are* the beginning of sorrows.

⁹"Then they will deliver you up to tribulation and kill you, and you will be hated by all nations for My name's sake. ¹⁰And then many will be offended, will betray one another, and will hate one another. ¹¹Then many false prophets will rise up and deceive many. ¹²And because lawlessness will abound, the love of many will grow cold.

24:6 ^aNU-Text omits *all*.   24:7 ^aNU-Text omits *pestilences*.

[13]But he who endures to the end shall be saved. [14]And this gospel of the kingdom will be preached in all the world as a witness to all the nations, and then the end will come.

The Great Tribulation

[15]"Therefore when you see the *'abomination of desolation,'*[a] spoken of by Daniel the prophet, standing in the holy place" (whoever reads, let him understand), [16]"then let those who are in Judea flee to the mountains. [17]Let him who is on the housetop not go down to take anything out of his house. [18]And let him who is in the field not go back to get his clothes. [19]But woe to those who are pregnant and to those who are nursing babies in those days! [20]And pray that your flight may not be in winter or on the Sabbath. [21]For then there will be great tribulation, such as has not been since the beginning of the world until this time, no, nor ever shall be. [22]And unless those days were shortened, no flesh would be saved; but for the elect's sake those days will be shortened.

[23]"Then if anyone says to you, 'Look, here is the Christ!' or 'There!' do not believe it. [24]For false christs and false prophets will rise and show great signs and wonders to deceive, if possible, even the elect. [25]See, I have told you beforehand.

[26]"Therefore if they say to you, 'Look, He is in the desert!' do not go out; *or* 'Look, *He is* in the inner rooms!' do not believe it. [27]For as the lightning comes from the east and flashes to the west, so also will the coming of the Son of Man be. [28]For wherever the carcass is, there the eagles will be gathered together.

24:15 [a]Daniel 11:31; 12:11

The Coming of the Son of Man

²⁹"Immediately after the tribulation of those days the sun will be darkened, and the moon will not give its light; the stars will fall from heaven, and the powers of the heavens will be shaken. ³⁰Then the sign of the Son of Man will appear in heaven, and then all the tribes of the earth will mourn, and they will see the Son of Man coming on the clouds of heaven with power and great glory. ³¹And He will send His angels with a great sound of a trumpet, and they will gather together His elect from the four winds, from one end of heaven to the other.

The Parable of the Fig Tree

³²"Now learn this parable from the fig tree: When its branch has already become tender and puts forth leaves, you know that summer is near. ³³So you also, when you see all these things, know that it[a] is near—at the doors! ³⁴Assuredly, I say to you, this generation will by no means pass away till all these things take place. ³⁵Heaven and earth will pass away, but My words will by no means pass away.

No One Knows the Day or Hour

³⁶"But of that day and hour no one knows, not even the angels of heaven,[a] but My Father only. ³⁷But as the days of Noah were, so also will the coming of the Son of Man be. ³⁸For as in the days before the flood, they were eating and drinking, marrying and giving in marriage, until the day that Noah entered the ark, ³⁹and did not know until the flood came and took them all away, so also will the coming of the Son of Man

24:33 ªOr He   24:36 ªNU-Text adds nor the Son.

be. ⁴⁰Then two *men* will be in the field: one will be taken and the other left. ⁴¹Two *women will be* grinding at the mill: one will be taken and the other left. ⁴²Watch therefore, for you do not know what hour^a your Lord is coming. ⁴³But know this, that if the master of the house had known what hour the thief would come, he would have watched and not allowed his house to be broken into. ⁴⁴Therefore you also be ready, for the Son of Man is coming at an hour you do not expect.

The Faithful Servant and the Evil Servant

⁴⁵"Who then is a faithful and wise servant, whom his master made ruler over his household, to give them food in due season? ⁴⁶Blessed *is* that servant whom his master, when he comes, will find so doing. ⁴⁷Assuredly, I say to you that he will make him ruler over all his goods. ⁴⁸But if that evil servant says in his heart, 'My master is delaying his coming,'^a ⁴⁹and begins to beat *his* fellow servants, and to eat and drink with the drunkards, ⁵⁰the master of that servant will come on a day when he is not looking for *him* and at an hour that he is not aware of, ⁵¹and will cut him in two and appoint *him* his portion with the hypocrites. There shall be weeping and gnashing of teeth.

The Parable of the Wise and Foolish Virgins

25 "Then the kingdom of heaven shall be likened to ten virgins who took their lamps and went out to meet the bridegroom.

24:42 ^aNU-Text reads *day.*   24:48 ^aNU-Text omits *his coming.*

²Now five of them were wise, and five *were* fool-ish. ³Those who *were* foolish took their lamps and took no oil with them, ⁴but the wise took oil in their vessels with their lamps. ⁵But while the bridegroom was delayed, they all slumbered and slept.

⁶"And at midnight a cry was *heard:* 'Behold, the bridegroom is coming;[a] go out to meet him!' ⁷Then all those virgins arose and trimmed their lamps. ⁸And the foolish said to the wise, 'Give us *some* of your oil, for our lamps are going out.' ⁹But the wise answered, saying, 'No, lest there should not be enough for us and you; but go rather to those who sell, and buy for yourselves.' ¹⁰And while they went to buy, the bridegroom came, and those who were ready went in with him to the wedding; and the door was shut.

¹¹"Afterward the other virgins came also, say-ing, 'Lord, Lord, open to us!' ¹²But he answered and said, 'Assuredly, I say to you, I do not know you.'

¹³"Watch therefore, for you know neither the day nor the hour[a] in which the Son of Man is coming.

The Parable of the Talents

¹⁴"For *the kingdom of heaven* is like a man trav-eling to a far country, *who* called his own servants and delivered his goods to them. ¹⁵And to one he gave five talents, to another two, and to another one, to each according to his own ability; and immediately he went on a journey. ¹⁶Then he who had received the five talents went and traded with them, and made another five talents. ¹⁷And like-

---

25:6 [a]NU-Text omits *is coming.*   25:13 [a]NU-Text omits the rest of this verse.

wise he who *had received* two gained two more also. ¹⁸But he who had received one went and dug in the ground, and hid his lord's money. ¹⁹After a long time the lord of those servants came and settled accounts with them.

²⁰"So he who had received five talents came and brought five other talents, saying, 'Lord, you delivered to me five talents; look, I have gained five more talents besides them.' ²¹His lord said to him, 'Well *done*, good and faithful servant; you were faithful over a few things, I will make you ruler over many things. Enter into the joy of your lord.' ²²He also who had received two talents came and said, 'Lord, you delivered to me two talents; look, I have gained two more talents besides them.' ²³His lord said to him, 'Well *done*, good and faithful servant; you have been faithful over a few things, I will make you ruler over many things. Enter into the joy of your lord.'

²⁴"Then he who had received the one talent came and said, 'Lord, I knew you to be a hard man, reaping where you have not sown, and gathering where you have not scattered seed. ²⁵And I was afraid, and went and hid your talent in the ground. Look, *there* you have *what is* yours.'

²⁶"But his lord answered and said to him, 'You wicked and lazy servant, you knew that I reap where I have not sown, and gather where I have not scattered seed. ²⁷So you ought to have deposited my money with the bankers, and at my coming I would have received back my own with interest. ²⁸So take the talent from him, and give *it* to him who has ten talents.

²⁹'For to everyone who has, more will be given, and he will have abundance; but from him

who does not have, even what he has will be taken away. ³⁰And cast the unprofitable servant into the outer darkness. There will be weeping and gnashing of teeth.'

The Son of Man Will Judge the Nations

³¹"When the Son of Man comes in His glory, and all the holy^a angels with Him, then He will sit on the throne of His glory. ³²All the nations will be gathered before Him, and He will separate them one from another, as a shepherd divides *his* sheep from the goats. ³³And He will set the sheep on His right hand, but the goats on the left. ³⁴Then the King will say to those on His right hand, 'Come, you blessed of My Father, inherit the kingdom prepared for you from the foundation of the world: ³⁵for I was hungry and you gave Me food; I was thirsty and you gave Me drink; I was a stranger and you took Me in; ³⁶I *was* naked and you clothed Me; I was sick and you visited Me; I was in prison and you came to Me.'

³⁷"Then the righteous will answer Him, saying, 'Lord, when did we see You hungry and feed *You,* or thirsty and give *You* drink? ³⁸When did we see You a stranger and take *You* in, or naked and clothe *You?* ³⁹Or when did we see You sick, or in prison, and come to You?' ⁴⁰And the King will answer and say to them, 'Assuredly, I say to you, inasmuch as you did *it* to one of the least of these My brethren, you did *it* to Me.'

⁴¹"Then He will also say to those on the left hand, 'Depart from Me, you cursed, into the everlasting fire prepared for the devil and his angels: ⁴²for I was hungry and you gave Me no

---

25:31 ^aNU-Text omits *holy.*

food; I was thirsty and you gave Me no drink; [43]I was a stranger and you did not take Me in, naked and you did not clothe Me, sick and in prison and you did not visit Me.'

[44]"Then they also will answer Him,[a] saying, 'Lord, when did we see You hungry or thirsty or a stranger or naked or sick or in prison, and did not minister to You?' [45]Then He will answer them, saying, 'Assuredly, I say to you, inasmuch as you did not do *it* to one of the least of these, you did not do *it* to Me.' [46]And these will go away into everlasting punishment, but the righteous into eternal life."

The Plot to Kill Jesus

26 Now it came to pass, when Jesus had finished all these sayings, *that* He said to His disciples, [2]"You know that after two days is the Passover, and the Son of Man will be delivered up to be crucified."

[3]Then the chief priests, the scribes,[a] and the elders of the people assembled at the palace of the high priest, who was called Caiaphas, [4]and plotted to take Jesus by trickery and kill *Him.* [5]But they said, "Not during the feast, lest there be an uproar among the people."

The Anointing at Bethany

[6]And when Jesus was in Bethany at the house of Simon the leper, [7]a woman came to Him having an alabaster flask of very costly fragrant oil, and she poured *it* on His head as He sat *at the table.* [8]But when His disciples saw *it,* they were indignant, saying, "Why this waste? [9]For this fra-

---

25:44 [a]NU-Text and M-Text omit *Him.* 26:3 [a]NU-Text omits *the scribes.*

grant oil might have been sold for much and given to *the* poor."

¹⁰But when Jesus was aware of *it,* He said to them, "Why do you trouble the woman? For she has done a good work for Me. ¹¹For you have the poor with you always, but Me you do not have always. ¹²For in pouring this fragrant oil on My body, she did *it* for My burial. ¹³Assuredly, I say to you, wherever this gospel is preached in the whole world, what this woman has done will also be told as a memorial to her."

Judas Agrees to Betray Jesus

¹⁴Then one of the twelve, called Judas Iscariot, went to the chief priests ¹⁵and said, "What are you willing to give me if I deliver Him to you?" And they counted out to him thirty pieces of silver. ¹⁶So from that time he sought opportunity to betray Him.

Jesus Celebrates Passover
with His Disciples

¹⁷Now on the first *day of the Feast* of the Unleavened Bread the disciples came to Jesus, saying to Him, "Where do You want us to prepare for You to eat the Passover?"

¹⁸And He said, "Go into the city to a certain man, and say to him, 'The Teacher says, "My time is at hand; I will keep the Passover at your house with My disciples." ' "

¹⁹So the disciples did as Jesus had directed them; and they prepared the Passover.

²⁰When evening had come, He sat down with the twelve. ²¹Now as they were eating, He said, "Assuredly, I say to you, one of you will betray Me."

²²And they were exceedingly sorrowful, and each of them began to say to Him, "Lord, is it I?"

²³He answered and said, "He who dipped *his* hand with Me in the dish will betray Me. ²⁴The Son of Man indeed goes just as it is written of Him, but woe to that man by whom the Son of Man is betrayed! It would have been good for that man if he had not been born."

²⁵Then Judas, who was betraying Him, answered and said, "Rabbi, is it I?"

He said to him, "You have said it."

Jesus Institutes the Lord's Supper

²⁶And as they were eating, Jesus took bread, blessed[a] and broke *it,* and gave *it* to the disciples and said, "Take, eat; this is My body."

²⁷Then He took the cup, and gave thanks, and gave *it* to them, saying, "Drink from it, all of you. ²⁸For this is My blood of the new[a] covenant, which is shed for many for the remission of sins. ²⁹But I say to you, I will not drink of this fruit of the vine from now on until that day when I drink it new with you in My Father's kingdom."

³⁰And when they had sung a hymn, they went out to the Mount of Olives.

Jesus Predicts Peter's Denial

³¹Then Jesus said to them, "All of you will be made to stumble because of Me this night, for it is written:

> '*I will strike the Shepherd,*
> *And the sheep of the flock will be*
> *scattered.*'[a]

26:26 [a]M-Text reads *gave thanks for.*   **26:28** [a]NU-Text omits *new.*
26:31 [a]Zechariah 13:7

³²But after I have been raised, I will go before you to Galilee."

³³Peter answered and said to Him, "Even if all are made to stumble because of You, I will never be made to stumble."

³⁴Jesus said to him, "Assuredly, I say to you that this night, before the rooster crows, you will deny Me three times."

³⁵Peter said to Him, "Even if I have to die with You, I will not deny You!"

And so said all the disciples.

The Prayer in the Garden

³⁶Then Jesus came with them to a place called Gethsemane, and said to the disciples, "Sit here while I go and pray over there." ³⁷And He took with Him Peter and the two sons of Zebedee, and He began to be sorrowful and deeply distressed. ³⁸Then He said to them, "My soul is exceedingly sorrowful, even to death. Stay here and watch with Me."

³⁹He went a little farther and fell on His face, and prayed, saying, "O My Father, if it is possible, let this cup pass from Me; nevertheless, not as I will, but as You *will*."

⁴⁰Then He came to the disciples and found them sleeping, and said to Peter, "What! Could you not watch with Me one hour? ⁴¹Watch and pray, lest you enter into temptation. The spirit indeed *is* willing, but the flesh *is* weak."

⁴²Again, a second time, He went away and prayed, saying, "O My Father, if this cup cannot pass away from Me unless[a] I drink it, Your will be done." ⁴³And He came and found them asleep again, for their eyes were heavy.

26:42 [a]NU-Text reads *if this may not pass away unless.*

[44]So He left them, went away again, and prayed the third time, saying the same words. [45]Then He came to His disciples and said to them, "Are *you* still sleeping and resting? Behold, the hour is at hand, and the Son of Man is being betrayed into the hands of sinners. [46]Rise, let us be going. See, My betrayer is at hand."

Betrayal and Arrest in Gethsemane

[47]And while He was still speaking, behold, Judas, one of the twelve, with a great multitude with swords and clubs, came from the chief priests and elders of the people.

[48]Now His betrayer had given them a sign, saying, "Whomever I kiss, He is the One; seize Him." [49]Immediately he went up to Jesus and said, "Greetings, Rabbi!" and kissed Him.

[50]But Jesus said to him, "Friend, why have you come?"

Then they came and laid hands on Jesus and took Him. [51]And suddenly, one of those *who were* with Jesus stretched out *his* hand and drew his sword, struck the servant of the high priest, and cut off his ear.

[52]But Jesus said to him, "Put your sword in its place, for all who take the sword will perish[a] by the sword. [53]Or do you think that I cannot now pray to My Father, and He will provide Me with more than twelve legions of angels? [54]How then could the Scriptures be fulfilled, that it must happen thus?"

[55]In that hour Jesus said to the multitudes, "Have you come out, as against a robber, with swords and clubs to take Me? I sat daily with you, teaching in the temple, and you did not

26:52 [a]M-Text reads *die.*

seize Me. ⁵⁶But all this was done that the Scriptures of the prophets might be fulfilled."

Then all the disciples forsook Him and fled.

Jesus Faces the Sanhedrin

⁵⁷And those who had laid hold of Jesus led *Him* away to Caiaphas the high priest, where the scribes and the elders were assembled. ⁵⁸But Peter followed Him at a distance to the high priest's courtyard. And he went in and sat with the servants to see the end.

⁵⁹Now the chief priests, the elders,ᵃ and all the council sought false testimony against Jesus to put Him to death, ⁶⁰but found none. Even though many false witnesses came forward, they found none.ᵃ But at last two false witnessesᵇ came forward ⁶¹and said, "This *fellow* said, 'I am able to destroy the temple of God and to build it in three days.' "

⁶²And the high priest arose and said to Him, "Do You answer nothing? What is *it* these men testify against You?" ⁶³But Jesus kept silent. And the high priest answered and said to Him, "I put You under oath by the living God: Tell us if You are the Christ, the Son of God!"

⁶⁴Jesus said to him, "*It is as* you said. Nevertheless, I say to you, hereafter you will see the Son of Man sitting at the right hand of the Power, and coming on the clouds of heaven."

⁶⁵Then the high priest tore his clothes, saying, "He has spoken blasphemy! What further need do we have of witnesses? Look, now you have heard His blasphemy! ⁶⁶What do you think?"

26:59 ᵃNU-Text omits *the elders*.   26:60 ᵃNU-Text puts a comma after *but found none,* does not capitalize *Even,* and omits *they found none.* ᵇNU-Text omits *false witnesses.*

How do you know the Bible is true?

There are many ways to know that the Bible is the Word of God. For example, it has amazing continuity. If you take any biblical theme (for example, the subject of "blood") and follow it from the Old Testament into the New Testament, you will find incredible continuity and harmony, even though the Scriptures were written over a period of 1,500 years by about 40 different people from all walks of life.

Or if you study the nature of the Creator—that He is perfect, holy, just, and good—you will find the same consistency throughout the Scriptures. This is because the Bible was written by one Author—God, who used men to write His words to mankind, just as you would use a pen to write a letter.

You can also know that the Bible is the Word of God because of its hundreds of fulfilled prophecies. Unlike other books, the Bible offers a multitude of detailed predictions—some thousands of years in advance—that have been literally fulfilled. No other religious text has specific, repeated, and unfailing fulfillment of predictions many years in advance of events over which the predictor had no control.

The Scriptures predicted the rise and fall of great empires, foretold the destruction of cities, and prophesied of the reign and death of national leaders. Even more important are the many prophecies of a coming Messiah. God said He would send someone to redeem mankind from sin, and He wanted there to be no mistake about who that Person would be. There are over three hundred prophecies that tell of the ancestry, birth, life, ministry, death, resurrection, and ascension of Jesus of Nazareth. All have been literally fulfilled to the smallest detail.

Only one who is omniscient can accurately predict details of events thousands of years in the future. God provided this evidence for us so we would know that the Scriptures have a divine Author. In all, over 25 percent of the entire Bible contains specific predictive prophecies that have been literally fulfilled. This is true of no other book in the world. And it is a sure sign of its divine origin.

In addition, archaeological evidence attests to the accuracy of the Scriptures. There have been over 25,000 archaeological finds that relate to people, places, and events in the Bible, and not one has ever refuted a biblical statement. The Bible is not only historically true, but it gives a purpose for history. History is not merely a series of unrelated events. The Bible tells us the beginning and shows a progression to an end, and promises that the world in which we live, with all its corruption, will one day be made into a new world without sin.

However, there is another way to know that the Bible is the Word of God. It speaks to the *experience* of the Christian.

Imagine if you were given a dry, complicated instruction book that didn't make much sense to you. Then someone gave you a very complex appliance that you had no idea how to operate.

You wondered if the instruction book was made by the appliance manufacturer, so you opened it with that in mind. It said to plug the appliance into an electrical outlet, and then to adjust three switches on the left, and a red light would come on. When you flicked the three switches, the red light came on.

It gave you fifteen more instructions, which you diligently carried out. You then flicked the main switch, a blue light came on as it said it should, and the appliance turned on and ran perfectly. Your experience proved to you that the instruction book in your hand was for the complex appliance.

You are the complex appliance, and the Bible is your instruction Book. Do what it says and you will find *by experience* that it was indeed written by the Manufacturer.

They answered and said, "He is deserving of death."

⁶⁷Then they spat in His face and beat Him; and others struck *Him* with the palms of their hands, ⁶⁸saying, "Prophesy to us, Christ! Who is the one who struck You?"

Peter Denies Jesus, and Weeps Bitterly

⁶⁹Now Peter sat outside in the courtyard. And a servant girl came to him, saying, "You also were with Jesus of Galilee."

⁷⁰But he denied it before *them* all, saying, "I do not know what you are saying."

⁷¹And when he had gone out to the gateway, another *girl* saw him and said to those *who were* there, "This *fellow* also was with Jesus of Nazareth."

⁷²But again he denied with an oath, "I do not know the Man!"

⁷³And a little later those who stood by came up and said to Peter, "Surely you also are *one* of them, for your speech betrays you."

⁷⁴Then he began to curse and swear, *saying,* "I do not know the Man!"

Immediately a rooster crowed. ⁷⁵And Peter remembered the word of Jesus who had said to him, "Before the rooster crows, you will deny Me three times." So he went out and wept bitterly.

Jesus Handed Over to Pontius Pilate

27 When morning came, all the chief priests and elders of the people plotted against Jesus to put Him to death. ²And when they had bound Him, they led Him away and delivered Him to Pontius[a] Pilate the governor.

27:2 [a]NU-Text omits *Pontius*.

Judas Hangs Himself

³Then Judas, His betrayer, seeing that He had been condemned, was remorseful and brought back the thirty pieces of silver to the chief priests and elders, ⁴saying, "I have sinned by betraying innocent blood."

And they said, "What *is that* to us? You see *to it!*"

⁵Then he threw down the pieces of silver in the temple and departed, and went and hanged himself.

⁶But the chief priests took the silver pieces and said, "It is not lawful to put them into the treasury, because they are the price of blood." ⁷And they consulted together and bought with them the potter's field, to bury strangers in. ⁸Therefore that field has been called the Field of Blood to this day.

⁹Then was fulfilled what was spoken by Jeremiah the prophet, saying, *"And they took the thirty pieces of silver, the value of Him who was priced, whom they of the children of Israel priced,* ¹⁰*and gave them for the potter's field, as the Lord directed me."*ᵃ

Jesus Faces Pilate

¹¹Now Jesus stood before the governor. And the governor asked Him, saying, "Are You the King of the Jews?"

Jesus said to him, *"It is as you say."* ¹²And while He was being accused by the chief priests and elders, He answered nothing.

¹³Then Pilate said to Him, "Do You not hear how many things they testify against You?" ¹⁴But He answered him not one word, so that the gov-

---

27:10 ᵃJeremiah 32:6–9

ernor marveled greatly.

Taking the Place of Barabbas

[15]Now at the feast the governor was accustomed to releasing to the multitude one prisoner whom they wished. [16]And at that time they had a notorious prisoner called Barabbas.[a] [17]Therefore, when they had gathered together, Pilate said to them, "Whom do you want me to release to you? Barabbas, or Jesus who is called Christ?" [18]For he knew that they had handed Him over because of envy.

[19]While he was sitting on the judgment seat, his wife sent to him, saying, "Have nothing to do with that just Man, for I have suffered many things today in a dream because of Him."

[20]But the chief priests and elders persuaded the multitudes that they should ask for Barabbas and destroy Jesus. [21]The governor answered and said to them, "Which of the two do you want me to release to you?"

They said, "Barabbas!"

[22]Pilate said to them, "What then shall I do with Jesus who is called Christ?"

They all said to him, "Let Him be crucified!"

[23]Then the governor said, "Why, what evil has He done?"

But they cried out all the more, saying, "Let Him be crucified!"

[24]When Pilate saw that he could not prevail at all, but rather *that* a tumult was rising, he took water and washed *his* hands before the multitude, saying, "I am innocent of the blood of this just Person.[a] You see *to it.*"

27:16 [a]NU-Text reads *Jesus Barabbas.* 27:24 [a]NU-Text omits *just.*

²⁵And all the people answered and said, "His blood *be* on us and on our children."

²⁶Then he released Barabbas to them; and when he had scourged Jesus, he delivered *Him* to be crucified.

The Soldiers Mock Jesus

²⁷Then the soldiers of the governor took Jesus into the Praetorium and gathered the whole garrison around Him. ²⁸And they stripped Him and put a scarlet robe on Him. ²⁹When they had twisted a crown of thorns, they put *it* on His head, and a reed in His right hand. And they bowed the knee before Him and mocked Him, saying, "Hail, King of the Jews!" ³⁰Then they spat on Him, and took the reed and struck Him on the head. ³¹And when they had mocked Him, they took the robe off Him, put His *own* clothes on Him, and led Him away to be crucified.

The King on a Cross

³²Now as they came out, they found a man of Cyrene, Simon by name. Him they compelled to bear His cross. ³³And when they had come to a place called Golgotha, that is to say, Place of a Skull, ³⁴they gave Him sourᵃ wine mingled with gall to drink. But when He had tasted *it*, He would not drink.

³⁵Then they crucified Him, and divided His garments, casting lots,ᵃ that it might be fulfilled which was spoken by the prophet:

> "They divided My garments among them,
> And for My clothing they cast lots."ᵇ

27:34 ᵃNU-Text omits *sour*.   27:35 ᵃNU-Text and M-Text omit the rest of this verse.   ᵇPsalm 22:18

³⁶Sitting down, they kept watch over Him there. ³⁷And they put up over His head the accusation written against Him:

THIS IS JESUS
THE KING OF THE JEWS.

³⁸Then two robbers were crucified with Him, one on the right and another on the left.

³⁹And those who passed by blasphemed Him, wagging their heads ⁴⁰and saying, "You who destroy the temple and build *it* in three days, save Yourself! If You are the Son of God, come down from the cross."

⁴¹Likewise the chief priests also, mocking with the scribes and elders,ᵃ said, ⁴²"He saved others; Himself He cannot save. If He is the King of Israel,ᵃ let Him now come down from the cross, and we will believe Him.ᵇ ⁴³He trusted in God; let Him deliver Him now if He will have Him; for He said, 'I am the Son of God.' "

⁴⁴Even the robbers who were crucified with Him reviled Him with the same thing.

Jesus Dies on the Cross

⁴⁵Now from the sixth hour until the ninth hour there was darkness over all the land. ⁴⁶And about the ninth hour Jesus cried out with a loud voice, saying, "Eli, Eli, lama sabachthani?" that is, *"My God, My God, why have You forsaken Me?"*ᵃ

⁴⁷Some of those who stood there, when they heard *that,* said, "This Man is calling for Elijah!" ⁴⁸Immediately one of them ran and took a

---

27:41 ᵃM-Text reads *with the scribes, the Pharisees, and the elders.* 27:42 ᵃNU-Text reads *He is the King of Israel!* ᵇNU-Text and M-Text read *we will believe in Him.* 27:46 ᵃPsalm 22:1

sponge, filled *it* with sour wine and put *it* on a reed, and offered it to Him to drink.

[49]The rest said, "Let Him alone; let us see if Elijah will come to save Him."

[50]And Jesus cried out again with a loud voice, and yielded up His spirit.

[51]Then, behold, the veil of the temple was torn in two from top to bottom; and the earth quaked, and the rocks were split, [52]and the graves were opened; and many bodies of the saints who had fallen asleep were raised; [53]and coming out of the graves after His resurrection, they went into the holy city and appeared to many.

[54]So when the centurion and those with him, who were guarding Jesus, saw the earthquake and the things that had happened, they feared greatly, saying, "Truly this was the Son of God!"

[55]And many women who followed Jesus from Galilee, ministering to Him, were there looking on from afar, [56]among whom were Mary Magdalene, Mary the mother of James and Joses,[a] and the mother of Zebedee's sons.

Jesus Buried in Joseph's Tomb

[57]Now when evening had come, there came a rich man from Arimathea, named Joseph, who himself had also become a disciple of Jesus. [58]This man went to Pilate and asked for the body of Jesus. Then Pilate commanded the body to be given to him. [59]When Joseph had taken the body, he wrapped it in a clean linen cloth, [60]and laid it in his new tomb which he had hewn out of the rock; and he rolled a large stone against the door of the tomb, and departed. [61]And Mary

---

27:56 [a]NU-Text reads *Joseph.*

Magdalene was there, and the other Mary, sitting opposite the tomb.

Pilate Sets a Guard

[62]On the next day, which followed the Day of Preparation, the chief priests and Pharisees gathered together to Pilate, [63]saying, "Sir, we remember, while He was still alive, how that deceiver said, 'After three days I will rise.' [64]Therefore command that the tomb be made secure until the third day, lest His disciples come by night[a] and steal Him *away,* and say to the people, 'He has risen from the dead.' So the last deception will be worse than the first."

[65]Pilate said to them, "You have a guard; go your way, make *it* as secure as you know how." [66]So they went and made the tomb secure, sealing the stone and setting the guard.

He Is Risen

28 Now after the Sabbath, as the first *day* of the week began to dawn, Mary Magdalene and the other Mary came to see the tomb. [2]And behold, there was a great earthquake; for an angel of the Lord descended from heaven, and came and rolled back the stone from the door,[a] and sat on it. [3]His countenance was like lightning, and his clothing as white as snow. [4]And the guards shook for fear of him, and became like dead *men.*

[5]But the angel answered and said to the women, "Do not be afraid, for I know that you seek Jesus who was crucified. [6]He is not here; for He is risen, as He said. Come, see the place where

27:64 [a]NU-Text omits *by night.*   28:2 [a]NU-Text omits *from the door.*

the Lord lay. [7]And go quickly and tell His disciples that He is risen from the dead, and indeed He is going before you into Galilee; there you will see Him. Behold, I have told you."

[8]So they went out quickly from the tomb with fear and great joy, and ran to bring His disciples word.

The Women Worship the Risen Lord

[9]And as they went to tell His disciples,[a] behold, Jesus met them, saying, "Rejoice!" So they came and held Him by the feet and worshiped Him. [10]Then Jesus said to them, "Do not be afraid. Go *and* tell My brethren to go to Galilee, and there they will see Me."

The Soldiers Are Bribed

[11]Now while they were going, behold, some of the guard came into the city and reported to the chief priests all the things that had happened. [12]When they had assembled with the elders and consulted together, they gave a large sum of money to the soldiers, [13]saying, "Tell them, 'His disciples came at night and stole Him *away* while we slept.' [14]And if this comes to the governor's ears, we will appease him and make you secure." [15]So they took the money and did as they were instructed; and this saying is commonly reported among the Jews until this day.

The Great Commission

[16]Then the eleven disciples went away into Galilee, to the mountain which Jesus had appointed for them. [17]When they saw Him, they worshiped Him; but some doubted.

28:9 [a]NU-Text omits the first clause of this verse.

¹⁸And Jesus came and spoke to them, saying, "All authority has been given to Me in heaven and on earth. ¹⁹Go therefore[a] and make disciples of all the nations, baptizing them in the name of the Father and of the Son and of the Holy Spirit, ²⁰teaching them to observe all things that I have commanded you; and lo, I am with you always, *even* to the end of the age." Amen.[a]

28:19 [a]M-Text omits *therefore*.   28:20 [a]NU-Text omits *Amen*.

Mark

John the Baptist Prepares the Way

1 The beginning of the gospel of Jesus Christ, the Son of God. ²As it is written in the Prophets:[a]

> "Behold, I send My messenger before Your
>   face,
>   Who will prepare Your way before You."[b]
> ³"The voice of one crying in the wilderness:
>   'Prepare the way of the LORD;
>   Make His paths straight.' "[a]

⁴John came baptizing in the wilderness and preaching a baptism of repentance for the remission of sins. ⁵Then all the land of Judea, and those from Jerusalem, went out to him and were all baptized by him in the Jordan River, confessing their sins.

⁶Now John was clothed with camel's hair and with a leather belt around his waist, and he ate locusts and wild honey. ⁷And he preached, saying, "There comes One after me who is mightier than I, whose sandal strap I am not worthy to stoop down and loose. ⁸I indeed baptized you with water, but He will baptize you with the Holy Spirit."

John Baptizes Jesus

⁹It came to pass in those days that Jesus came from Nazareth of Galilee, and was baptized by John in the Jordan. ¹⁰And immediately, coming

---

1:2 ᵃNU-Text reads *Isaiah the prophet.* ᵇMalachi 3:1   1:3 ᵃIsaiah 40:3

up from[a] the water, He saw the heavens parting and the Spirit descending upon Him like a dove. [11]Then a voice came from heaven, "You are My beloved Son, in whom I am well pleased."

Satan Tempts Jesus

[12]Immediately the Spirit drove Him into the wilderness. [13]And He was there in the wilderness forty days, tempted by Satan, and was with the wild beasts; and the angels ministered to Him.

Jesus Begins His Galilean Ministry

[14]Now after John was put in prison, Jesus came to Galilee, preaching the gospel of the kingdom[a] of God, [15]and saying, "The time is fulfilled, and the kingdom of God is at hand. Repent, and believe in the gospel."

Four Fishermen Called as Disciples

[16]And as He walked by the Sea of Galilee, He saw Simon and Andrew his brother casting a net into the sea; for they were fishermen. [17]Then Jesus said to them, "Follow Me, and I will make you become fishers of men." [18]They immediately left their nets and followed Him.

[19]When He had gone a little farther from there, He saw James the *son* of Zebedee, and John his brother, who also *were* in the boat mending their nets. [20]And immediately He called them, and they left their father Zebedee in the boat with the hired servants, and went after Him.

Jesus Casts Out an Unclean Spirit

[21]Then they went into Capernaum, and im-

1:10 [a]NU-Text reads *out of.* **1:14** [a]NU-Text omits *of the kingdom.*

mediately on the Sabbath He entered the synagogue and taught. ²²And they were astonished at His teaching, for He taught them as one having authority, and not as the scribes.

²³Now there was a man in their synagogue with an unclean spirit. And he cried out, ²⁴saying, "Let *us* alone! What have we to do with You, Jesus of Nazareth? Did You come to destroy us? I know who You are—the Holy One of God!"

²⁵But Jesus rebuked him, saying, "Be quiet, and come out of him!" ²⁶And when the unclean spirit had convulsed him and cried out with a loud voice, he came out of him. ²⁷Then they were all amazed, so that they questioned among themselves, saying, "What is this? What new doctrine is this? For with authority^a He commands even the unclean spirits, and they obey Him." ²⁸And immediately His fame spread throughout all the region around Galilee.

Peter's Mother-in-Law Healed

²⁹Now as soon as they had come out of the synagogue, they entered the house of Simon and Andrew, with James and John. ³⁰But Simon's wife's mother lay sick with a fever, and they told Him about her at once. ³¹So He came and took her by the hand and lifted her up, and immediately the fever left her. And she served them.

Many Healed After Sabbath Sunset

³²At evening, when the sun had set, they brought to Him all who were sick and those who were demon-possessed. ³³And the whole city was gathered together at the door. ³⁴Then He healed many who were sick with various diseases, and

1:27 ^aNU-Text reads *What is this? A new doctrine with authority.*

cast out many demons; and He did not allow the demons to speak, because they knew Him.

Preaching in Galilee

[35]Now in the morning, having risen a long while before daylight, He went out and departed to a solitary place; and there He prayed. [36]And Simon and those *who were* with Him searched for Him. [37]When they found Him, they said to Him, "Everyone is looking for You."

[38]But He said to them, "Let us go into the next towns, that I may preach there also, because for this purpose I have come forth."

[39]And He was preaching in their synagogues throughout all Galilee, and casting out demons.

Jesus Cleanses a Leper

[40]Now a leper came to Him, imploring Him, kneeling down to Him and saying to Him, "If You are willing, You can make me clean."

[41]Then Jesus, moved with compassion, stretched out *His* hand and touched him, and said to him, "I am willing; be cleansed." [42]As soon as He had spoken, immediately the leprosy left him, and he was cleansed. [43]And He strictly warned him and sent him away at once, [44]and said to him, "See that you say nothing to anyone; but go your way, show yourself to the priest, and offer for your cleansing those things which Moses commanded, as a testimony to them."

[45]However, he went out and began to proclaim *it* freely, and to spread the matter, so that Jesus could no longer openly enter the city, but was outside in deserted places; and they came to Him from every direction.

Jesus Forgives and Heals a Paralytic

2And again He entered Capernaum after *some* days, and it was heard that He was in the house. [2]Immediately[a] many gathered together, so that there was no longer room to receive *them*, not even near the door. And He preached the word to them. [3]Then they came to Him, bringing a paralytic who was carried by four *men.* [4]And when they could not come near Him because of the crowd, they uncovered the roof where He was. So when they had broken through, they let down the bed on which the paralytic was lying.

[5]When Jesus saw their faith, He said to the paralytic, "Son, your sins are forgiven you."

[6]And some of the scribes were sitting there and reasoning in their hearts, [7]"Why does this *Man* speak blasphemies like this? Who can forgive sins but God alone?"

[8]But immediately, when Jesus perceived in His spirit that they reasoned thus within themselves, He said to them, "Why do you reason about these things in your hearts? [9]Which is easier, to say to the paralytic, '*Your* sins are forgiven you,' or to say, 'Arise, take up your bed and walk'? [10]But that you may know that the Son of Man has power on earth to forgive sins"—He said to the paralytic, [11]"I say to you, arise, take up your bed, and go to your house." [12]Immediately he arose, took up the bed, and went out in the presence of them all, so that all were amazed and glorified God, saying, "We never saw *anything* like this!"

Matthew the Tax Collector

[13]Then He went out again by the sea; and all the multitude came to Him, and He taught them.

2:2 [a]NU-Text omits *Immediately.*

[14]As He passed by, He saw Levi the *son* of Alphaeus sitting at the tax office. And He said to him, "Follow Me." So he arose and followed Him.

[15]Now it happened, as He was dining in *Levi's* house, that many tax collectors and sinners also sat together with Jesus and His disciples; for there were many, and they followed Him. [16]And when the scribes and[a] Pharisees saw Him eating with the tax collectors and sinners, they said to His disciples, "How *is it* that He eats and drinks with tax collectors and sinners?"

[17]When Jesus heard *it,* He said to them, "Those who are well have no need of a physician, but those who are sick. I did not come to call *the* righteous, but sinners, to repentance."[a]

Jesus Is Questioned About Fasting

[18]The disciples of John and of the Pharisees were fasting. Then they came and said to Him, "Why do the disciples of John and of the Pharisees fast, but Your disciples do not fast?"

[19]And Jesus said to them, "Can the friends of the bridegroom fast while the bridegroom is with them? As long as they have the bridegroom with them they cannot fast. [20]But the days will come when the bridegroom will be taken away from them, and then they will fast in those days. [21]No one sews a piece of unshrunk cloth on an old garment; or else the new piece pulls away from the old, and the tear is made worse. [22]And no one puts new wine into old wineskins; or else the new wine bursts the wineskins, the wine is spilled, and the wineskins are ruined. But new wine must be put into new wineskins."

2:16 [a]NU-Text reads *of the.*   2:17 [a]NU-Text omits *to repentance.*

Jesus Is Lord of the Sabbath

²³Now it happened that He went through the grainfields on the Sabbath; and as they went His disciples began to pluck the heads of grain. ²⁴And the Pharisees said to Him, "Look, why do they do what is not lawful on the Sabbath?"

²⁵But He said to them, "Have you never read what David did when he was in need and hungry, he and those with him: ²⁶how he went into the house of God *in the days* of Abiathar the high priest, and ate the showbread, which is not lawful to eat except for the priests, and also gave some to those who were with him?"

²⁷And He said to them, "The Sabbath was made for man, and not man for the Sabbath. ²⁸Therefore the Son of Man is also Lord of the Sabbath."

Healing on the Sabbath

3 And He entered the synagogue again, and a man was there who had a withered hand. ²So they watched Him closely, whether He would heal him on the Sabbath, so that they might accuse Him. ³And He said to the man who had the withered hand, "Step forward." ⁴Then He said to them, "Is it lawful on the Sabbath to do good or to do evil, to save life or to kill?" But they kept silent. ⁵And when He had looked around at them with anger, being grieved by the hardness of their hearts, He said to the man, "Stretch out your hand." And he stretched *it* out, and his hand was restored as whole as the other.ᵃ ⁶Then the Pharisees went out and immediately plotted with the Herodians against Him, how they might destroy Him.

3:5 ᵃNU-Text omits *as whole as the other.*

A Great Multitude Follows Jesus

[7]But Jesus withdrew with His disciples to the sea. And a great multitude from Galilee followed Him, and from Judea [8]and Jerusalem and Idumea and beyond the Jordan; and those from Tyre and Sidon, a great multitude, when they heard how many things He was doing, came to Him. [9]So He told His disciples that a small boat should be kept ready for Him because of the multitude, lest they should crush Him. [10]For He healed many, so that as many as had afflictions pressed about Him to touch Him. [11]And the unclean spirits, whenever they saw Him, fell down before Him and cried out, saying, "You are the Son of God." [12]But He sternly warned them that they should not make Him known.

The Twelve Apostles

[13]And He went up on the mountain and called to *Him* those He Himself wanted. And they came to Him. [14]Then He appointed twelve,[a] that they might be with Him and that He might send them out to preach, [15]and to have power to heal sicknesses and[a] to cast out demons: [16]Simon,[a] to whom He gave the name Peter; [17]James the *son* of Zebedee and John the brother of James, to whom He gave the name Boanerges, that is, "Sons of Thunder"; [18]Andrew, Philip, Bartholomew, Matthew, Thomas, James the *son* of Alphaeus, Thaddaeus, Simon the Cananite; [19]and Judas Iscariot, who also betrayed Him. And they went into a house.

3:14 [a]NU-Text adds *whom He also named apostles.*   3:15 [a]NU-Text omits *to heal sicknesses and.*   3:16 [a]NU-Text reads *and He appointed the twelve: Simon. . . .*

A House Divided Cannot Stand

[20]Then the multitude came together again, so that they could not so much as eat bread. [21]But when His own people heard *about this*, they went out to lay hold of Him, for they said, "He is out of His mind."

[22]And the scribes who came down from Jerusalem said, "He has Beelzebub," and, "By the ruler of the demons He casts out demons."

[23]So He called them to *Himself* and said to them in parables: "How can Satan cast out Satan? [24]If a kingdom is divided against itself, that kingdom cannot stand. [25]And if a house is divided against itself, that house cannot stand. [26]And if Satan has risen up against himself, and is divided, he cannot stand, but has an end. [27]No one can enter a strong man's house and plunder his goods, unless he first binds the strong man. And then he will plunder his house.

The Unpardonable Sin

[28]"Assuredly, I say to you, all sins will be forgiven the sons of men, and whatever blasphemies they may utter; [29]but he who blasphemes against the Holy Spirit never has forgiveness, but is subject to eternal condemnation"— [30]because they said, "He has an unclean spirit."

Jesus' Mother and Brothers Send for Him

[31]Then His brothers and His mother came, and standing outside they sent to Him, calling Him. [32]And a multitude was sitting around Him; and they said to Him, "Look, Your mother and Your brothers[a] are outside seeking You."

3:32 [a]NU-Text and M-Text add *and Your sisters*.

³³But He answered them, saying, "Who is My mother, or My brothers?" ³⁴And He looked around in a circle at those who sat about Him, and said, "Here are My mother and My brothers! ³⁵For whoever does the will of God is My brother and My sister and mother."

The Parable of the Sower

4 And again He began to teach by the sea. And a great multitude was gathered to Him, so that He got into a boat and sat *in it* on the sea; and the whole multitude was on the land facing the sea. ²Then He taught them many things by parables, and said to them in His teaching:

³"Listen! Behold, a sower went out to sow. ⁴And it happened, as he sowed, *that* some *seed* fell by the wayside; and the birds of the air[a] came and devoured it. ⁵Some fell on stony ground, where it did not have much earth; and immediately it sprang up because it had no depth of earth. ⁶But when the sun was up it was scorched, and because it had no root it withered away. ⁷And some *seed* fell among thorns; and the thorns grew up and choked it, and it yielded no crop. ⁸But other *seed* fell on good ground and yielded a crop that sprang up, increased and produced: some thirtyfold, some sixty, and some a hundred."

⁹And He said to them,[a] "He who has ears to hear, let him hear!"

The Purpose of Parables

¹⁰But when He was alone, those around Him with the twelve asked Him about the parable.

4:4 [a]NU-Text and M-Text omit *of the air.*   4:9 [a]NU-Text and M-Text omit *to them.*

[11]And He said to them, "To you it has been given to know the mystery of the kingdom of God; but to those who are outside, all things come in parables, [12]so that

'Seeing they may see and not perceive,
And hearing they may hear and not
    understand;
Lest they should turn,
And their sins be forgiven them.' "[a]

The Parable of the Sower Explained

[13]And He said to them, "Do you not understand this parable? How then will you understand all the parables? [14]The sower sows the word. [15]And these are the ones by the wayside where the word is sown. When they hear, Satan comes immediately and takes away the word that was sown in their hearts. [16]These likewise are the ones sown on stony ground who, when they hear the word, immediately receive it with gladness; [17]and they have no root in themselves, and so endure only for a time. Afterward, when tribulation or persecution arises for the word's sake, immediately they stumble. [18]Now these are the ones sown among thorns; *they are* the ones who hear the word, [19]and the cares of this world, the deceitfulness of riches, and the desires for other things entering in choke the word, and it becomes unfruitful. [20]But these are the ones sown on good ground, those who hear the word, accept *it,* and bear fruit: some thirtyfold, some sixty, and some a hundred."

4:12 [a]Isaiah 6:9, 10

Light Under a Basket

²¹Also He said to them, "Is a lamp brought to be put under a basket or under a bed? Is it not to be set on a lampstand? ²²For there is nothing hidden which will not be revealed, nor has anything been kept secret but that it should come to light. ²³If anyone has ears to hear, let him hear."

²⁴Then He said to them, "Take heed what you hear. With the same measure you use, it will be measured to you; and to you who hear, more will be given. ²⁵For whoever has, to him more will be given; but whoever does not have, even what he has will be taken away from him."

The Parable of the Growing Seed

²⁶And He said, "The kingdom of God is as if a man should scatter seed on the ground, ²⁷and should sleep by night and rise by day, and the seed should sprout and grow, he himself does not know how. ²⁸For the earth yields crops by itself: first the blade, then the head, after that the full grain in the head. ²⁹But when the grain ripens, immediately he puts in the sickle, because the harvest has come."

The Parable of the Mustard Seed

³⁰Then He said, "To what shall we liken the kingdom of God? Or with what parable shall we picture it? ³¹It is like a mustard seed which, when it is sown on the ground, is smaller than all the seeds on earth; ³²but when it is sown, it grows up and becomes greater than all herbs, and shoots out large branches, so that the birds of the air may nest under its shade."

Jesus' Use of Parables

[33]And with many such parables He spoke the word to them as they were able to hear *it*. [34]But without a parable He did not speak to them. And when they were alone, He explained all things to His disciples.

Wind and Wave Obey Jesus

[35]On the same day, when evening had come, He said to them, "Let us cross over to the other side." [36]Now when they had left the multitude, they took Him along in the boat as He was. And other little boats were also with Him. [37]And a great windstorm arose, and the waves beat into the boat, so that it was already filling. [38]But He was in the stern, asleep on a pillow. And they awoke Him and said to Him, "Teacher, do You not care that we are perishing?"

[39]Then He arose and rebuked the wind, and said to the sea, "Peace, be still!" And the wind ceased and there was a great calm. [40]But He said to them, "Why are you so fearful? How *is it* that you have no faith?"[a] [41]And they feared exceedingly, and said to one another, "Who can this be, that even the wind and the sea obey Him!"

A Demon-Possessed Man Healed

5 Then they came to the other side of the sea, to the country of the Gadarenes.[a] [2]And when He had come out of the boat, immediately there met Him out of the tombs a man with an unclean spirit, [3]who had *his* dwelling among the tombs; and no one could bind him,[a] not even with chains, [4]because he had often been bound with

4:40 [a]NU-Text reads *Have you still no faith?* 5:1 [a]NU-Text reads *Gerasenes.* 5:3 [a]NU-Text adds *anymore.*

shackles and chains. And the chains had been pulled apart by him, and the shackles broken in pieces; neither could anyone tame him. [5]And always, night and day, he was in the mountains and in the tombs, crying out and cutting himself with stones.

[6]When he saw Jesus from afar, he ran and worshiped Him. [7]And he cried out with a loud voice and said, "What have I to do with You, Jesus, Son of the Most High God? I implore You by God that You do not torment me."

[8]For He said to him, "Come out of the man, unclean spirit!" [9]Then He asked him, "What *is* your name?"

And he answered, saying, "My name *is* Legion; for we are many." [10]Also he begged Him earnestly that He would not send them out of the country.

[11]Now a large herd of swine was feeding there near the mountains. [12]So all the demons begged Him, saying, "Send us to the swine, that we may enter them." [13]And at once Jesus[a] gave them permission. Then the unclean spirits went out and entered the swine (there were about two thousand); and the herd ran violently down the steep place into the sea, and drowned in the sea.

[14]So those who fed the swine fled, and they told *it* in the city and in the country. And they went out to see what it was that had happened. [15]Then they came to Jesus, and saw the one *who had been* demon-possessed and had the legion, sitting and clothed and in his right mind. And they were afraid. [16]And those who saw it told them how it happened to him *who had been* demon-possessed, and about the swine. [17]Then

---

5:13 [a]NU-Text reads *And He gave.*

they began to plead with Him to depart from their region.

¹⁸And when He got into the boat, he who had been demon-possessed begged Him that he might be with Him. ¹⁹However, Jesus did not permit him, but said to him, "Go home to your friends, and tell them what great things the Lord has done for you, and how He has had compassion on you." ²⁰And he departed and began to proclaim in Decapolis all that Jesus had done for him; and all marveled.

A Girl Restored to Life and a Woman Healed

²¹Now when Jesus had crossed over again by boat to the other side, a great multitude gathered to Him; and He was by the sea. ²²And behold, one of the rulers of the synagogue came, Jairus by name. And when he saw Him, he fell at His feet ²³and begged Him earnestly, saying, "My little daughter lies at the point of death. Come and lay Your hands on her, that she may be healed, and she will live." ²⁴So *Jesus* went with him, and a great multitude followed Him and thronged Him.

²⁵Now a certain woman had a flow of blood for twelve years, ²⁶and had suffered many things from many physicians. She had spent all that she had and was no better, but rather grew worse. ²⁷When she heard about Jesus, she came behind *Him* in the crowd and touched His garment. ²⁸For she said, "If only I may touch His clothes, I shall be made well."

²⁹Immediately the fountain of her blood was dried up, and she felt in *her* body that she was healed of the affliction. ³⁰And Jesus, immediately knowing in Himself that power had gone out of

Him, turned around in the crowd and said, "Who touched My clothes?"

³¹But His disciples said to Him, "You see the multitude thronging You, and You say, 'Who touched Me?' "

³²And He looked around to see her who had done this thing. ³³But the woman, fearing and trembling, knowing what had happened to her, came and fell down before Him and told Him the whole truth. ³⁴And He said to her, "Daughter, your faith has made you well. Go in peace, and be healed of your affliction."

³⁵While He was still speaking, *some* came from the ruler of the synagogue's *house* who said, "Your daughter is dead. Why trouble the Teacher any further?"

³⁶As soon as Jesus heard the word that was spoken, He said to the ruler of the synagogue, "Do not be afraid; only believe." ³⁷And He permitted no one to follow Him except Peter, James, and John the brother of James. ³⁸Then He came to the house of the ruler of the synagogue, and saw a tumult and those who wept and wailed loudly. ³⁹When He came in, He said to them, "Why make this commotion and weep? The child is not dead, but sleeping."

⁴⁰And they ridiculed Him. But when He had put them all outside, He took the father and the mother of the child, and those *who were* with Him, and entered where the child was lying. ⁴¹Then He took the child by the hand, and said to her, "Talitha, cumi," which is translated, "Little girl, I say to you, arise." ⁴²Immediately the girl arose and walked, for she was twelve years *of age.* And they were overcome with great amazement. ⁴³But He commanded them strictly that no one

should know it, and said that *something* should
be given her to eat.

Jesus Rejected at Nazareth

6 Then He went out from there and came to
His own country, and His disciples followed
Him. [2]And when the Sabbath had come, He began to teach in the synagogue. And many hearing *Him* were astonished, saying, "Where *did* this
Man *get* these things? And what wisdom *is* this
which is given to Him, that such mighty works
are performed by His hands! [3]Is this not the carpenter, the Son of Mary, and brother of James,
Joses, Judas, and Simon? And are not His sisters
here with us?" So they were offended at Him.

[4]But Jesus said to them, "A prophet is not
without honor except in his own country, among
his own relatives, and in his own house." [5]Now
He could do no mighty work there, except that
He laid His hands on a few sick people and
healed *them*. [6]And He marveled because of their
unbelief. Then He went about the villages in a
circuit, teaching.

Sending Out the Twelve

[7]And He called the twelve to *Himself*, and began to send them out two *by* two, and gave them
power over unclean spirits. [8]He commanded
them to take nothing for the journey except a
staff—no bag, no bread, no copper in *their*
money belts— [9]but to wear sandals, and not to
put on two tunics.

[10]Also He said to them, "In whatever place
you enter a house, stay there till you depart from
that place. [11]And whoever[a] will not receive you

6:11 [a]NU-Text reads *whatever place.*

nor hear you, when you depart from there, shake off the dust under your feet as a testimony against them.[b] Assuredly, I say to you, it will be more tolerable for Sodom and Gomorrah in the day of judgment than for that city!"

[12]So they went out and preached that *people* should repent. [13]And they cast out many demons, and anointed with oil many who were sick, and healed *them*.

John the Baptist Beheaded

[14]Now King Herod heard *of Him,* for His name had become well known. And he said, "John the Baptist is risen from the dead, and therefore these powers are at work in him."

[15]Others said, "It is Elijah."

And others said, "It is the Prophet, or[a] like one of the prophets."

[16]But when Herod heard, he said, "This is John, whom I beheaded; he has been raised from the dead!" [17]For Herod himself had sent and laid hold of John, and bound him in prison for the sake of Herodias, his brother Philip's wife; for he had married her. [18]Because John had said to Herod, "It is not lawful for you to have your brother's wife."

[19]Therefore Herodias held it against him and wanted to kill him, but she could not; [20]for Herod feared John, knowing that he *was* a just and holy man, and he protected him. And when he heard him, he did many things, and heard him gladly.

[21]Then an opportune day came when Herod on his birthday gave a feast for his nobles, the

---

6:11 [b]NU-Text omits the rest of this verse.   6:15 [a]NU-Text and M-Text omit *or.*

high officers, and the chief *men* of Galilee. ²²And when Herodias' daughter herself came in and danced, and pleased Herod and those who sat with him, the king said to the girl, "Ask me whatever you want, and I will give *it* to you." ²³He also swore to her, "Whatever you ask me, I will give you, up to half my kingdom."

²⁴So she went out and said to her mother, "What shall I ask?"

And she said, "The head of John the Baptist!"

²⁵Immediately she came in with haste to the king and asked, saying, "I want you to give me at once the head of John the Baptist on a platter."

²⁶And the king was exceedingly sorry; *yet,* because of the oaths and because of those who sat with him, he did not want to refuse her. ²⁷Immediately the king sent an executioner and commanded his head to be brought. And he went and beheaded him in prison, ²⁸brought his head on a platter, and gave it to the girl; and the girl gave it to her mother. ²⁹When his disciples heard *of it,* they came and took away his corpse and laid it in a tomb.

Feeding the Five Thousand

³⁰Then the apostles gathered to Jesus and told Him all things, both what they had done and what they had taught. ³¹And He said to them, "Come aside by yourselves to a deserted place and rest a while." For there were many coming and going, and they did not even have time to eat. ³²So they departed to a deserted place in the boat by themselves.

³³But the multitudes[a] saw them departing, and many knew Him and ran there on foot from

---

6:33 ᵃNU-Text and M-Text read *they.*

all the cities. They arrived before them and came together to Him. ³⁴And Jesus, when He came out, saw a great multitude and was moved with compassion for them, because they were like sheep not having a shepherd. So He began to teach them many things. ³⁵When the day was now far spent, His disciples came to Him and said, "This is a deserted place, and already the hour is late. ³⁶Send them away, that they may go into the surrounding country and villages and buy themselves bread;ᵃ for they have nothing to eat."

³⁷But He answered and said to them, "You give them something to eat."

And they said to Him, "Shall we go and buy two hundred denarii worth of bread and give them *something* to eat?"

³⁸But He said to them, "How many loaves do you have? Go and see."

And when they found out they said, "Five, and two fish."

³⁹Then He commanded them to make them all sit down in groups on the green grass. ⁴⁰So they sat down in ranks, in hundreds and in fifties. ⁴¹And when He had taken the five loaves and the two fish, He looked up to heaven, blessed and broke the loaves, and gave *them* to His disciples to set before them; and the two fish He divided among *them* all. ⁴²So they all ate and were filled. ⁴³And they took up twelve baskets full of fragments and of the fish. ⁴⁴Now those who had eaten the loaves were aboutᵃ five thousand men.

Jesus Walks on the Sea

⁴⁵Immediately He made His disciples get into

6:36 ᵃNU-Text reads *something to eat* and omits the rest of this verse.   6:44 ᵃNU-Text and M-Text omit *about*.

the boat and go before Him to the other side, to Bethsaida, while He sent the multitude away. ⁴⁶And when He had sent them away, He departed to the mountain to pray. ⁴⁷Now when evening came, the boat was in the middle of the sea; and He *was* alone on the land. ⁴⁸Then He saw them straining at rowing, for the wind was against them. Now about the fourth watch of the night He came to them, walking on the sea, and would have passed them by. ⁴⁹And when they saw Him walking on the sea, they supposed it was a ghost, and cried out; ⁵⁰for they all saw Him and were troubled. But immediately He talked with them and said to them, "Be of good cheer! It is I; do not be afraid." ⁵¹Then He went up into the boat to them, and the wind ceased. And they were greatly amazed in themselves beyond measure, and marveled. ⁵²For they had not understood about the loaves, because their heart was hardened.

Many Touch Him and Are Made Well

⁵³When they had crossed over, they came to the land of Gennesaret and anchored there. ⁵⁴And when they came out of the boat, immediately the people recognized Him, ⁵⁵ran through that whole surrounding region, and began to carry about on beds those who were sick to wherever they heard He was. ⁵⁶Wherever He entered, into villages, cities, or the country, they laid the sick in the marketplaces, and begged Him that they might just touch the hem of His garment. And as many as touched Him were made well.

Defilement Comes from Within

7 Then the Pharisees and some of the scribes came together to Him, having come from

Jerusalem. [2]Now when[a] they saw some of His disciples eat bread with defiled, that is, with unwashed hands, they found fault. [3]For the Pharisees and all the Jews do not eat unless they wash *their* hands in a special way, holding the tradition of the elders. [4]*When they come* from the marketplace, they do not eat unless they wash. And there are many other things which they have received and hold, *like* the washing of cups, pitchers, copper vessels, and couches.

[5]Then the Pharisees and scribes asked Him, "Why do Your disciples not walk according to the tradition of the elders, but eat bread with unwashed hands?"

[6]He answered and said to them, "Well did Isaiah prophesy of you hypocrites, as it is written:

'This people honors Me with their lips,
   But their heart is far from Me.
[7] And in vain they worship Me,
   Teaching as doctrines the commandments of
       men.'[a]

[8]For laying aside the commandment of God, you hold the tradition of men[a]—the washing of pitchers and cups, and many other such things you do."

[9]He said to them, "*All too* well you reject the commandment of God, that you may keep your tradition. [10]For Moses said, '*Honor your father and your mother*';[a] and, '*He who curses father or mother, let him be put to death.*'[b] [11]But you say, 'If a man says to his father or mother, "Whatever

---

7:2 [a]NU-Text omits *when* and *they found fault.*   7:7 [a]Isaiah 29:13
7:8 [a]NU-Text omits the rest of this verse.   7:10 [a]Exodus 20:12;
Deuteronomy 5:16 [b]Exodus 21:17

profit you might have received from me *is* Corban"—' (that is, a gift *to God*), [12]then you no longer let him do anything for his father or his mother, [13]making the word of God of no effect through your tradition which you have handed down. And many such things you do."

[14]When He had called all the multitude to *Himself,* He said to them, "Hear Me, everyone, and understand: [15]There is nothing that enters a man from outside which can defile him; but the things which come out of him, those are the things that defile a man. [16]If anyone has ears to hear, let him hear!"[a]

[17]When He had entered a house away from the crowd, His disciples asked Him concerning the parable. [18]So He said to them, "Are you thus without understanding also? Do you not perceive that whatever enters a man from outside cannot defile him, [19]because it does not enter his heart but his stomach, and is eliminated, *thus* purifying all foods?"[a] [20]And He said, "What comes out of a man, that defiles a man. [21]For from within, out of the heart of men, proceed evil thoughts, adulteries, fornications, murders, [22]thefts, covetousness, wickedness, deceit, lewdness, an evil eye, blasphemy, pride, foolishness. [23]All these evil things come from within and defile a man."

A Gentile Shows Her Faith

[24]From there He arose and went to the region of Tyre and Sidon.[a] And He entered a house and wanted no one to know *it,* but He could not be hidden. [25]For a woman whose young daughter

---

7:16 [a]NU-Text omits this verse.   7:19 [a]NU-Text ends quotation with *eliminated,* setting off the final clause as Mark's comment that Jesus has declared all foods clean.   7:24 [a]NU-Text omits *and Sidon.*

What about Bible contradictions?

The Bible has many *seeming* contradictions within its pages. For example, the four Gospels give four differing accounts as to what was written on the sign that hung on the cross. Matthew said, "This is Jesus the King of the Jews" (27:37). However, Mark contradicts that with "The King of the Jews" (15:26). Luke says something different: "This is the King of the Jews" (23:38), and John maintains that the sign said "Jesus of Nazareth, the King of the Jews" (19:19).

Those who are looking for contradictions may therefore say, "See, the Bible is full of mistakes!" and choose to reject it entirely as being untrustworthy. However, those who trust God have no problem harmonizing the Gospels. There is no contradiction if the sign simply said, "This is Jesus of Nazareth, the King of the Jews."

The godly base their confidence on two truths: 1) "All Scripture is given by inspiration of God" (2 Timothy 3:16); and 2) any seeming contradictions are included in God's Word to "snare" the proud. He has "hidden" things from the "wise and prudent and revealed them to babes" (Luke 10:21), purposely choosing foolish things to confound those who are wise in their own eyes (see 1 Corinthians 1:27).

If an ungodly man refuses to humble himself and obey the gospel, and instead desires to build a case against the Bible, God gives him enough material to build his own gallows.

This incredible principle is clearly illustrated in the account of the capture of Zedekiah, king of Judah. The prophet Jeremiah told Zedekiah that God would judge him. He would be "delivered into the hand of the king of Babylon" and "see him eye to eye" (Jeremiah 32:4). This is confirmed in Jeremiah 39:5–7 where we are told that he was captured and brought to King Nebuchadnezzar, then they "bound him with bronze fetters to carry him off to Babylon." However, in Ezekiel 12:13, God Himself warned, "I will bring him to Babylon, . . . yet *he shall not see it*, though he shall die there" (emphasis added).

Here is material to build a case against the Bible! It is an *obvious* mistake. The Bible says that the king would go to Babylon, yet in another place it says that he would not see Babylon. How can someone be taken somewhere and not see it? It makes no sense at all—unless Zedekiah was blinded.

And that is precisely what happened. Zedekiah saw Nebuchadnezzar face to face, saw his sons killed before his eyes, then "the king of Babylon . . . put out Zedekiah's eyes" before taking him to Babylon (see Jeremiah 39:6,7).

This is the underlying principle behind the many "contradictions" of Holy Scripture (such as the hour at which Jesus was crucified, who was the first to arrive at the tomb after the resurrection of Jesus, etc.). God has turned the tables on proud, arrogant, self-righteous men, who smugly stand outside of the kingdom of God and seek to justify their sinfulness through evidence that they think discredits the Bible. They don't realize that God has simply lowered the door of life, so that only those willing to exercise childlike faith, and bow in humility, may enter.

The professed atheist looks at the Scriptures the same way an extremely nearsighted man would look at the Mona Lisa. To him, the painting is nothing but a meaningless blur, so he approaches it and studies the canvas from a distance of one inch (the only distance at which he can see anything in focus).

Naturally, he concludes that the painting is horrible. This is because the only way he will ever appreciate its beauty and harmony is to step back and see the whole picture. The same is true of Scripture. The Bible is intended to be read as a whole; when the complete picture is viewed, it makes perfect sense and its flawless beauty and amazing harmony can be seen.

had an unclean spirit heard about Him, and she came and fell at His feet. ²⁶The woman was a Greek, a Syro-Phoenician by birth, and she kept asking Him to cast the demon out of her daughter. ²⁷But Jesus said to her, "Let the children be filled first, for it is not good to take the children's bread and throw *it* to the little dogs."

²⁸And she answered and said to Him, "Yes, Lord, yet even the little dogs under the table eat from the children's crumbs."

²⁹Then He said to her, "For this saying go your way; the demon has gone out of your daughter."

³⁰And when she had come to her house, she found the demon gone out, and her daughter lying on the bed.

Jesus Heals a Deaf-Mute

³¹Again, departing from the region of Tyre and Sidon, He came through the midst of the region of Decapolis to the Sea of Galilee. ³²Then they brought to Him one who was deaf and had an impediment in his speech, and they begged Him to put His hand on him. ³³And He took him aside from the multitude, and put His fingers in his ears, and He spat and touched his tongue. ³⁴Then, looking up to heaven, He sighed, and said to him, "Ephphatha," that is, "Be opened." ³⁵Immediately his ears were opened, and the impediment of his tongue was loosed, and he spoke plainly. ³⁶Then He commanded them that they should tell no one; but the more He commanded them, the more widely they proclaimed it. ³⁷And they were astonished beyond measure, saying, "He has done all things well. He makes both the deaf to hear and the mute to speak."

Feeding the Four Thousand

8 In those days, the multitude being very great and having nothing to eat, Jesus called His disciples *to Him* and said to them, ²"I have compassion on the multitude, because they have now continued with Me three days and have nothing to eat. ³And if I send them away hungry to their own houses, they will faint on the way; for some of them have come from afar."

⁴Then His disciples answered Him, "How can one satisfy these people with bread here in the wilderness?"

⁵He asked them, "How many loaves do you have?"

And they said, "Seven."

⁶So He commanded the multitude to sit down on the ground. And He took the seven loaves and gave thanks, broke *them* and gave *them* to His disciples to set before *them;* and they set *them* before the multitude. ⁷They also had a few small fish; and having blessed them, He said to set them also before *them.* ⁸So they ate and were filled, and they took up seven large baskets of leftover fragments. ⁹Now those who had eaten were about four thousand. And He sent them away, ¹⁰immediately got into the boat with His disciples, and came to the region of Dalmanutha.

The Pharisees Seek a Sign

¹¹Then the Pharisees came out and began to dispute with Him, seeking from Him a sign from heaven, testing Him. ¹²But He sighed deeply in His spirit, and said, "Why does this generation seek a sign? Assuredly, I say to you, no sign shall be given to this generation."

Beware of the Leaven of the Pharisees and Herod

[13]And He left them, and getting into the boat again, departed to the other side. [14]Now the disciples[a] had forgotten to take bread, and they did not have more than one loaf with them in the boat. [15]Then He charged them, saying, "Take heed, beware of the leaven of the Pharisees and the leaven of Herod."

[16]And they reasoned among themselves, saying, "It is because we have no bread."

[17]But Jesus, being aware of it, said to them, "Why do you reason because you have no bread? Do you not yet perceive nor understand? Is your heart still[a] hardened? [18]Having eyes, do you not see? And having ears, do you not hear? And do you not remember? [19]When I broke the five loaves for the five thousand, how many baskets full of fragments did you take up?"

They said to Him, "Twelve."

[20]"Also, when I broke the seven for the four thousand, how many large baskets full of fragments did you take up?"

And they said, "Seven."

[21]So He said to them, "How is it you do not understand?"

A Blind Man Healed at Bethsaida

[22]Then He came to Bethsaida; and they brought a blind man to Him, and begged Him to touch him. [23]So He took the blind man by the hand and led him out of the town. And when He had spit on his eyes and put His hands on him, He asked him if he saw anything.

8:14 [a]NU-Text and M-Text read *they*.   8:17 [a]NU-Text omits *still*.

²⁴And he looked up and said, "I see men like trees, walking."

²⁵Then He put *His* hands on his eyes again and made him look up. And he was restored and saw everyone clearly. ²⁶Then He sent him away to his house, saying, "Neither go into the town, nor tell anyone in the town."ᵃ

Peter Confesses Jesus as the Christ

²⁷Now Jesus and His disciples went out to the towns of Caesarea Philippi; and on the road He asked His disciples, saying to them, "Who do men say that I am?"

²⁸So they answered, "John the Baptist; but some *say,* Elijah; and others, one of the prophets."

²⁹He said to them, "But who do you say that I am?"

Peter answered and said to Him, "You are the Christ."

³⁰Then He strictly warned them that they should tell no one about Him.

Jesus Predicts His Death and Resurrection

³¹And He began to teach them that the Son of Man must suffer many things, and be rejected by the elders and chief priests and scribes, and be killed, and after three days rise again. ³²He spoke this word openly. Then Peter took Him aside and began to rebuke Him. ³³But when He had turned around and looked at His disciples, He rebuked Peter, saying, "Get behind Me, Satan! For you are not mindful of the things of God, but the things of men."

8:26 ᵃNU-Text reads *"Do not even go into the town."*

Take Up the Cross and Follow Him

³⁴When He had called the people to *Himself,* with His disciples also, He said to them, "Whoever desires to come after Me, let him deny himself, and take up his cross, and follow Me. ³⁵For whoever desires to save his life will lose it, but whoever loses his life for My sake and the gospel's will save it. ³⁶For what will it profit a man if he gains the whole world, and loses his own soul? ³⁷Or what will a man give in exchange for his soul? ³⁸For whoever is ashamed of Me and My words in this adulterous and sinful generation, of him the Son of Man also will be ashamed when He comes in the glory of His Father with the holy angels."

Jesus Transfigured on the Mount

9 And He said to them, "Assuredly, I say to you that there are some standing here who will not taste death till they see the kingdom of God present with power."

²Now after six days Jesus took Peter, James, and John, and led them up on a high mountain apart by themselves; and He was transfigured before them. ³His clothes became shining, exceedingly white, like snow, such as no launderer on earth can whiten them. ⁴And Elijah appeared to them with Moses, and they were talking with Jesus. ⁵Then Peter answered and said to Jesus, "Rabbi, it is good for us to be here; and let us make three tabernacles: one for You, one for Moses, and one for Elijah"— ⁶because he did not know what to say, for they were greatly afraid.

⁷And a cloud came and overshadowed them; and a voice came out of the cloud, saying, "This is My beloved Son. Hear Him!" ⁸Suddenly, when

they had looked around, they saw no one anymore, but only Jesus with themselves.

⁹Now as they came down from the mountain,
He commanded them that they should tell no
one the things they had seen, till the Son of Man
had risen from the dead. ¹⁰So they kept this
word to themselves, questioning what the rising
from the dead meant.

¹¹And they asked Him, saying, "Why do the
scribes say that Elijah must come first?"

¹²Then He answered and told them, "Indeed,
Elijah is coming first and restores all things. And
how is it written concerning the Son of Man, that
He must suffer many things and be treated with
contempt? ¹³But I say to you that Elijah has also
come, and they did to him whatever they wished,
as it is written of him."

A Boy Is Healed

¹⁴And when He came to the disciples, He saw
a great multitude around them, and scribes dis-
puting with them. ¹⁵Immediately, when they saw
Him, all the people were greatly amazed, and
running to *Him,* greeted Him. ¹⁶And He asked
the scribes, "What are you discussing with them?"

¹⁷Then one of the crowd answered and said,
"Teacher, I brought You my son, who has a mute
spirit. ¹⁸And wherever it seizes him, it throws
him down; he foams at the mouth, gnashes his
teeth, and becomes rigid. So I spoke to Your disciples, that they should cast it out, but they
could not."

¹⁹He answered him and said, "O faithless
generation, how long shall I be with you? How
long shall I bear with you? Bring him to Me."
²⁰Then they brought him to Him. And when he

saw Him, immediately the spirit convulsed him, and he fell on the ground and wallowed, foaming at the mouth.

21So He asked his father, "How long has this been happening to him?"

And he said, "From childhood. 22And often he has thrown him both into the fire and into the water to destroy him. But if You can do anything, have compassion on us and help us."

23Jesus said to him, "If you can believe,a all things *are* possible to him who believes."

24Immediately the father of the child cried out and said with tears, "Lord, I believe; help my unbelief!"

25When Jesus saw that the people came running together, He rebuked the unclean spirit, saying to it, "Deaf and dumb spirit, I command you, come out of him and enter him no more!" 26Then *the spirit* cried out, convulsed him greatly, and came out of him. And he became as one dead, so that many said, "He is dead." 27But Jesus took him by the hand and lifted him up, and he arose.

28And when He had come into the house, His disciples asked Him privately, "Why could we not cast it out?"

29So He said to them, "This kind can come out by nothing but prayer and fasting."a

Jesus Again Predicts His Death and Resurrection

30Then they departed from there and passed through Galilee, and He did not want anyone to know *it.* 31For He taught His disciples and said

---

9:23 aNU-Text reads "'If *You* can!' All things. . . ." 9:29 aNU-Text omits *and fasting.*

to them, "The Son of Man is being betrayed into the hands of men, and they will kill Him. And after He is killed, He will rise the third day." [32]But they did not understand this saying, and were afraid to ask Him.

Who Is the Greatest?

[33]Then He came to Capernaum. And when He was in the house He asked them, "What was it you disputed among yourselves on the road?" [34]But they kept silent, for on the road they had disputed among themselves who *would be the* greatest. [35]And He sat down, called the twelve, and said to them, "If anyone desires to be first, he shall be last of all and servant of all." [36]Then He took a little child and set him in the midst of them. And when He had taken him in His arms, He said to them, [37]"Whoever receives one of these little children in My name receives Me; and whoever receives Me, receives not Me but Him who sent Me."

Jesus Forbids Sectarianism

[38]Now John answered Him, saying, "Teacher, we saw someone who does not follow us casting out demons in Your name, and we forbade him because he does not follow us."

[39]But Jesus said, "Do not forbid him, for no one who works a miracle in My name can soon afterward speak evil of Me. [40]For he who is not against us is on our[a] side. [41]For whoever gives you a cup of water to drink in My name, because you belong to Christ, assuredly, I say to you, he will by no means lose his reward.

9:40 [a]M-Text reads *against you is on your side.*

Jesus Warns of Offenses

⁴²"But whoever causes one of these little ones who believe in Me to stumble, it would be better for him if a millstone were hung around his neck, and he were thrown into the sea. ⁴³If your hand causes you to sin, cut it off. It is better for you to enter into life maimed, rather than having two hands, to go to hell, into the fire that shall never be quenched— ⁴⁴where

> *Their worm does not die
> And the fire is not quenched.'*ᵃ

⁴⁵And if your foot causes you to sin, cut it off. It is better for you to enter life lame, rather than having two feet, to be cast into hell, into the fire that shall never be quenched— ⁴⁶where

> *Their worm does not die
> And the fire is not quenched.'*ᵃ

⁴⁷And if your eye causes you to sin, pluck it out. It is better for you to enter the kingdom of God with one eye, rather than having two eyes, to be cast into hell fire— ⁴⁸where

> *Their worm does not die
> And the fire is not quenched.'*ᵃ

Tasteless Salt Is Worthless

⁴⁹"For everyone will be seasoned with fire,ᵃ and every sacrifice will be seasoned with salt. ⁵⁰Salt is good, but if the salt loses its flavor, how

---

9:44 ᵃNU-Text omits this verse.   9:46 ᵃNU-Text omits the last clause of verse 45 and all of verse 46.   9:48 ᵃIsaiah 66:24   9:49 ᵃNU-Text omits the rest of this verse.

will you season it? Have salt in yourselves, and have peace with one another."

Marriage and Divorce

10 Then He arose from there and came to the region of Judea by the other side of the Jordan. And multitudes gathered to Him again, and as He was accustomed, He taught them again.

2The Pharisees came and asked Him, "Is it lawful for a man to divorce *his* wife?" testing Him.

3And He answered and said to them, "What did Moses command you?"

4They said, "Moses permitted *a man* to write a certificate of divorce, and to dismiss *her*."

5And Jesus answered and said to them, "Because of the hardness of your heart he wrote you this precept. 6But from the beginning of the creation, God *'made them male and female.'*a 7*'For this reason a man shall leave his father and mother and be joined to his wife,* 8*and the two shall become one flesh';*a so then they are no longer two, but one flesh. 9Therefore what God has joined together, let not man separate."

10In the house His disciples also asked Him again about the same *matter.* 11So He said to them, "Whoever divorces his wife and marries another commits adultery against her. 12And if a woman divorces her husband and marries another, she commits adultery."

Jesus Blesses Little Children

13Then they brought little children to Him, that He might touch them; but the disciples re-

---

10:6 aGenesis 1:27; 5:2   10:8 aGenesis 2:24

buked those who brought *them*. ¹⁴But when Jesus saw *it*, He was greatly displeased and said to them, "Let the little children come to Me, and do not forbid them; for of such is the kingdom of God. ¹⁵Assuredly, I say to you, whoever does not receive the kingdom of God as a little child will by no means enter it." ¹⁶And He took them up in His arms, laid *His* hands on them, and blessed them.

Jesus Counsels the Rich Young Ruler

¹⁷Now as He was going out on the road, one came running, knelt before Him, and asked Him, "Good Teacher, what shall I do that I may inherit eternal life?"

¹⁸So Jesus said to him, "Why do you call Me good? No one *is* good but One, *that is,* God. ¹⁹You know the commandments: *'Do not commit adultery,' 'Do not murder,' 'Do not steal,' 'Do not bear false witness,'* 'Do not defraud,' *'Honor your father and your mother.'* "ª

²⁰And he answered and said to Him, "Teacher, all these things I have kept from my youth."

²¹Then Jesus, looking at him, loved him, and said to him, "One thing you lack: Go your way, sell whatever you have and give to the poor, and you will have treasure in heaven; and come, take up the cross, and follow Me."

²²But he was sad at this word, and went away sorrowful, for he had great possessions.

With God All Things Are Possible

²³Then Jesus looked around and said to His disciples, "How hard it is for those who have

10:19 ªExodus 20:12–16; Deuteronomy 5:16–20

riches to enter the kingdom of God!" ²⁴And the disciples were astonished at His words. But Jesus answered again and said to them, "Children, how hard it is for those who trust in riches[a] to enter the kingdom of God! ²⁵It is easier for a camel to go through the eye of a needle than for a rich man to enter the kingdom of God."

²⁶And they were greatly astonished, saying among themselves, "Who then can be saved?"

²⁷But Jesus looked at them and said, "With men *it is* impossible, but not with God; for with God all things are possible."

²⁸Then Peter began to say to Him, "See, we have left all and followed You."

²⁹So Jesus answered and said, "Assuredly, I say to you, there is no one who has left house or brothers or sisters or father or mother or wife[a] or children or lands, for My sake and the gospel's, ³⁰who shall not receive a hundredfold now in this time—houses and brothers and sisters and mothers and children and lands, with persecutions—and in the age to come, eternal life. ³¹But many *who are* first will be last, and the last first."

Jesus a Third Time Predicts His Death and Resurrection

³²Now they were on the road, going up to Jerusalem, and Jesus was going before them; and they were amazed. And as they followed they were afraid. Then He took the twelve aside again and began to tell them the things that would happen to Him: ³³"Behold, we are going up to Jerusalem, and the Son of Man will be betrayed to the chief priests and to the scribes; and they

10:24 [a]NU-Text omits *for those who trust in riches.* 10:29 [a]NU-Text omits *or wife.*

will condemn Him to death and deliver Him to the Gentiles; ³⁴and they will mock Him, and scourge Him, and spit on Him, and kill Him. And the third day He will rise again."

Greatness Is Serving

³⁵Then James and John, the sons of Zebedee, came to Him, saying, "Teacher, we want You to do for us whatever we ask."

³⁶And He said to them, "What do you want Me to do for you?"

³⁷They said to Him, "Grant us that we may sit, one on Your right hand and the other on Your left, in Your glory."

³⁸But Jesus said to them, "You do not know what you ask. Are you able to drink the cup that I drink, and be baptized with the baptism that I am baptized with?"

³⁹They said to Him, "We are able."

So Jesus said to them, "You will indeed drink the cup that I drink, and with the baptism I am baptized with you will be baptized; ⁴⁰but to sit on My right hand and on My left is not Mine to give, but *it is for those* for whom it is prepared."

⁴¹And when the ten heard *it*, they began to be greatly displeased with James and John. ⁴²But Jesus called them to *Himself* and said to them, "You know that those who are considered rulers over the Gentiles lord it over them, and their great ones exercise authority over them. ⁴³Yet it shall not be so among you; but whoever desires to become great among you shall be your servant. ⁴⁴And whoever of you desires to be first shall be slave of all. ⁴⁵For even the Son of Man did not come to be served, but to serve, and to give His life a ransom for many."

Jesus Heals Blind Bartimaeus

[46]Now they came to Jericho. As He went out of Jericho with His disciples and a great multitude, blind Bartimaeus, the son of Timaeus, sat by the road begging. [47]And when he heard that it was Jesus of Nazareth, he began to cry out and say, "Jesus, Son of David, have mercy on me!"

[48]Then many warned him to be quiet; but he cried out all the more, "Son of David, have mercy on me!"

[49]So Jesus stood still and commanded him to be called.

Then they called the blind man, saying to him, "Be of good cheer. Rise, He is calling you."

[50]And throwing aside his garment, he rose and came to Jesus.

[51]So Jesus answered and said to him, "What do you want Me to do for you?"

The blind man said to Him, "Rabboni, that I may receive my sight."

[52]Then Jesus said to him, "Go your way; your faith has made you well." And immediately he received his sight and followed Jesus on the road.

The Triumphal Entry

11 Now when they drew near Jerusalem, to Bethphage[a] and Bethany, at the Mount of Olives, He sent two of His disciples; [2]and He said to them, "Go into the village opposite you; and as soon as you have entered it you will find a colt tied, on which no one has sat. Loose it and bring *it*. [3]And if anyone says to you, 'Why are you doing this?' say, 'The Lord has need of it,' and immediately he will send it here."

11:1 [a]M-Text reads *Bethsphage*.

⁴So they went their way, and found the colt tied by the door outside on the street, and they loosed it. ⁵But some of those who stood there said to them, "What are you doing, loosing the colt?" ⁶And they spoke to them just as Jesus had commanded. So they let them go. ⁷Then they brought the colt to Jesus and threw their clothes on it, and He sat on it. ⁸And many spread their clothes on the road, and others cut down leafy branches from the trees and spread *them* on the road. ⁹Then those who went before and those who followed cried out, saying:

"Hosanna!
'Blessed is He who comes in the name of the Lord!'ᵃ
¹⁰Blessed is the kingdom of our father David
That comes in the name of the Lord!ᵃ
Hosanna in the highest!"

¹¹And Jesus went into Jerusalem and into the temple. So when He had looked around at all things, as the hour was already late, He went out to Bethany with the twelve.

The Fig Tree Withered

¹²Now the next day, when they had come out from Bethany, He was hungry. ¹³And seeing from afar a fig tree having leaves, He went to see if perhaps He would find something on it. When He came to it, He found nothing but leaves, for it was not the season for figs. ¹⁴In response Jesus said to it, "Let no one eat fruit from you ever again."

And His disciples heard *it*.

11:4 ᵃNU-Text and M-Text read *a*. 11:9 ᵃPsalm 118:26 11:10 ᵃNU-Text omits *in the name of the Lord.*

Jesus Cleanses the Temple

[15]So they came to Jerusalem. Then Jesus went into the temple and began to drive out those who bought and sold in the temple, and overturned the tables of the money changers and the seats of those who sold doves. [16]And He would not allow anyone to carry wares through the temple. [17]Then He taught, saying to them, "Is it not written, *'My house shall be called a house of prayer for all nations'?*[a] But you have made it a *'den of thieves.' "*[b]

[18]And the scribes and chief priests heard it and sought how they might destroy Him; for they feared Him, because all the people were astonished at His teaching. [19]When evening had come, He went out of the city.

The Lesson of the Withered Fig Tree

[20]Now in the morning, as they passed by, they saw the fig tree dried up from the roots. [21]And Peter, remembering, said to Him, "Rabbi, look! The fig tree which You cursed has withered away."

[22]So Jesus answered and said to them, "Have faith in God. [23]For assuredly, I say to you, whoever says to this mountain, 'Be removed and be cast into the sea,' and does not doubt in his heart, but believes that those things he says will be done, he will have whatever he says. [24]Therefore I say to you, whatever things you ask when you pray, believe that you receive *them,* and you will have *them.*

Forgiveness and Prayer

[25]"And whenever you stand praying, if you have anything against anyone, forgive him, that

11:17 [a]Isaiah 56:7   [b]Jeremiah 7:11

your Father in heaven may also forgive you your trespasses. [26]But if you do not forgive, neither will your Father in heaven forgive your trespasses."[a]

Jesus' Authority Questioned

[27]Then they came again to Jerusalem. And as He was walking in the temple, the chief priests, the scribes, and the elders came to Him. [28]And they said to Him, "By what authority are You doing these things? And who gave You this authority to do these things?"

[29]But Jesus answered and said to them, "I also will ask you one question; then answer Me, and I will tell you by what authority I do these things: [30]The baptism of John—was it from heaven or from men? Answer Me."

[31]And they reasoned among themselves, saying, "If we say, 'From heaven,' He will say, 'Why then did you not believe him?' [32]But if we say, 'From men' "—they feared the people, for all counted John to have been a prophet indeed. [33]So they answered and said to Jesus, "We do not know."

And Jesus answered and said to them, "Neither will I tell you by what authority I do these things."

The Parable of the Wicked Vinedressers

12 Then He began to speak to them in parables: "A man planted a vineyard and set a hedge around it, dug *a place for* the wine vat and built a tower. And he leased it to vinedressers and went into a far country. [2]Now at vintage-time he sent a servant to the vinedressers, that he might receive some of the fruit of the vineyard

---

11:26 [a]NU-Text omits this verse.

from the vinedressers. ³And they took *him* and beat him and sent *him* away empty-handed. ⁴Again he sent them another servant, and at him they threw stones,ᵃ wounded *him* in the head, and sent *him* away shamefully treated. ⁵And again he sent another, and him they killed; and many others, beating some and killing some. ⁶Therefore still having one son, his beloved, he also sent him to them last, saying, 'They will respect my son.' ⁷But those vinedressers said among themselves, 'This is the heir. Come, let us kill him, and the inheritance will be ours.' ⁸So they took him and killed *him* and cast *him* out of the vineyard.

⁹"Therefore what will the owner of the vineyard do? He will come and destroy the vinedressers, and give the vineyard to others. ¹⁰Have you not even read this Scripture:

> 'The stone which the builders rejected
> Has become the chief cornerstone.
> ¹¹ This was the Lord's doing,
> And it is marvelous in our eyes'? "ᵃ

¹²And they sought to lay hands on Him, but feared the multitude, for they knew He had spoken the parable against them. So they left Him and went away.

The Pharisees: Is It Lawful to Pay Taxes to Caesar?

¹³Then they sent to Him some of the Pharisees and the Herodians, to catch Him in *His* words. ¹⁴When they had come, they said to Him, "Teacher, we know that You are true, and care about no one; for You do not regard the person

---

12:4 ᵃNU-Text omits *and at him they threw stones.*   12:11 ᵃPsalm 118:22, 23

of men, but teach the way of God in truth. Is it lawful to pay taxes to Caesar, or not? [15]Shall we pay, or shall we not pay?"

But He, knowing their hypocrisy, said to them, "Why do you test Me? Bring Me a denarius that I may see *it*." [16]So they brought *it*.

And He said to them, "Whose image and inscription *is* this?" They said to Him, "Caesar's."

[17]And Jesus answered and said to them, "Render to Caesar the things that are Caesar's, and to God the things that are God's."

And they marveled at Him.

The Sadducees: What About the Resurrection?

[18]Then *some* Sadducees, who say there is no resurrection, came to Him; and they asked Him, saying: [19]"Teacher, Moses wrote to us that if a man's brother dies, and leaves *his* wife behind, and leaves no children, his brother should take his wife and raise up offspring for his brother. [20]Now there were seven brothers. The first took a wife; and dying, he left no offspring. [21]And the second took her, and he died; nor did he leave any offspring. And the third likewise. [22]So the seven had her and left no offspring. Last of all the woman died also. [23]Therefore, in the resurrection, when they rise, whose wife will she be? For all seven had her as wife."

[24]Jesus answered and said to them, "Are you not therefore mistaken, because you do not know the Scriptures nor the power of God? [25]For when they rise from the dead, they neither marry nor are given in marriage, but are like angels in heaven. [26]But concerning the dead, that they rise, have you not read in the book of Moses, in

the *burning* bush *passage,* how God spoke to him, saying, *'I am the God of Abraham, the God of Isaac, and the God of Jacob'?*[a] [27]He is not the God of the dead, but the God of the living. You are therefore greatly mistaken."

The Scribes: Which Is the First Commandment of All?

[28]Then one of the scribes came, and having heard them reasoning together, perceiving[a] that He had answered them well, asked Him, "Which is the first commandment of all?"

[29]Jesus answered him, "The first of all the commandments is: *'Hear, O Israel, the* LORD *our God, the* LORD *is one.* [30] *And you shall love the* LORD *your God with all your heart, with all your soul, with all your mind, and with all your strength.'*[a] This is the first commandment.[b] [31]And the second, like *it,* is this: *'You shall love your neighbor as yourself.'*[a] There is no other commandment greater than these."

[32]So the scribe said to Him, "Well *said,* Teacher. You have spoken the truth, for there is one God, and there is no other but He. [33]And to love Him with all the heart, with all the understanding, with all the soul,[a] and with all the strength, and to love one's neighbor as oneself, is more than all the whole burnt offerings and sacrifices."

[34]Now when Jesus saw that he answered wisely, He said to him, "You are not far from the kingdom of God."

But after that no one dared question Him.

12:26 [a]Exodus 3:6, 15   12:28 [a]NU-Text reads *seeing.*   12:30
[a]Deuteronomy 6:4, 5   [b]NU-Text omits this sentence.   12:31
[a]Leviticus 19:18   12:33 [a]NU-Text omits *with all the soul.*

Jesus: How Can David Call His Descendant Lord?

[35]Then Jesus answered and said, while He taught in the temple, "How *is it* that the scribes say that the Christ is the Son of David? [36]For David himself said by the Holy Spirit:

> 'The LORD said to my Lord,
> "Sit at My right hand,
> Till I make Your enemies Your footstool." '[a]

[37]Therefore David himself calls Him *'Lord'*; how is He *then* his Son?"

And the common people heard Him gladly.

Beware of the Scribes

[38]Then He said to them in His teaching, "Beware of the scribes, who desire to go around in long robes, *love* greetings in the marketplaces, [39]the best seats in the synagogues, and the best places at feasts, [40]who devour widows' houses, and for a pretense make long prayers. These will receive greater condemnation."

The Widow's Two Mites

[41]Now Jesus sat opposite the treasury and saw how the people put money into the treasury. And many *who were* rich put in much. [42]Then one poor widow came and threw in two mites,[a] which make a quadrans. [43]So He called His disciples to *Himself* and said to them, "Assuredly, I say to you that this poor widow has put in more than all those who have given to the treasury; [44]for they all put in out of their abundance, but

---

12:36 [a]Psalm 110:1   12:42 [a]Greek *lepta*, very small copper coins worth a fraction of a penny

she out of her poverty put in all that she had, her whole livelihood."

Jesus Predicts the Destruction the Temple

13 Then as He went out of the temple, one of His disciples said to Him, "Teacher, see what manner of stones and what buildings *are here!*"

²And Jesus answered and said to him, "Do you see these great buildings? Not *one* stone shall be left upon another, that shall not be thrown down."

The Signs of the Times and the End of the Age

³Now as He sat on the Mount of Olives opposite the temple, Peter, James, John, and Andrew asked Him privately, ⁴"Tell us, when will these things be? And what *will be* the sign when all these things will be fulfilled?"

⁵And Jesus, answering them, began to say: "Take heed that no one deceives you. ⁶For many will come in My name, saying, 'I am He,' and will deceive many. ⁷But when you hear of wars and rumors of wars, do not be troubled; for *such things* must happen, but the end is not yet. ⁸For nation will rise against nation, and kingdom against kingdom. And there will be earthquakes in various places, and there will be famines and troubles.ᵃ These *are* the beginnings of sorrows.

⁹"But watch out for yourselves, for they will deliver you up to councils, and you will be beaten in the synagogues. You will be broughtᵃ

13:8 ᵃNU-Text omits *and troubles.*   13:9 ᵃNU-Text and M-Text read *will stand.*

before rulers and kings for My sake, for a testimony to them. [10]And the gospel must first be preached to all the nations. [11]But when they arrest *you* and deliver you up, do not worry beforehand, or premeditate[a] what you will speak. But whatever is given you in that hour, speak that; for it is not you who speak, but the Holy Spirit. [12]Now brother will betray brother to death, and a father *his* child; and children will rise up against parents and cause them to be put to death. [13]And you will be hated by all for My name's sake. But he who endures to the end shall be saved.

The Great Tribulation

[14]"So when you see the *'abomination of desolation,'*[a] spoken of by Daniel the prophet,[b] standing where it ought not" (let the reader understand), "then let those who are in Judea flee to the mountains. [15]Let him who is on the housetop not go down into the house, nor enter to take anything out of his house. [16]And let him who is in the field not go back to get his clothes. [17]But woe to those who are pregnant and to those who are nursing babies in those days! [18]And pray that your flight may not be in winter. [19]For *in* those days there will be tribulation, such as has not been since the beginning of the creation which God created until this time, nor ever shall be. [20]And unless the Lord had shortened those days, no flesh would be saved; but for the elect's sake, whom He chose, He shortened the days.

[21]"Then if anyone says to you, 'Look, here *is* the Christ!' or, 'Look, *He is* there!' do not believe

13:11 [a]NU-Text omits *or premeditate*.   13:14 [a]Daniel 11:31; 12:11 [b]NU-Text omits *spoken of by Daniel the prophet*.

it. 22For false christs and false prophets will rise and show signs and wonders to deceive, if possible, even the elect. 23But take heed; see, I have told you all things beforehand.

The Coming of the Son of Man

24"But in those days, after that tribulation, the sun will be darkened, and the moon will not give its light; 25the stars of heaven will fall, and the powers in the heavens will be shaken. 26Then they will see the Son of Man coming in the clouds with great power and glory. 27And then He will send His angels, and gather together His elect from the four winds, from the farthest part of earth to the farthest part of heaven.

The Parable of the Fig Tree

28"Now learn this parable from the fig tree: When its branch has already become tender, and puts forth leaves, you know that summer is near. 29So you also, when you see these things happening, know that it[a] is near—at the doors! 30Assuredly, I say to you, this generation will by no means pass away till all these things take place. 31Heaven and earth will pass away, but My words will by no means pass away.

No One Knows the Day or Hour

32"But of that day and hour no one knows, not even the angels in heaven, nor the Son, but only the Father. 33Take heed, watch and pray; for you do not know when the time is. 34It is like a man going to a far country, who left his house and gave authority to his servants, and to each his work, and commanded the doorkeeper to watch.

13:29 aOr *He*

³⁵Watch therefore, for you do not know when the master of the house is coming—in the evening, at midnight, at the crowing of the rooster, or in the morning— ³⁶lest, coming suddenly, he find you sleeping. ³⁷And what I say to you, I say to all: Watch!"

The Plot to Kill Jesus

14 After two days it was the Passover and *the Feast* of Unleavened Bread. And the chief priests and the scribes sought how they might take Him by trickery and put *Him* to death. ²But they said, "Not during the feast, lest there be an uproar of the people."

The Anointing at Bethany

³And being in Bethany at the house of Simon the leper, as He sat at the table, a woman came having an alabaster flask of very costly oil of spikenard. Then she broke the flask and poured *it* on His head. ⁴But there were some who were indignant among themselves, and said, "Why was this fragrant oil wasted? ⁵For it might have been sold for more than three hundred denarii and given to the poor." And they criticized her sharply.

⁶But Jesus said, "Let her alone. Why do you trouble her? She has done a good work for Me. ⁷For you have the poor with you always, and whenever you wish you may do them good; but Me you do not have always. ⁸She has done what she could. She has come beforehand to anoint My body for burial. ⁹Assuredly, I say to you, wherever this gospel is preached in the whole world, what this woman has done will also be told as a memorial to her."

Judas Agrees to Betray Jesus

[10]Then Judas Iscariot, one of the twelve, went to the chief priests to betray Him to them. [11]And when they heard *it,* they were glad, and promised to give him money. So he sought how he might conveniently betray Him.

Jesus Celebrates the Passover with His Disciples

[12]Now on the first day of Unleavened Bread, when they killed the Passover *lamb,* His disciples said to Him, "Where do You want us to go and prepare, that You may eat the Passover?"

[13]And He sent out two of His disciples and said to them, "Go into the city, and a man will meet you carrying a pitcher of water; follow him. [14]Wherever he goes in, say to the master of the house, 'The Teacher says, "Where is the guest room in which I may eat the Passover with My disciples?"' [15]Then he will show you a large upper room, furnished *and* prepared; there make ready for us."

[16]So His disciples went out, and came into the city, and found it just as He had said to them; and they prepared the Passover.

[17]In the evening He came with the twelve. [18]Now as they sat and ate, Jesus said, "Assuredly, I say to you, one of you who eats with Me will betray Me."

[19]And they began to be sorrowful, and to say to Him one by one, "Is it I?" And another *said,* "Is it I?"[a]

[20]He answered and said to them, "*It is* one of the twelve, who dips with Me in the dish. [21]The

---

14:19 [a]NU-Text omits this sentence.

Son of Man indeed goes just as it is written of Him, but woe to that man by whom the Son of Man is betrayed! It would have been good for that man if he had never been born."

Jesus Institutes the Lord's Supper

²²And as they were eating, Jesus took bread, blessed and broke *it*, and gave *it* to them and said, "Take, eat;ᵃ this is My body."

²³Then He took the cup, and when He had given thanks He gave *it* to them, and they all drank from it. ²⁴And He said to them, "This is My blood of the newᵃ covenant, which is shed for many. ²⁵Assuredly, I say to you, I will no longer drink of the fruit of the vine until that day when I drink it new in the kingdom of God."

²⁶And when they had sung a hymn, they went out to the Mount of Olives.

Jesus Predicts Peter's Denial

²⁷Then Jesus said to them, "All of you will be made to stumble because of Me this night,ᵃ for it is written:

'I will strike the Shepherd,
*And the sheep will be scattered.'*ᵇ

²⁸"But after I have been raised, I will go before you to Galilee."

²⁹Peter said to Him, "Even if all are made to stumble, yet I *will* not *be*."

³⁰Jesus said to him, "Assuredly, I say to you that today, *even* this night, before the rooster crows twice, you will deny Me three times."

14:22 ᵃNU-Text omits *eat*. 14:24 ᵃNU-Text omits *new*. 14:27 ᵃNU-Text omits *because of Me this night*. ᵇZechariah 13:7

[31]But he spoke more vehemently, "If I have to die with You, I will not deny You!"

And they all said likewise.

The Prayer in the Garden

[32]Then they came to a place which was named Gethsemane; and He said to His disciples, "Sit here while I pray." [33]And He took Peter, James, and John with Him, and He began to be troubled and deeply distressed. [34]Then He said to them, "My soul is exceedingly sorrowful, *even* to death. Stay here and watch."

[35]He went a little farther, and fell on the ground, and prayed that if it were possible, the hour might pass from Him. [36]And He said, "Abba, Father, all things *are* possible for You. Take this cup away from Me; nevertheless, not what I will, but what You *will*."

[37]Then He came and found them sleeping, and said to Peter, "Simon, are you sleeping? Could you not watch one hour? [38]Watch and pray, lest you enter into temptation. The spirit indeed is willing, but the flesh *is* weak."

[39]Again He went away and prayed, and spoke the same words. [40]And when He returned, He found them asleep again, for their eyes were heavy; and they did not know what to answer Him.

[41]Then He came the third time and said to them, "Are you still sleeping and resting? It is enough! The hour has come; behold, the Son of Man is being betrayed into the hands of sinners. [42]Rise, let us be going. See, My betrayer is at hand."

Betrayal and Arrest in Gethsemane

[43]And immediately, while He was still speaking, Judas, one of the twelve, with a great multi-

tude with swords and clubs, came from the chief priests and the scribes and the elders. [44]Now His betrayer had given them a signal, saying, "Whomever I kiss, He is the One; seize Him and lead *Him* away safely."

[45]As soon as he had come, immediately he went up to Him and said to Him, "Rabbi, Rabbi!" and kissed Him.

[46]Then they laid their hands on Him and took Him. [47]And one of those who stood by drew his sword and struck the servant of the high priest, and cut off his ear.

[48]Then Jesus answered and said to them, "Have you come out, as against a robber, with swords and clubs to take Me? [49]I was daily with you in the temple teaching, and you did not seize Me. But the Scriptures must be fulfilled."

[50]Then they all forsook Him and fled.

A Young Man Flees Naked

[51]Now a certain young man followed Him, having a linen cloth thrown around *his* naked *body*. And the young men laid hold of him, [52]and he left the linen cloth and fled from them naked.

Jesus Faces the Sanhedrin

[53]And they led Jesus away to the high priest; and with him were assembled all the chief priests, the elders, and the scribes. [54]But Peter followed Him at a distance, right into the courtyard of the high priest. And he sat with the servants and warmed himself at the fire.

[55]Now the chief priests and all the council sought testimony against Jesus to put Him to death, but found none. [56]For many bore false witness against Him, but their testimonies did not agree.

⁵⁷Then some rose up and bore false witness against Him, saying, ⁵⁸"We heard Him say, 'I will destroy this temple made with hands, and within three days I will build another made without hands.' " ⁵⁹But not even then did their testimony agree.

⁶⁰And the high priest stood up in the midst and asked Jesus, saying, "Do You answer nothing? What *is it* these men testify against You?" ⁶¹But He kept silent and answered nothing.

Again the high priest asked Him, saying to Him, "Are You the Christ, the Son of the Blessed?"

⁶²Jesus said, "I am. And you will see the Son of Man sitting at the right hand of the Power, and coming with the clouds of heaven."

⁶³Then the high priest tore his clothes and said, "What further need do we have of witnesses? ⁶⁴You have heard the blasphemy! What do you think?"

And they all condemned Him to be deserving of death.

⁶⁵Then some began to spit on Him, and to blindfold Him, and to beat Him, and to say to Him, "Prophesy!" And the officers struck Him with the palms of their hands.ᵃ

Peter Denies Jesus, and Weeps

⁶⁶Now as Peter was below in the courtyard, one of the servant girls of the high priest came. ⁶⁷And when she saw Peter warming himself, she looked at him and said, "You also were with Jesus of Nazareth."

⁶⁸But he denied it, saying, "I neither know nor understand what you are saying." And he went out on the porch, and a rooster crowed.

14:65 ᵃNU-Text reads *received Him with slaps.*

⁶⁹And the servant girl saw him again, and began to say to those who stood by, "This is *one* of them." ⁷⁰But he denied it again.

And a little later those who stood by said to Peter again, "Surely you are *one* of them; for you are a Galilean, and your speech shows *it.*"ᵃ

⁷¹Then he began to curse and swear, "I do not know this Man of whom you speak!"

⁷²A second time *the* rooster crowed. Then Peter called to mind the word that Jesus had said to him, "Before the rooster crows twice, you will deny Me three times." And when he thought about it, he wept.

Jesus Faces Pilate

15 Immediately, in the morning, the chief priests held a consultation with the elders and scribes and the whole council; and they bound Jesus, led *Him* away, and delivered *Him* to Pilate. ²Then Pilate asked Him, "Are You the King of the Jews?"

He answered and said to him, "*It is as* you say."

³And the chief priests accused Him of many things, but He answered nothing. ⁴Then Pilate asked Him again, saying, "Do You answer nothing? See how many things they testify against You!"ᵃ ⁵But Jesus still answered nothing, so that Pilate marveled.

Taking the Place of Barabbas

⁶Now at the feast he was accustomed to releasing one prisoner to them, whomever they requested. ⁷And there was one named Barabbas, *who was* chained with his fellow rebels; they had

---

14:70 ᵃNU-Text omits *and your speech shows it.* 15:4 ᵃNU-Text reads *of which they accuse You.*

committed murder in the rebellion. [8]Then the multitude, crying aloud,[a] began to ask *him to do* just as he had always done for them. [9]But Pilate answered them, saying, "Do you want me to release to you the King of the Jews?" [10]For he knew that the chief priests had handed Him over because of envy.

[11]But the chief priests stirred up the crowd, so that he should rather release Barabbas to them. [12]Pilate answered and said to them again, "What then do you want me to do *with Him* whom you call the King of the Jews?"

[13]So they cried out again, "Crucify Him!"

[14]Then Pilate said to them, "Why, what evil has He done?"

But they cried out all the more, "Crucify Him!"

[15]So Pilate, wanting to gratify the crowd, released Barabbas to them; and he delivered Jesus, after he had scourged *Him,* to be crucified.

The Soldiers Mock Jesus

[16]Then the soldiers led Him away into the hall called Praetorium, and they called together the whole garrison. [17]And they clothed Him with purple; and they twisted a crown of thorns, put it on His *head,* [18]and began to salute Him, "Hail, King of the Jews!" [19]Then they struck Him on the head with a reed and spat on Him; and bowing the knee, they worshiped Him. [20]And when they had mocked Him, they took the purple off Him, put His own clothes on Him, and led Him out to crucify Him.

The King on a Cross

[21]Then they compelled a certain man, Simon

15:8 [a]NU-Text reads *going up.*

If the Bible is reliable, why so many translations?

True, there are many different versions of the Bible. There are versions in Chinese for the Chinese. There are versions in Russian for the Russian people. There are actually thousands of versions of the Bible—some are in modern languages, some in foreign languages, and some in old English. In fact, the Bible is the most translated book in the world, with at least portions of it available in over 2,400 languages, representing approximately 98% of the world's population. Few, in the printing age, can claim that they don't have access to the Scriptures in their own language. However, each translation is based on the original biblical texts. Due to the Dead Sea Scrolls, we can know that these texts are reliable.

In the spring of 1947, the Dead Sea Scrolls were discovered in a cave near Jerusalem. Called "the greatest manuscript discovery of all times," these manuscripts are the oldest Old Testament copies ever found, and consist of portions of every book of the Old Testament except for Esther. Dating from the third century BC to the first century AD, these manuscripts are about a thousand years older than any other existing copies. Study of the scrolls has revealed that the Bible hasn't changed in content down through the ages as many skeptics had surmised.

We can now obtain access to computer programs that give the original Hebrew and Greek words, and see that the only "changes" have been made for clarity. For example, the old English translation of 2 Corinthians 12:8 is "For this thing I besought the Lord thrice...," while a contemporary translation is "Concerning this thing I pleaded with the Lord three times..." We can have confidence that the same God who inspired men to record His message to humanity has preserved His Word down through the ages.

What about people who have never heard of Jesus?

Skeptics often ask, "What about ignorant tribes in the deepest jungle who've never heard the gospel?" The inference is that those who have never heard the gospel are basically good people, and that God would be unjust to send them to Hell. They will be fine on Judgment Day—*if* they are good people.

However, in God's eyes a good person is one who is morally perfect in thought, word, and deed. That means that they will be in trouble with God if they have ever lied, stolen, committed adultery (lusted), murdered (hated someone), etc. God will do what is right and just, and will punish wrongdoing no matter where it's found. If they have broken even one Law, they will get what's coming to them. (This is dealt with in the first three chapters of the Book of Romans.) A person goes to Hell not because he hasn't heard of Jesus, but because he's sinned against the Lord.

In addition, God's attributes, power, and divine nature are "clearly seen" in creation so that all of mankind is "without excuse" (Romans 1:20; see also Romans 10:17,18). But the Bible also tells us that our compassionate God has given light to every man, and that He "desires all men to be saved and to come to the knowledge of the truth" (1 Timothy 2:4). God knows those whose hearts are truly seeking Him, and He ensures that they hear the gospel, no matter where they are located. He can reveal Himself to people even in the midst of Hindu, Muslim, or animist cultures, so they can put their trust in the Savior.

Now, what about you? On Judgment Day, will you be able to say that you've never heard of Jesus? If you really care about the lost, you should get right with God yourself, then become a missionary and take the good news of God's forgiveness in Christ to them.

a Cyrenian, the father of Alexander and Rufus, as he was coming out of the country and passing by, to bear His cross. ²²And they brought Him to the place Golgotha, which is translated, Place of a Skull. ²³Then they gave Him wine mingled with myrrh to drink, but He did not take *it*. ²⁴And when they crucified Him, they divided His garments, casting lots for them to determine what every man should take.

²⁵Now it was the third hour, and they crucified Him. ²⁶And the inscription of His accusation was written above:

THE KING OF THE JEWS.

²⁷With Him they also crucified two robbers, one on His right and the other on His left. ²⁸So the Scripture was fulfilled[a] which says, *"And He was numbered with the transgressors."*[b]

²⁹And those who passed by blasphemed Him, wagging their heads and saying, "Aha! *You* who destroy the temple and build *it* in three days, ³⁰save Yourself, and come down from the cross!"

³¹Likewise the chief priests also, mocking among themselves with the scribes, said, "He saved others; Himself He cannot save. ³²Let the Christ, the King of Israel, descend now from the cross, that we may see and believe."[a]

Even those who were crucified with Him reviled Him.

Jesus Dies on the Cross

³³Now when the sixth hour had come, there was darkness over the whole land until the ninth hour. ³⁴And at the ninth hour Jesus cried out

15:28 [a]Isaiah 53:12 [b]NU-Text omits this verse. 15:32 [a]M-Text reads *believe Him.*

with a loud voice, saying, "Eloi, Eloi, lama sabachthani?" which is translated, *"My God, My God, why have You forsaken Me?"*[a]

³⁵Some of those who stood by, when they heard *that,* said, "Look, He is calling for Elijah!" ³⁶Then someone ran and filled a sponge full of sour wine, put *it* on a reed, and offered *it* to Him to drink, saying, "Let Him alone; let us see if Elijah will come to take Him down."

³⁷And Jesus cried out with a loud voice, and breathed His last.

³⁸Then the veil of the temple was torn in two from top to bottom. ³⁹So when the centurion, who stood opposite Him, saw that He cried out like this and breathed His last,[a] he said, "Truly this Man was the Son of God!"

⁴⁰There were also women looking on from afar, among whom were Mary Magdalene, Mary the mother of James the Less and of Joses, and Salome, ⁴¹who also followed Him and ministered to Him when He was in Galilee, and many other women who came up with Him to Jerusalem.

Jesus Buried in Joseph's Tomb

⁴²Now when evening had come, because it was the Preparation Day, that is, the day before the Sabbath, ⁴³Joseph of Arimathea, a prominent council member, who was himself waiting for the kingdom of God, coming and taking courage, went in to Pilate and asked for the body of Jesus. ⁴⁴Pilate marveled that He was already dead; and summoning the centurion, he asked him if He had been dead for some time. ⁴⁵So when he found out from the centurion, he granted the body to

---

15:34 ªPsalm 22:1   15:39 ªNU-Text reads *that He thus breathed His last.*

Joseph. [46]Then he bought fine linen, took Him down, and wrapped Him in the linen. And he laid Him in a tomb which had been hewn out of the rock, and rolled a stone against the door of the tomb. [47]And Mary Magdalene and Mary *the mother* of Joses observed where He was laid.

He Is Risen

16 Now when the Sabbath was past, Mary Magdalene, Mary *the mother* of James, and Salome bought spices, that they might come and anoint Him. [2]Very early in the morning, on the first *day* of the week, they came to the tomb when the sun had risen. [3]And they said among themselves, "Who will roll away the stone from the door of the tomb for us?" [4]But when they looked up, they saw that the stone had been rolled away— for it was very large. [5]And entering the tomb, they saw a young man clothed in a long white robe sitting on the right side; and they were alarmed.

[6]But he said to them, "Do not be alarmed. You seek Jesus of Nazareth, who was crucified. He is risen! He is not here. See the place where they laid Him. [7]But go, tell His disciples—and Peter —that He is going before you into Galilee; there you will see Him, as He said to you."

[8]So they went out quickly[a] and fled from the tomb, for they trembled and were amazed. And they said nothing to anyone, for they were afraid.

Mary Magdalene Sees the Risen Lord

[9]Now when *He* rose early on the first *day* of the week, He appeared first to Mary Magdalene, out of whom He had cast seven demons. [10]She went and told those who had been with Him, as they

---

16:8 [a]NU-Text and M-Text omit *quickly*.

mourned and wept. [11]And when they heard that He was alive and had been seen by her, they did not believe.

Jesus Appears to Two Disciples

[12]After that, He appeared in another form to two of them as they walked and went into the country. [13]And they went and told *it* to the rest, *but* they did not believe them either.

The Great Commission

[14]Later He appeared to the eleven as they sat at the table; and He rebuked their unbelief and hardness of heart, because they did not believe those who had seen Him after He had risen. [15]And He said to them, "Go into all the world and preach the gospel to every creature. [16]He who believes and is baptized will be saved; but he who does not believe will be condemned. [17]And these signs will follow those who believe: In My name they will cast out demons; they will speak with new tongues; [18]they[a] will take up serpents; and if they drink anything deadly, it will by no means hurt them; they will lay hands on the sick, and they will recover."

Christ Ascends to God's Right Hand

[19]So then, after the Lord had spoken to them, He was received up into heaven, and sat down at the right hand of God. [20]And they went out and preached everywhere, the Lord working with *them* and confirming the word through the accompanying signs. Amen.[a]

16:18 [a]NU-Text reads *and in their hands they will.*   16:20 [a]Verses 9–20 are bracketed in NU-Text as not original. They are lacking in Codex Sinaiticus and Codex Vaticanus, although nearly all other manuscripts of Mark contain them.

Luke

Dedication to Theophilus

1 Inasmuch as many have taken in hand to set in order a narrative of those things which have been fulfilled[a] among us, ²just as those who from the beginning were eyewitnesses and ministers of the word delivered them to us, ³it seemed good to me also, having had perfect understanding of all things from the very first, to write to you an orderly account, most excellent Theophilus, ⁴that you may know the certainty of those things in which you were instructed.

John's Birth Announced to Zacharias

⁵There was in the days of Herod, the king of Judea, a certain priest named Zacharias, of the division of Abijah. His wife *was* of the daughters of Aaron, and her name *was* Elizabeth. ⁶And they were both righteous before God, walking in all the commandments and ordinances of the Lord blameless. ⁷But they had no child, because Elizabeth was barren, and they were both well advanced in years.

⁸So it was, that while he was serving as priest before God in the order of his division, ⁹according to the custom of the priesthood, his lot fell to burn incense when he went into the temple of the Lord. ¹⁰And the whole multitude of the people was praying outside at the hour of incense. ¹¹Then an angel of the Lord appeared to him, standing on the right side of the altar of incense. ¹²And when Zacharias saw *him*, he was troubled,

---

1:1 ªOr *are most surely believed*

and fear fell upon him.

¹³But the angel said to him, "Do not be afraid, Zacharias, for your prayer is heard; and your wife Elizabeth will bear you a son, and you shall call his name John. ¹⁴And you will have joy and gladness, and many will rejoice at his birth. ¹⁵For he will be great in the sight of the Lord, and shall drink neither wine nor strong drink. He will also be filled with the Holy Spirit, even from his mother's womb. ¹⁶And he will turn many of the children of Israel to the Lord their God. ¹⁷He will also go before Him in the spirit and power of Elijah, *'to turn the hearts of the fathers to the children,*[a] and the disobedient to the wisdom of the just, to make ready a people prepared for the Lord."

¹⁸And Zacharias said to the angel, "How shall I know this? For I am an old man, and my wife is well advanced in years."

¹⁹And the angel answered and said to him, "I am Gabriel, who stands in the presence of God, and was sent to speak to you and bring you these glad tidings. ²⁰But behold, you will be mute and not able to speak until the day these things take place, because you did not believe my words which will be fulfilled in their own time."

²¹And the people waited for Zacharias, and marveled that he lingered so long in the temple. ²²But when he came out, he could not speak to them; and they perceived that he had seen a vision in the temple, for he beckoned to them and remained speechless.

²³So it was, as soon as the days of his service were completed, that he departed to his own house. ²⁴Now after those days his wife Elizabeth conceived; and she hid herself five months, say-

---

1:17 [a]Malachi 4:5, 6

ing, ^{25}"Thus the Lord has dealt with me, in the days when He looked on *me*, to take away my reproach among people."

Christ's Birth Announced to Mary

^{26}Now in the sixth month the angel Gabriel was sent by God to a city of Galilee named Nazareth, ^{27}to a virgin betrothed to a man whose name was Joseph, of the house of David. The virgin's name *was* Mary. ^{28}And having come in, the angel said to her, "Rejoice, highly favored *one*, the Lord *is* with you; blessed *are* you among women!"^{a}

^{29}But when she saw *him*,^{a} she was troubled at his saying, and considered what manner of greeting this was. ^{30}Then the angel said to her, "Do not be afraid, Mary, for you have found favor with God. ^{31}And behold, you will conceive in your womb and bring forth a Son, and shall call His name JESUS. ^{32}He will be great, and will be called the Son of the Highest; and the Lord God will give Him the throne of His father David. ^{33}And He will reign over the house of Jacob forever, and of His kingdom there will be no end."

^{34}Then Mary said to the angel, "How can this be, since I do not know a man?"

^{35}And the angel answered and said to her, "*The* Holy Spirit will come upon you, and the power of the Highest will overshadow you; therefore, also, that Holy One who is to be born will be called the Son of God. ^{36}Now indeed, Elizabeth your relative has also conceived a son in her old age; and this is now the sixth month for her who was called barren. ^{37}For with God nothing will be impossible."

1:28 ^{a}NU-Text omits *blessed are you among women.*   **1:29** ^{a}NU-Text omits *when she saw him.*

³⁸Then Mary said, "Behold the maidservant of the Lord! Let it be to me according to your word." And the angel departed from her.

Mary Visits Elizabeth

³⁹Now Mary arose in those days and went into the hill country with haste, to a city of Judah, ⁴⁰and entered the house of Zacharias and greeted Elizabeth. ⁴¹And it happened, when Elizabeth heard the greeting of Mary, that the babe leaped in her womb; and Elizabeth was filled with the Holy Spirit. ⁴²Then she spoke out with a loud voice and said, "Blessed *are* you among women, and blessed *is* the fruit of your womb! ⁴³But why *is* this *granted* to me, that the mother of my Lord should come to me? ⁴⁴For indeed, as soon as the voice of your greeting sounded in my ears, the babe leaped in my womb for joy. ⁴⁵Blessed *is* she who believed, for there will be a fulfillment of those things which were told her from the Lord."

The Song of Mary

⁴⁶And Mary said:

"My soul magnifies the Lord,
⁴⁷And my spirit has rejoiced in God my Savior.
⁴⁸For He has regarded the lowly state of His
      maidservant;
  For behold, henceforth all generations will
      call me blessed.
⁴⁹For He who is mighty has done great things
      for me,
  And holy *is* His name.
⁵⁰And His mercy *is* on those who fear Him
  From generation to generation.

⁵¹He has shown strength with His arm;
He has scattered *the* proud in the
imagination of their hearts.
⁵²He has put down the mighty from *their*
thrones,
And exalted *the* lowly.
⁵³He has filled *the* hungry with good things,
And *the* rich He has sent away empty.
⁵⁴He has helped His servant Israel,
In remembrance of *His* mercy,
⁵⁵As He spoke to our fathers,
To Abraham and to his seed forever."

⁵⁶And Mary remained with her about three months, and returned to her house.

Birth of John the Baptist

⁵⁷Now Elizabeth's full time came for her to be delivered, and she brought forth a son. ⁵⁸When her neighbors and relatives heard how the Lord had shown great mercy to her, they rejoiced with her.

Circumcision of John the Baptist

⁵⁹So it was, on the eighth day, that they came to circumcise the child; and they would have called him by the name of his father, Zacharias. ⁶⁰His mother answered and said, "No; he shall be called John."

⁶¹But they said to her, "There is no one among your relatives who is called by this name." ⁶²So they made signs to his father—what he would have him called.

⁶³And he asked for a writing tablet, and wrote, saying, "His name is John." So they all marveled. ⁶⁴Immediately his mouth was opened and his

tongue *loosed,* and he spoke, praising God. ⁶⁵Then fear came on all who dwelt around them; and all these sayings were discussed throughout all the hill country of Judea. ⁶⁶And all those who heard *them* kept *them* in their hearts, saying, "What kind of child will this be?" And the hand of the Lord was with him.

Zacharias' Prophecy

⁶⁷Now his father Zacharias was filled with the Holy Spirit, and prophesied, saying:

⁶⁸"Blessed *is* the Lord God of Israel,
    For He has visited and redeemed His people,
⁶⁹And has raised up a horn of salvation for us
    In the house of His servant David,
⁷⁰As He spoke by the mouth of His holy
       prophets,
    Who *have been* since the world began,
⁷¹That we should be saved from our enemies
    And from the hand of all who hate us,
⁷²To perform the mercy *promised* to our fathers
    And to remember His holy covenant,
⁷³The oath which He swore to our father
       Abraham:
⁷⁴To grant us that we,
    Being delivered from the hand of our
       enemies,
    Might serve Him without fear,
⁷⁵In holiness and righteousness before Him all
       the days of our life.

⁷⁶"And you, child, will be called the prophet of
       the Highest;
    For you will go before the face of the Lord to
       prepare His ways,

⁷⁷To give knowledge of salvation to His people
By the remission of their sins,
⁷⁸Through the tender mercy of our God,
With which the Dayspring from on high has
visitedᵃ us;
⁷⁹To give light to those who sit in darkness
and the shadow of death,
To guide our feet into the way of peace."

⁸⁰So the child grew and became strong in
spirit, and was in the deserts till the day of his
manifestation to Israel.

Christ Born of Mary

2 And it came to pass in those days *that* a de-
cree went out from Caesar Augustus that all
the world should be registered. ²This census first
took place while Quirinius was governing Syria.
³So all went to be registered, everyone to his own
city.

⁴Joseph also went up from Galilee, out of the
city of Nazareth, into Judea, to the city of David,
which is called Bethlehem, because he was of the
house and lineage of David, ⁵to be registered with
Mary, his betrothed wife,ᵃ who was with child.
⁶So it was, that while they were there, the days
were completed for her to be delivered. ⁷And she
brought forth her firstborn Son, and wrapped
Him in swaddling cloths, and laid Him in a
manger, because there was no room for them in
the inn.

Glory in the Highest

⁸Now there were in the same country shepherds living out in the fields, keeping watch over

---

1:78 ᵃNU-Text reads *shall visit.*   2:5 ᵃNU-Text omits *wife.*

their flock by night. [9]And behold,[a] an angel of the Lord stood before them, and the glory of the Lord shone around them, and they were greatly afraid. [10]Then the angel said to them, "Do not be afraid, for behold, I bring you good tidings of great joy which will be to all people. [11]For there is born to you this day in the city of David a Savior, who is Christ the Lord. [12]And this *will be* the sign to you: You will find a Babe wrapped in swaddling cloths, lying in a manger."

[13]And suddenly there was with the angel a multitude of the heavenly host praising God and saying:

[14]"Glory to God in the highest,
  And on earth peace, goodwill toward men!"[a]

[15]So it was, when the angels had gone away from them into heaven, that the shepherds said to one another, "Let us now go to Bethlehem and see this thing that has come to pass, which the Lord has made known to us." [16]And they came with haste and found Mary and Joseph, and the Babe lying in a manger. [17]Now when they had seen *Him*, they made widely[a] known the saying which was told them concerning this Child. [18]And all those who heard *it* marveled at those things which were told them by the shepherds. [19]But Mary kept all these things and pondered *them* in her heart. [20]Then the shepherds returned, glorifying and praising God for all the things that they had heard and seen, as it was told them.

2:9 [a]NU-Text omits *behold*.   2:14 [a]NU-Text reads *toward men of goodwill*.   2:17 [a]NU-Text omits *widely*.

Circumcision of Jesus

[21]And when eight days were completed for the circumcision of the Child,[a] His name was called Jesus, the name given by the angel before He was conceived in the womb.

Jesus Presented in the Temple

[22]Now when the days of her purification according to the law of Moses were completed, they brought Him to Jerusalem to present *Him* to the Lord [23](as it is written in the law of the Lord, *"Every male who opens the womb shall be called holy to the Lord"*),[a] [24]and to offer a sacrifice according to what is said in the law of the Lord, *"A pair of turtledoves or two young pigeons."*[a]

Simeon Sees God's Salvation

[25]And behold, there was a man in Jerusalem whose name *was* Simeon, and this man *was* just and devout, waiting for the Consolation of Israel, and the Holy Spirit was upon him. [26]And it had been revealed to him by the Holy Spirit that he would not see death before he had seen the Lord's Christ. [27]So he came by the Spirit into the temple. And when the parents brought in the Child Jesus, to do for Him according to the custom of the law, [28]he took Him up in his arms and blessed God and said:

[29]"Lord, now You are letting Your servant
          depart in peace,
     According to Your word;
[30]For my eyes have seen Your salvation
[31]Which You have prepared before the face of
          all peoples,

2:21 [a]NU-Text reads *for His circumcision.*   2:23 [a]Exodus 13:2, 12, 15   2:24 [a]Leviticus 12:8

³²A light to *bring* revelation to the Gentiles,
  And the glory of Your people Israel."

³³And Joseph and His mother^a marveled at
those things which were spoken of Him. ³⁴Then
Simeon blessed them, and said to Mary His
mother, "Behold, this *Child* is destined for the fall
and rising of many in Israel, and for a sign which
will be spoken against ³⁵(yes, a sword will pierce
through your own soul also), that the thoughts of
many hearts may be revealed."

Anna Bears Witness to the Redeemer

³⁶Now there was one, Anna, a prophetess, the
daughter of Phanuel, of the tribe of Asher. She
was of a great age, and had lived with a husband
seven years from her virginity; ³⁷and this woman
was a widow of about eighty-four years,^a who
did not depart from the temple, but served *God*
with fastings and prayers night and day. ³⁸And
coming in that instant she gave thanks to the
Lord,^a and spoke of Him to all those who looked
for redemption in Jerusalem.

The Family Returns to Nazareth

³⁹So when they had performed all things according to the law of the Lord, they returned to
Galilee, to their *own* city, Nazareth. ⁴⁰And the
Child grew and became strong in spirit,^a filled with
wisdom; and the grace of God was upon Him.

The Boy Jesus Amazes the Scholars

⁴¹His parents went to Jerusalem every year at

2:33 ^aNU-Text reads *And His father and mother.*   2:37 ^aNU-Text
reads *a widow until she was eighty-four.*   2:38 ^aNU-Text reads *to
God.*   2:40 ^aNU-Text omits *in spirit.*

the Feast of the Passover. [42]And when He was twelve years old, they went up to Jerusalem according to the custom of the feast. [43]When they had finished the days, as they returned, the Boy Jesus lingered behind in Jerusalem. And Joseph and His mother[a] did not know *it*; [44]but supposing Him to have been in the company, they went a day's journey, and sought Him among *their* relatives and acquaintances. [45]So when they did not find Him, they returned to Jerusalem, seeking Him. [46]Now so it was *that* after three days they found Him in the temple, sitting in the midst of the teachers, both listening to them and asking them questions. [47]And all who heard Him were astonished at His understanding and answers. [48]So when they saw Him, they were amazed; and His mother said to Him, "Son, why have You done this to us? Look, Your father and I have sought You anxiously."

[49]And He said to them, "Why did you seek Me? Did you not know that I must be about My Father's business?" [50]But they did not understand the statement which He spoke to them.

Jesus Advances in Wisdom and Favor

[51]Then He went down with them and came to Nazareth, and was subject to them, but His mother kept all these things in her heart. [52]And Jesus increased in wisdom and stature, and in favor with God and men.

John the Baptist Prepares the Way

3 Now in the fifteenth year of the reign of Tiberius Caesar, Pontius Pilate being governor of Judea, Herod being tetrarch of Galilee, his

---

2:43 [a]NU-Text reads *And His parents.*

brother Philip tetrarch of Iturea and the region of Trachonitis, and Lysanias tetrarch of Abilene, [2]while Annas and Caiaphas were high priests,[a] the word of God came to John the son of Zacharias in the wilderness. [3]And he went into all the region around the Jordan, preaching a baptism of repentance for the remission of sins, [4]as it is written in the book of the words of Isaiah the prophet, saying:

"The voice of one crying in the wilderness:
    'Prepare the way of the Lord;
    Make His paths straight.
[5]Every valley shall be filled
    And every mountain and hill brought low;
    The crooked places shall be made straight
    And the rough ways smooth;
[6]And all flesh shall see the salvation of God.' "[a]

John Preaches to the People

[7]Then he said to the multitudes that came out to be baptized by him, "Brood of vipers! Who warned you to flee from the wrath to come? [8]Therefore bear fruits worthy of repentance, and do not begin to say to yourselves, 'We have Abraham as *our* father.' For I say to you that God is able to raise up children to Abraham from these stones. [9]And even now the ax is laid to the root of the trees. Therefore every tree which does not bear good fruit is cut down and thrown into the fire."

[10]So the people asked him, saying, "What shall we do then?"

[11]He answered and said to them, "He who

3:2 [a]NU-Text and M-Text read *in the high priesthood of Annas and Caiaphas.* 3:6 [a]Isaiah 40:3–5

has two tunics, let him give to him who has none; and he who has food, let him do likewise."

¹²Then tax collectors also came to be baptized, and said to him, "Teacher, what shall we do?".

¹³And he said to them, "Collect no more than what is appointed for you."

¹⁴Likewise the soldiers asked him, saying, "And what shall we do?"

So he said to them, "Do not intimidate anyone or accuse falsely, and be content with your wages."

¹⁵Now as the people were in expectation, and all reasoned in their hearts about John, whether he was the Christ *or* not, ¹⁶John answered, saying to all, "I indeed baptize you with water; but One mightier than I is coming, whose sandal strap I am not worthy to loose. He will baptize you with the Holy Spirit and fire. ¹⁷His winnowing fan *is* in His hand, and He will thoroughly clean out His threshing floor, and gather the wheat into His barn; but the chaff He will burn with unquenchable fire."

¹⁸And with many other exhortations he preached to the people. ¹⁹But Herod the tetrarch, being rebuked by him concerning Herodias, his brother Philip's wife,[a] and for all the evils which Herod had done, ²⁰also added this, above all, that he shut John up in prison.

John Baptizes Jesus

²¹When all the people were baptized, it came to pass that Jesus also was baptized; and while He prayed, the heaven was opened. ²²And the Holy Spirit descended in bodily form like a dove

---

3:19 ªNU-Text reads *his brother's wife.*

upon Him, and a voice came from heaven which said, "You are My beloved Son; in You I am well pleased."

The Genealogy of Jesus Christ

23Now Jesus Himself began *His ministry at* about thirty years of age, being (as was supposed) *the* son of Joseph, *the* son of Heli, 24*the son* of Matthat,[a] *the son* of Levi, *the* son of Melchi, *the* son of Janna, *the* son of Joseph, 25*the son of* Mattathiah, *the son* of Amos, *the* son of Nahum, *the* son of Esli, *the son* of Naggai, 26*the son* of Maath, *the* son of Mattathiah, *the son* of Semei, *the son* of Joseph, *the son* of Judah, 27*the son* of Joannas, *the* son of Rhesa, *the son* of Zerubbabel, *the son* of Shealtiel, *the son* of Neri, 28*the son* of Melchi, *the* son of Addi, *the son* of Cosam, *the son* of Elmodam, *the son* of Er, 29*the son* of Jose, *the son* of Eliezer, *the son* of Jorim, *the son* of Matthat, *the* son of Levi, 30*the son* of Simeon, *the son* of Judah, *the son* of Joseph, *the son* of Jonan, *the son* of Eliakim, 31*the son* of Melea, *the son* of Menan, *the son* of Mattathah, *the son* of Nathan, *the son* of David, 32*the son* of Jesse, *the son* of Obed, *the son* of Boaz, *the son* of Salmon, *the son* of Nahshon, 33*the son* of Amminadab, *the son* of Ram, *the son* of Hezron, *the son* of Perez, *the son* of Judah, 34*the son* of Jacob, *the son* of Isaac, *the son* of Abraham, *the son* of Terah, *the son* of Nahor, 35*the son* of Serug, *the* son of Reu, *the son* of Peleg, *the son* of Eber, *the son* of Shelah, 36*the son* of Cainan, *the son* of Arphaxad, *the son* of Shem, *the son* of Noah, *the*

3:24 [a]This and several other names in the genealogy are spelled somewhat differently in the NU-Text. Since the New King James Version uses the Old Testament spelling for persons mentioned in the New Testament, these variations, which come from the Greek, have not been footnoted.

son of Lamech, [37]*the son* of Methuselah, *the son* of Enoch, *the son* of Jared, *the son* of Mahalalel, *the son* of Cainan, [38]*the son* of Enosh, *the son* of Seth, *the son* of Adam, *the son* of God.

Satan Tempts Jesus

4 Then Jesus, being filled with the Holy Spirit, returned from the Jordan and was led by the Spirit into[a] the wilderness, [2]being tempted for forty days by the devil. And in those days He ate nothing, and afterward, when they had ended, He was hungry.

[3]And the devil said to Him, "If You are the Son of God, command this stone to become bread."

[4]But Jesus answered him, saying,[a] "It is written, *'Man shall not live by bread alone, but by every word of God.'* "[b]

[5]Then the devil, taking Him up on a high mountain, showed Him[a] all the kingdoms of the world in a moment of time. [6]And the devil said to Him, "All this authority I will give You, and their glory; for *this* has been delivered to me, and I give it to whomever I wish. [7]Therefore, if You will worship before me, all will be Yours."

[8]And Jesus answered and said to him, "Get behind Me, Satan![a] For[b] it is written, *'You shall worship the Lord your God, and Him only you shall serve.'* "[c]

[9]Then he brought Him to Jerusalem, set Him on the pinnacle of the temple, and said to Him, "If You are the Son of God, throw Yourself down

---

4:1 [a]NU-Text reads *in.*   4:4 [a]Deuteronomy 8:3   [b]NU-Text omits *but by every word of God.*   4:5 [a]NU-Text reads *And taking Him up, he showed Him.*   4:8 [a]NU-Text omits *Get behind Me, Satan.* [b]NU-Text and M-Text omit *For.* [c]Deuteronomy 6:13

from here. [10]For it is written:

> 'He shall give His angels charge over you,
> To keep you,'

[11]and,

> 'In their hands they shall bear you up,
> Lest you dash your foot against a stone.'"[a]

[12]And Jesus answered and said to him, "It has been said, 'You shall not tempt the Lord your God.'"[a]

[13]Now when the devil had ended every temptation, he departed from Him until an opportune time.

Jesus Begins His Galilean Ministry

[14]Then Jesus returned in the power of the Spirit to Galilee, and news of Him went out through all the surrounding region. [15]And He taught in their synagogues, being glorified by all.

Jesus Rejected at Nazareth

[16]So He came to Nazareth, where He had been brought up. And as His custom was, He went into the synagogue on the Sabbath day, and stood up to read. [17]And He was handed the book of the prophet Isaiah. And when He had opened the book, He found the place where it was written:

> [18]"The Spirit of the LORD is upon Me,
> Because He has anointed Me
> To preach the gospel to the poor;

4:11 [a]Psalm 91:11, 12   4:12 [a]Deuteronomy 6:16

He has sent Me to heal the brokenhearted,[a]
To proclaim liberty to the captives
And recovery of sight to the blind,
To set at liberty those who are oppressed;
[19] *To proclaim the acceptable year of the*
        LORD."[a]

[20]Then He closed the book, and gave *it* back to the attendant and sat down. And the eyes of all who were in the synagogue were fixed on Him. [21]And He began to say to them, "Today this Scripture is fulfilled in your hearing." [22]So all bore witness to Him, and marveled at the gracious words which proceeded out of His mouth. And they said, "Is this not Joseph's son?"

[23]He said to them, "You will surely say this proverb to Me, 'Physician, heal yourself! Whatever we have heard done in Capernaum,[a] do also here in Your country.' " [24]Then He said, "Assuredly, I say to you, no prophet is accepted in his own country. [25]But I tell you truly, many widows were in Israel in the days of Elijah, when the heaven was shut up three years and six months, and there was a great famine throughout all the land; [26]but to none of them was Elijah sent except to Zarephath,[a] *in the region* of Sidon, to a woman *who was* a widow. [27]And many lepers were in Israel in the time of Elisha the prophet, and none of them was cleansed except Naaman the Syrian."

[28]So all those in the synagogue, when they heard these things, were filled with wrath, [29]and rose up and thrust Him out of the city; and they

---

4:18 [a]NU-Text omits *to heal the brokenhearted.*   **4:19** [a]Isaiah 61:1, 2   **4:23** [a]Here and elsewhere the NU-Text spelling is *Capharnaum.*   **4:26** [a]Greek *Sarepta*

led Him to the brow of the hill on which their city was built, that they might throw Him down over the cliff. ³⁰Then passing through the midst of them, He went His way.

Jesus Casts Out an Unclean Spirit

³¹Then He went down to Capernaum, a city of Galilee, and was teaching them on the Sabbaths. ³²And they were astonished at His teaching, for His word was with authority. ³³Now in the synagogue there was a man who had a spirit of an unclean demon. And he cried out with a loud voice, ³⁴saying, "Let *us* alone! What have we to do with You, Jesus of Nazareth? Did You come to destroy us? I know who You are—the Holy One of God!"

³⁵But Jesus rebuked him, saying, "Be quiet, and come out of him!" And when the demon had thrown him in *their* midst, it came out of him and did not hurt him. ³⁶Then they were all amazed and spoke among themselves, saying, "What a word this *is!* For with authority and power He commands the unclean spirits, and they come out." ³⁷And the report about Him went out into every place in the surrounding region.

Peter's Mother-in-Law Healed

³⁸Now He arose from the synagogue and entered Simon's house. But Simon's wife's mother was sick with a high fever, and they made request of Him concerning her. ³⁹So He stood over her and rebuked the fever, and it left her. And immediately she arose and served them.

Many Healed After Sabbath Sunset

⁴⁰When the sun was setting, all those who had any that were sick with various diseases

brought them to Him; and He laid His hands on every one of them and healed them. ⁴¹And demons also came out of many, crying out and saying, "You are the Christ,ᵃ the Son of God!"

And He, rebuking *them,* did not allow them to speak, for they knew that He was the Christ.

Jesus Preaches in Galilee

⁴²Now when it was day, He departed and went into a deserted place. And the crowd sought Him and came to Him, and tried to keep Him from leaving them; ⁴³but He said to them, "I must preach the kingdom of God to the other cities also, because for this purpose I have been sent." ⁴⁴And He was preaching in the synagogues of Galilee.ᵃ

Four Fishermen Called as Disciples

5 So it was, as the multitude pressed about Him to hear the word of God, that He stood by the Lake of Gennesaret, ²and saw two boats standing by the lake; but the fishermen had gone from them and were washing *their* nets. ³Then He got into one of the boats, which was Simon's, and asked him to put out a little from the land. And He sat down and taught the multitudes from the boat.

⁴When He had stopped speaking, He said to Simon, "Launch out into the deep and let down your nets for a catch."

⁵But Simon answered and said to Him, "Master, we have toiled all night and caught nothing; nevertheless at Your word I will let down the net." ⁶And when they had done this, they caught a great number of fish, and their net was breaking.

4:41 ᵃNU-Text omits *the Christ.*   4:44 ᵃNU-Text reads *Judea.*

⁷So they signaled to *their* partners in the other boat to come and help them. And they came and filled both the boats, so that they began to sink. ⁸When Simon Peter saw it, he fell down at Jesus' knees, saying, "Depart from me, for I am a sinful man, O Lord!"

⁹For he and all who were with him were astonished at the catch of fish which they had taken; ¹⁰and so also *were* James and John, the sons of Zebedee, who were partners with Simon. And Jesus said to Simon, "Do not be afraid. From now on you will catch men." ¹¹So when they had brought their boats to land, they forsook all and followed Him.

Jesus Cleanses a Leper

¹²And it happened when He was in a certain city, that behold, a man who was full of leprosy saw Jesus; and he fell on *his* face and implored Him, saying, "Lord, if You are willing, You can make me clean."

¹³Then He put out *His* hand and touched him, saying, "I am willing; be cleansed." Immediately the leprosy left him. ¹⁴And He charged him to tell no one, "But go and show yourself to the priest, and make an offering for your cleansing, as a testimony to them, just as Moses commanded."

¹⁵However, the report went around concerning Him all the more; and great multitudes came together to hear, and to be healed by Him of their infirmities. ¹⁶So He Himself *often* withdrew into the wilderness and prayed.

Jesus Forgives and Heals a Paralytic

¹⁷Now it happened on a certain day, as He was teaching, that there were Pharisees and teachers

of the law sitting by, who had come out of every town of Galilee, Judea, and Jerusalem. And the power of the Lord was *present* to heal them.[a] [18]Then behold, men brought on a bed a man who was paralyzed, whom they sought to bring in and lay before Him. [19]And when they could not find how they might bring him in, because of the crowd, they went up on the housetop and let him down with *his* bed through the tiling into the midst before Jesus.

[20]When He saw their faith, He said to him, "Man, your sins are forgiven you."

[21]And the scribes and the Pharisees began to reason, saying, "Who is this who speaks blasphemies? Who can forgive sins but God alone?"

[22]But when Jesus perceived their thoughts, He answered and said to them, "Why are you reasoning in your hearts? [23]Which is easier, to say, 'Your sins are forgiven you,' or to say, 'Rise up and walk'? [24]But that you may know that the Son of Man has power on earth to forgive sins"—He said to the man who was paralyzed, "I say to you, arise, take up your bed, and go to your house."

[25]Immediately he rose up before them, took up what he had been lying on, and departed to his own house, glorifying God. [26]And they were all amazed, and they glorified God and were filled with fear, saying, "We have seen strange things today!"

Matthew the Tax Collector

[27]After these things He went out and saw a tax collector named Levi, sitting at the tax office. And He said to him, "Follow Me." [28]So he left all, rose up, and followed Him.

5:17 [a]NU-Text reads *present with Him to heal.*

²⁹Then Levi gave Him a great feast in his own house. And there were a great number of tax collectors and others who sat down with them. ³⁰And their scribes and the Pharisees[a] complained against His disciples, saying, "Why do You eat and drink with tax collectors and sinners?"

³¹Jesus answered and said to them, "Those who are well have no need of a physician, but those who are sick. ³²I have not come to call *the* righteous, but sinners, to repentance."

Jesus Is Questioned About Fasting

³³Then they said to Him, "Why do[a] the disciples of John fast often and make prayers, and likewise those of the Pharisees, but Yours eat and drink?"

³⁴And He said to them, "Can you make the friends of the bridegroom fast while the bridegroom is with them? ³⁵But the days will come when the bridegroom will be taken away from them; then they will fast in those days."

³⁶Then He spoke a parable to them: "No one puts a piece from a new garment on an old one;[a] otherwise the new makes a tear, and also the piece that was *taken* out of the new does not match the old. ³⁷And no one puts new wine into old wineskins; or else the new wine will burst the wineskins and be spilled, and the wineskins will be ruined. ³⁸But new wine must be put into new wineskins, and both are preserved.[a] ³⁹And no one, having drunk old *wine*, immediately[a] desires new; for he says, 'The old is better.' "[b]

5:30 [a]NU-Text reads *But the Pharisees and their scribes.*   5:33 [a]NU-Text omits *Why do,* making the verse a statement.   5:36 [a]NU-Text omits *No one tears a piece from a new garment and puts it on an old one.*   5:38 [a]NU-Text omits *and both are preserved.* 5:39 [a]NU-Text omits *immediately.*   [b]NU-Text reads *good.*

Jesus Is Lord of the Sabbath

6 Now it happened on the second Sabbath after the first[a] that He went through the grain-fields. And His disciples plucked the heads of grain and ate *them,* rubbing *them* in *their* hands. [2]And some of the Pharisees said to them, "Why are you doing what is not lawful to do on the Sabbath?"

[3]But Jesus answering them said, "Have you not even read this, what David did when he was hungry, he and those who were with him: [4]how he went into the house of God, took and ate the showbread, and also gave some to those with him, which is not lawful for any but the priests to eat?" [5]And He said to them, "The Son of Man is also Lord of the Sabbath."

Healing on the Sabbath

[6]Now it happened on another Sabbath, also, that He entered the synagogue and taught. And a man was there whose right hand was withered. [7]So the scribes and Pharisees watched Him closely, whether He would heal on the Sabbath, that they might find an accusation against Him. [8]But He knew their thoughts, and said to the man who had the withered hand, "Arise and stand here." And he arose and stood. [9]Then Jesus said to them, "I will ask you one thing: Is it lawful on the Sabbath to do good or to do evil, to save life or to destroy?"[a] [10]And when He had looked around at them all, He said to the man,[a] "Stretch out your hand." And he did so, and his hand was restored as whole as the other.[b] [11]But

---

6:1 [a]NU-Text reads *on a Sabbath.*   6:9 [a]M-Text reads *to kill.*
6:10 [a]NU-Text and M-Text read *to him.*   [b]NU-Text omits *as whole as the other.*

they were filled with rage, and discussed with one another what they might do to Jesus.

The Twelve Apostles

¹²Now it came to pass in those days that He went out to the mountain to pray, and continued all night in prayer to God. ¹³And when it was day, He called His disciples to *Himself;* and from them He chose twelve whom He also named apostles: ¹⁴Simon, whom He also named Peter, and Andrew his brother; James and John; Philip and Bartholomew; ¹⁵Matthew and Thomas; James the *son* of Alphaeus, and Simon called the Zealot; ¹⁶Judas *the son* of James, and Judas Iscariot who also became a traitor.

Jesus Heals a Great Multitude

¹⁷And He came down with them and stood on a level place with a crowd of His disciples and a great multitude of people from all Judea and Jerusalem, and from the seacoast of Tyre and Sidon, who came to hear Him and be healed of their diseases, ¹⁸as well as those who were tormented with unclean spirits. And they were healed. ¹⁹And the whole multitude sought to touch Him, for power went out from Him and healed *them* all.

The Beatitudes

²⁰Then He lifted up His eyes toward His disciples, and said:

"Blessed *are you* poor,
    For yours is the kingdom of God.
²¹Blessed *are you* who hunger now,
    For you shall be filled.

Blessed *are you* who weep now,
    For you shall laugh.
²²Blessed are you when men hate you,
    And when they exclude you,
    And revile *you,* and cast out your name as
        evil,
    For the Son of Man's sake.
²³Rejoice in that day and leap for joy!
    For indeed your reward is great in heaven,
    For in like manner their fathers did to the
        prophets.

Jesus Pronounces Woes

²⁴"But woe to you who are rich,
    For you have received your consolation.
²⁵Woe to you who are full,
    For you shall hunger.
Woe to you who laugh now,
    For you shall mourn and weep.
²⁶Woe to you[a] when all[b] men speak well of you,
    For so did their fathers to the false prophets.

Love Your Enemies

²⁷"But I say to you who hear: Love your enemies, do good to those who hate you, ²⁸bless
those who curse you, and pray for those who
spitefully use you. ²⁹To him who strikes you on
the *one* cheek, offer the other also. And from him
who takes away your cloak, do not withhold
your tunic either. ³⁰Give to everyone who asks of
you. And from him who takes away your goods
do not ask *them* back. ³¹And just as you want men
to do to you, you also do to them likewise.

³²"But if you love those who love you, what
credit is that to you? For even sinners love those

6:26 [a]NU-Text and M-Text omit *to you.* [b]M-Text omits *all.*

who love them. ³³And if you do good to those who do good to you, what credit is that to you? For even sinners do the same. ³⁴And if you lend *to those* from whom you hope to receive back, what credit is that to you? For even sinners lend to sinners to receive as much back. ³⁵But love your enemies, do good, and lend, hoping for nothing in return; and your reward will be great, and you will be sons of the Most High. For He is kind to the unthankful and evil. ³⁶Therefore be merciful, just as your Father also is merciful.

Do Not Judge

³⁷"Judge not, and you shall not be judged. Condemn not, and you shall not be condemned. Forgive, and you will be forgiven. ³⁸Give, and it will be given to you: good measure, pressed down, shaken together, and running over will be put into your bosom. For with the same measure that you use, it will be measured back to you."

³⁹And He spoke a parable to them: "Can the blind lead the blind? Will they not both fall into the ditch? ⁴⁰A disciple is not above his teacher, but everyone who is perfectly trained will be like his teacher. ⁴¹And why do you look at the speck in your brother's eye, but do not perceive the plank in your own eye? ⁴²Or how can you say to your brother, 'Brother, let me remove the speck that is in your eye,' when you yourself do not see the plank that is in your own eye? Hypocrite! First remove the plank from your own eye, and then you will see clearly to remove the speck that is in your brother's eye.

A Tree Is Known by Its Fruit

⁴³"For a good tree does not bear bad fruit, nor

does a bad tree bear good fruit. ⁴⁴For every tree is known by its own fruit. For *men* do not gather figs from thorns, nor do they gather grapes from a bramble bush. ⁴⁵A good man out of the good treasure of his heart brings forth good; and an evil man out of the evil treasure of his heartᵃ brings forth evil. For out of the abundance of the heart his mouth speaks.

Build on the Rock

⁴⁶"But why do you call Me 'Lord, Lord,' and not do the things which I say? ⁴⁷Whoever comes to Me, and hears My sayings and does them, I will show you whom he is like: ⁴⁸He is like a man building a house, who dug deep and laid the foundation on the rock. And when the flood arose, the stream beat vehemently against that house, and could not shake it, for it was founded on the rock.ᵃ ⁴⁹But he who heard and did nothing is like a man who built a house on the earth without a foundation, against which the stream beat vehemently; and immediately it fell.ᵃ And the ruin of that house was great."

Jesus Heals a Centurion's Servant

7 Now when He concluded all His sayings in the hearing of the people, He entered Capernaum. ²And a certain centurion's servant, who was dear to him, was sick and ready to die. ³So when he heard about Jesus, he sent elders of the Jews to Him, pleading with Him to come and heal his servant. ⁴And when they came to Jesus, they begged Him earnestly, saying that the one for whom He should do this was deserving, ⁵"for

---

6:45 ᵃNU-Text omits *treasure of his heart*.   6:48 ᵃNU-Text reads *for it was well built*.   6:49 ᵃNU-Text reads *collapsed*.

he loves our nation, and has built us a synagogue."

⁶Then Jesus went with them. And when He was already not far from the house, the centurion sent friends to Him, saying to Him, "Lord, do not trouble Yourself, for I am not worthy that You should enter under my roof. ⁷Therefore I did not even think myself worthy to come to You. But say the word, and my servant will be healed. ⁸For I also am a man placed under authority, having soldiers under me. And I say to one, 'Go,' and he goes; and to another, 'Come,' and he comes; and to my servant, 'Do this,' and he does *it*."

⁹When Jesus heard these things, He marveled at him, and turned around and said to the crowd that followed Him, "I say to you, I have not found such great faith, not even in Israel!" ¹⁰And those who were sent, returning to the house, found the servant well who had been sick.[a]

Jesus Raises the Son of the Widow of Nain

¹¹Now it happened, the day after, *that* He went into a city called Nain; and many of His disciples went with Him, and a large crowd. ¹²And when He came near the gate of the city, behold, a dead man was being carried out, the only son of his mother; and she was a widow. And a large crowd from the city was with her. ¹³When the Lord saw her, He had compassion on her and said to her, "Do not weep." ¹⁴Then He came and touched the open coffin, and those who carried *him* stood still. And He said, "Young man, I say to you, arise." ¹⁵So he who was dead sat up and began to speak. And He presented him to his mother.

7:10 ᵃNU-Text omits *who had been sick.*

Why worry about Hell?
All my friends will be there.

Obviously, those who flippantly say such things don't believe in the biblical concept of Hell. They might like to think that life as we know it couldn't get any worse, but the sufferings in this life will be Heaven compared to the suffering in the next life—for those who die in their sins. This life is the closest thing to Hell that Christians will ever know, and the closest thing to Heaven that sinners will ever know.

Skeptics try to dismiss the reality of Hell, picturing it as a fun, hedonistic, pleasure-filled place where they can engage in all the sensual sins that are forbidden here. Others accept that Hell is a place of punishment, but believe that the punishment is to be annihilated—to cease conscious existence. Because they can't conceive that a loving God would punish people in eternal torment, they believe Hell is just a metaphor for the grave. If they are correct, then a man like Adolph Hitler, who was responsible for the deaths of millions, is being "punished" merely with eternal sleep. His fate is simply to return to the nonexistent state he was in before he was born, where he doesn't even know that he is being punished.

But since our souls are eternal, this punishment will be eternal. It will also be conscious. Scripture tells us of the rich man who found himself in Hell (Luke 16:19–31). He was conscious and was able to feel pain, to thirst, and to experience remorse. He wasn't asleep in the grave; he was in a place of "torment."

We tend to forget what pain is like when we don't have it. Can you imagine how terrible it would be to be in agony, with no hope of relief? Many humans go insane if they are merely isolated for a long time from other people. Imagine how terrible it would be if God simply withdrew all the things we hold so dear—friendship, love, color, light, peace, joy, laughter. Hell isn't just a place with an absence of

God's blessings; it is punishment for sin. It is literal torment, forever. That's why the Bible warns that it is a fearful thing to fall into the hands of the living God. The fate of the unsaved is described with such fearful words as the following:

- "Shame and everlasting contempt" (Daniel 12:2)
- "Everlasting punishment" (Matthew 25:46)
- "Weeping and gnashing of teeth" (Matthew 24:51)
- "Unquenchable fire" (Luke 3:17)
- "Indignation and wrath, tribulation and anguish" (Romans 2:8,9)
- "Everlasting destruction from the presence of the Lord" (2 Thessalonians 1:9)
- "Eternal fire...the blackness of darkness forever" (Jude 7,13)

Revelation 14:10,11 tells us the final, eternal destiny of the sinner: "He shall be tormented with fire and brimstone... And the smoke of their torment ascends forever and ever; and they have no rest day or night..."

Scripture is quite clear: Hell is a very real place. It is not mere unconsciousness. It is not temporal. It is eternal torment. If Hell is a place of knowing nothing or a reference to the grave into which we go at death, Jesus' statements about Hell make no sense. He said that if your hand, foot, or eye causes you to sin, it would be better to remove it than to "be cast into hell fire—where 'their worm does not die, and the fire is not quenched'" (Mark 9:43–48).

Jesus spoke more of Hell than of Heaven and spent much time warning people not to go there. After all, if people just stopped existing, why warn them? If Hell were temporal, they'd get out in a while. But because it is eternal and conscious, we must heed His warning.

[16]Then fear came upon all, and they glorified God, saying, "A great prophet has risen up among us"; and, "God has visited His people." [17]And this report about Him went throughout all Judea and all the surrounding region.

John the Baptist Sends Messengers to Jesus

[18]Then the disciples of John reported to him concerning all these things. [19]And John, calling two of his disciples to *him,* sent *them* to Jesus,[a] saying, "Are You the Coming One, or do we look for another?"

[20]When the men had come to Him, they said, "John the Baptist has sent us to You, saying, 'Are You the Coming One, or do we look for another?' " [21]And that very hour He cured many of infirmities, afflictions, and evil spirits; and to many blind He gave sight.

[22]Jesus answered and said to them, "Go and tell John the things you have seen and heard: that *the* blind see, *the* lame walk, *the* lepers are cleansed, *the* deaf hear, *the* dead are raised, *the* poor have the gospel preached to them. [23]And blessed is *he* who is not offended because of Me."

[24]When the messengers of John had departed, He began to speak to the multitudes concerning John: "What did you go out into the wilderness to see? A reed shaken by the wind? [25]But what did you go out to see? A man clothed in soft garments? Indeed those who are gorgeously appareled and live in luxury are in kings' courts. [26]But what did you go out to see? A prophet? Yes, I say to you, and more than a prophet. [27]This is *he* of whom it is written:

7:19 [a]NU-Text reads *the Lord.*

> 'Behold, I send My messenger before Your
>   face,
> Who will prepare Your way before You. [a]

28For I say to you, among those born of women there is not a greater prophet than John the Baptist;[a] but he who is least in the kingdom of God is greater than he."

29And when all the people heard *Him*, even the tax collectors justified God, having been baptized with the baptism of John. 30But the Pharisees and lawyers rejected the will of God for themselves, not having been baptized by him.

31And the Lord said,[a] "To what then shall I liken the men of this generation, and what are they like? 32They are like children sitting in the marketplace and calling to one another, saying:

> 'We played the flute for you,
>   And you did not dance;
> We mourned to you,
>   And you did not weep.'

33For John the Baptist came neither eating bread nor drinking wine, and you say, 'He has a demon.' 34The Son of Man has come eating and drinking, and you say, 'Look, a glutton and a winebibber, a friend of tax collectors and sinners!' 35But wisdom is justified by all her children."

A Sinful Woman Forgiven

36Then one of the Pharisees asked Him to eat with him. And He went to the Pharisee's house, and sat down to eat. 37And behold, a woman in

---

7:27 [a]Malachi 3:1   7:28 [a]NU-Text reads *there is none greater than John.*   7:31 [a]NU-Text and M-Text omit *And the Lord said.*

the city who was a sinner, when she knew that *Jesus* sat at the table in the Pharisee's house, brought an alabaster flask of fragrant oil, ³⁸and stood at His feet behind *Him* weeping; and she began to wash His feet with her tears, and wiped *them* with the hair of her head; and she kissed His feet and anointed *them* with the fragrant oil. ³⁹Now when the Pharisee who had invited Him saw *this*, he spoke to himself, saying, "This Man, if He were a prophet, would know who and what manner of woman *this is* who is touching Him, for she is a sinner."

⁴⁰And Jesus answered and said to him, "Simon, I have something to say to you."

So he said, "Teacher, say it."

⁴¹"There was a certain creditor who had two debtors. One owed five hundred denarii, and the other fifty. ⁴²And when they had nothing with which to repay, he freely forgave them both. Tell Me, therefore, which of them will love him more?"

⁴³Simon answered and said, "I suppose the *one* whom he forgave more."

And He said to him, "You have rightly judged." ⁴⁴Then He turned to the woman and said to Simon, "Do you see this woman? I entered your house; you gave Me no water for My feet, but she has washed My feet with her tears and wiped *them* with the hair of her head. ⁴⁵You gave Me no kiss, but this woman has not ceased to kiss My feet since the time I came in. ⁴⁶You did not anoint My head with oil, but this woman has anointed My feet with fragrant oil. ⁴⁷Therefore I say to you, her sins, *which are* many, are forgiven, for she loved much. But to whom little is forgiven, *the same* loves little."

⁴⁸Then He said to her, "Your sins are forgiven."

⁴⁹And those who sat at the table with Him began to say to themselves, "Who is this who even forgives sins?"

⁵⁰Then He said to the woman, "Your faith has saved you. Go in peace."

Many Women Minister to Jesus

8 Now it came to pass, afterward, that He went through every city and village, preaching and bringing the glad tidings of the kingdom of God. And the twelve *were* with Him, ²and certain women who had been healed of evil spirits and infirmities—Mary called Magdalene, out of whom had come seven demons, ³and Joanna the wife of Chuza, Herod's steward, and Susanna, and many others who provided for Him[a] from their substance.

The Parable of the Sower

⁴And when a great multitude had gathered, and they had come to Him from every city, He spoke by a parable: ⁵"A sower went out to sow his seed. And as he sowed, some fell by the wayside; and it was trampled down, and the birds of the air devoured it. ⁶Some fell on rock; and as soon as it sprang up, it withered away because it lacked moisture. ⁷And some fell among thorns, and the thorns sprang up with it and choked it. ⁸But others fell on good ground, sprang up, and yielded a crop a hundredfold." When He had said these things He cried, "He who has ears to hear, let him hear!"

8:3 ᵃNU-Text and M-Text read *them*.

The Purpose of Parables

[9]Then His disciples asked Him, saying, "What does this parable mean?"

[10]And He said, "To you it has been given to know the mysteries of the kingdom of God, but to the rest *it is given* in parables, that

> *'Seeing they may not see,*
> *And hearing they may not understand.* [a]

The Parable of the Sower Explained

[11]"Now the parable is this: The seed is the word of God. [12]Those by the wayside are the ones who hear; then the devil comes and takes away the word out of their hearts, lest they should believe and be saved. [13]But the ones on the rock *are those* who, when they hear, receive the word with joy; and these have no root, who believe for a while and in time of temptation fall away. [14]Now the ones *that* fell among thorns are those who, when they have heard, go out and are choked with cares, riches, and pleasures of life, and bring no fruit to maturity. [15]But the ones *that* fell on the good ground are those who, having heard the word with a noble and good heart, keep *it* and bear fruit with patience.

The Parable of the Revealed Light

[16]"No one, when he has lit a lamp, covers it with a vessel or puts *it* under a bed, but sets *it* on a lampstand, that those who enter may see the light. [17]For nothing is secret that will not be revealed, nor *anything* hidden that will not be known and come to light. [18]Therefore take heed how you hear. For whoever has, to him *more* will

8:10 [a]Isaiah 6:9

be given; and whoever does not have, even what he seems to have will be taken from him."

Jesus' Mother and Brothers Come to Him

[19]Then His mother and brothers came to Him, and could not approach Him because of the crowd. [20]And it was told Him *by some,* who said, "Your mother and Your brothers are standing outside, desiring to see You."

[21]But He answered and said to them, "My mother and My brothers are these who hear the word of God and do it."

Wind and Wave Obey Jesus

[22]Now it happened, on a certain day, that He got into a boat with His disciples. And He said to them, "Let us cross over to the other side of the lake." And they launched out. [23]But as they sailed He fell asleep. And a windstorm came down on the lake, and they were filling *with water,* and were in jeopardy. [24]And they came to Him and awoke Him, saying, "Master, Master, we are perishing!"

Then He arose and rebuked the wind and the raging of the water. And they ceased, and there was a calm. [25]But He said to them, "Where is your faith?"

And they were afraid, and marveled, saying to one another, "Who can this be? For He commands even the winds and water, and they obey Him!"

A Demon-Possessed Man Healed

[26]Then they sailed to the country of the Gada-renes,[a] which is opposite Galilee. [27]And when He stepped out on the land, there met Him a cer-

---

8:26 [a]NU-Text reads *Gerasenes.*

tain man from the city who had demons for a long time. And he wore no clothes,[a] nor did he live in a house but in the tombs. [28]When he saw Jesus, he cried out, fell down before Him, and with a loud voice said, "What have I to do with You, Jesus, Son of the Most High God? I beg You, do not torment me!" [29]For He had commanded the unclean spirit to come out of the man. For it had often seized him, and he was kept under guard, bound with chains and shackles; and he broke the bonds and was driven by the demon into the wilderness.

[30]Jesus asked him, saying, "What is your name?"

And he said, "Legion," because many demons had entered him. [31]And they begged Him that He would not command them to go out into the abyss.

[32]Now a herd of many swine was feeding there on the mountain. So they begged Him that He would permit them to enter them. And He permitted them. [33]Then the demons went out of the man and entered the swine, and the herd ran violently down the steep place into the lake and drowned.

[34]When those who fed them saw what had happened, they fled and told it in the city and in the country. [35]Then they went out to see what had happened, and came to Jesus, and found the man from whom the demons had departed, sitting at the feet of Jesus, clothed and in his right mind. And they were afraid. [36]They also who had seen it told them by what means he who had been demon-possessed was healed. [37]Then the

---

8:27 [a]NU-Text reads who had demons and for a long time wore no clothes.

whole multitude of the surrounding region of the Gadarenes[a] asked Him to depart from them, for they were seized with great fear. And He got into the boat and returned.

[38]Now the man from whom the demons had departed begged Him that he might be with Him. But Jesus sent him away, saying, [39]"Return to your own house, and tell what great things God has done for you." And he went his way and proclaimed throughout the whole city what great things Jesus had done for him.

A Girl Restored to Life and a Woman Healed

[40]So it was, when Jesus returned, that the multitude welcomed Him, for they were all waiting for Him. [41]And behold, there came a man named Jairus, and he was a ruler of the synagogue. And he fell down at Jesus' feet and begged Him to come to his house, [42]for he had an only daughter about twelve years of age, and she was dying.

But as He went, the multitudes thronged Him. [43]Now a woman, having a flow of blood for twelve years, who had spent all her livelihood on physicians and could not be healed by any, [44]came from behind and touched the border of His garment. And immediately her flow of blood stopped.

[45]And Jesus said, "Who touched Me?"

When all denied it, Peter and those with him[a] said, "Master, the multitudes throng and press You, and You say, 'Who touched Me?' "[b]

[46]But Jesus said, "Somebody touched Me, for I perceived power going out from Me." [47]Now

8:37 [a]NU-Text reads *Gerasenes.*   8:45 [a]NU-Text omits *and those with him.* [b]NU-Text omits *and you say, 'Who touched Me?'*

when the woman saw that she was not hidden, she came trembling; and falling down before Him, she declared to Him in the presence of all the people the reason she had touched Him and how she was healed immediately.

⁴⁸And He said to her, "Daughter, be of good cheer;ᵃ your faith has made you well. Go in peace."

⁴⁹While He was still speaking, someone came from the ruler of the synagogue's *house,* saying to him, "Your daughter is dead. Do not trouble the Teacher."ᵃ

⁵⁰But when Jesus heard *it,* He answered him, saying, "Do not be afraid; only believe, and she will be made well." ⁵¹When He came into the house, He permitted no one to go inᵃ except Peter, James, and John,ᵇ and the father and mother of the girl. ⁵²Now all wept and mourned for her; but He said, "Do not weep; she is not dead, but sleeping." ⁵³And they ridiculed Him, knowing that she was dead.

⁵⁴But He put them all outside,ᵃ took her by the hand and called, saying, "Little girl, arise." ⁵⁵Then her spirit returned, and she arose immediately. And He commanded that she be given *something* to eat. ⁵⁶And her parents were astonished, but He charged them to tell no one what had happened.

Sending Out the Twelve

9 Then He called His twelve disciples together and gave them power and authority over all demons, and to cure diseases. ²He sent them to preach the kingdom of God and to heal the sick.

8:48 ᵃNU-Text omits *be of good cheer.*   8:49 ᵃNU-Text adds *any-more.*   8:51 ᵃNU-Text adds *with Him.*   ᵇNU-Text and M-Text read *Peter, John, and James.*   8:54 ᵃNU-Text omits *put them all outside.*

³And He said to them, "Take nothing for the journey, neither staffs nor bag nor bread nor money; and do not have two tunics apiece.

⁴"Whatever house you enter, stay there, and from there depart. ⁵And whoever will not receive you, when you go out of that city, shake off the very dust from your feet as a testimony against them."

⁶So they departed and went through the towns, preaching the gospel and healing everywhere.

Herod Seeks to See Jesus

⁷Now Herod the tetrarch heard of all that was done by Him; and he was perplexed, because it was said by some that John had risen from the dead, ⁸and by some that Elijah had appeared, and by others that one of the old prophets had risen again. ⁹Herod said, "John I have beheaded, but who is this of whom I hear such things?" So he sought to see Him.

Feeding the Five Thousand

¹⁰And the apostles, when they had returned, told Him all that they had done. Then He took them and went aside privately into a deserted place belonging to the city called Bethsaida. ¹¹But when the multitudes knew *it*, they followed Him; and He received them and spoke to them about the kingdom of God, and healed those who had need of healing. ¹²When the day began to wear away, the twelve came and said to Him, "Send the multitude away, that they may go into the surrounding towns and country, and lodge and get provisions; for we are in a deserted place here."

¹³But He said to them, "You give them some-

thing to eat."

And they said, "We have no more than five loaves and two fish, unless we go and buy food for all these people." ¹⁴For there were about five thousand men.

Then He said to His disciples, "Make them sit down in groups of fifty." ¹⁵And they did so, and made them all sit down.

¹⁶Then He took the five loaves and the two fish, and looking up to heaven, He blessed and broke *them*, and gave *them* to the disciples to set before the multitude. ¹⁷So they all ate and were filled, and twelve baskets of the leftover fragments were taken up by them.

Peter Confesses Jesus as the Christ

¹⁸And it happened, as He was alone praying, *that* His disciples joined Him, and He asked them, saying, "Who do the crowds say that I am?"

¹⁹So they answered and said, "John the Baptist, but some *say* Elijah; and others *say* that one of the old prophets has risen again."

²⁰He said to them, "But who do you say that I am?"

Peter answered and said, "The Christ of God."

Jesus Predicts His Death and Resurrection

²¹And He strictly warned and commanded them to tell this to no one, ²²saying, "The Son of Man must suffer many things, and be rejected by the elders and chief priests and scribes, and be killed, and be raised the third day."

Take Up the Cross and Follow Him

²³Then He said to *them* all, "If anyone desires

to come after Me, let him deny himself, and take up his cross daily,[a] and follow Me. [24]For whoever desires to save his life will lose it, but whoever loses his life for My sake will save it. [25]For what profit is it to a man if he gains the whole world, and is himself destroyed or lost? [26]For whoever is ashamed of Me and My words, of him the Son of Man will be ashamed when He comes in His *own* glory, and *in His* Father's, and of the holy angels.

Jesus Transfigured on the Mount

[27]But I tell you truly, there are some standing here who shall not taste death till they see the kingdom of God."

[28]Now it came to pass, about eight days after these sayings, that He took Peter, John, and James and went up on the mountain to pray. [29]As He prayed, the appearance of His face was altered, and His robe *became* white *and* glistening. [30]And behold, two men talked with Him, who were Moses and Elijah, [31]who appeared in glory and spoke of His decease which He was about to accomplish at Jerusalem. [32]But Peter and those with him were heavy with sleep; and when they were fully awake, they saw His glory and the two men who stood with Him. [33]Then it happened, as they were parting from Him, *that* Peter said to Jesus, "Master, it is good for us to be here; and let us make three tabernacles: one for You, one for Moses, and one for Elijah"—not knowing what he said.

[34]While he was saying this, a cloud came and overshadowed them; and they were fearful as they entered the cloud. [35]And a voice came out

9:23 [a]M-Text omits *daily.*

of the cloud, saying, "This is My beloved Son.[a] Hear Him!" [36]When the voice had ceased, Jesus was found alone. But they kept quiet, and told no one in those days any of the things they had seen.

A Boy Is Healed

[37]Now it happened on the next day, when they had come down from the mountain, that a great multitude met Him. [38]Suddenly a man from the multitude cried out, saying, "Teacher, I implore You, look on my son, for he is my only child. [39]And behold, a spirit seizes him, and he suddenly cries out; it convulses him so that he foams *at the mouth;* and it departs from him with great difficulty, bruising him. [40]So I implored Your disciples to cast it out, but they could not."

[41]Then Jesus answered and said, "O faithless and perverse generation, how long shall I be with you and bear with you? Bring your son here." [42]And as he was still coming, the demon threw him down and convulsed *him.* Then Jesus rebuked the unclean spirit, healed the child, and gave him back to his father.

Jesus Again Predicts His Death

[43]And they were all amazed at the majesty of God.

But while everyone marveled at all the things which Jesus did, He said to His disciples; [44]"Let these words sink down into your ears, for the Son of Man is about to be betrayed into the hands of men." [45]But they did not understand this saying, and it was hidden from them so that they did not perceive it; and they were afraid to

9:35 [a]NU-Text reads *This is My Son, the Chosen One.*

ask Him about this saying.

Who Is the Greatest?

⁴⁶Then a dispute arose among them as to which of them would be greatest. ⁴⁷And Jesus, perceiving the thought of their heart, took a little child and set him by Him, ⁴⁸and said to them, "Whoever receives this little child in My name receives Me; and whoever receives Me receives Him who sent Me. For he who is least among you all will be great."

Jesus Forbids Sectarianism

⁴⁹Now John answered and said, "Master, we saw someone casting out demons in Your name, and we forbade him because he does not follow with us."

⁵⁰But Jesus said to him, "Do not forbid *him*, for he who is not against us[a] is on our[b] side."

A Samaritan Village Rejects the Savior

⁵¹Now it came to pass, when the time had come for Him to be received up, that He steadfastly set His face to go to Jerusalem, ⁵²and sent messengers before His face. And as they went, they entered a village of the Samaritans, to prepare for Him. ⁵³But they did not receive Him, because His face was *set* for the journey to Jerusalem. ⁵⁴And when His disciples James and John saw *this*, they said, "Lord, do You want us to command fire to come down from heaven and consume them, just as Elijah did?"[a]

⁵⁵But He turned and rebuked them,[a] and

9:50 ᵃNU-Text reads *you*. ᵇNU-Text reads *your*. 9:54 ᵃNU-Text omits *just as Elijah did*. 9:55 ᵃNU-Text omits the rest of this verse.

said, "You do not know what manner of spirit you are of. [56]For the Son of Man did not come to destroy men's lives but to save *them*."[a] And they went to another village.

The Cost of Discipleship

[57]Now it happened as they journeyed on the road, *that* someone said to Him, "Lord, I will follow You wherever You go."

[58]And Jesus said to him, "Foxes have holes and birds of the air *have* nests, but the Son of Man has nowhere to lay *His* head."

[59]Then He said to another, "Follow Me."

But he said, "Lord, let me first go and bury my father."

[60]Jesus said to him, "Let the dead bury their own dead, but you go and preach the kingdom of God."

[61]And another also said, "Lord, I will follow You, but let me first go *and* bid them farewell who are at my house."

[62]But Jesus said to him, "No one, having put his hand to the plow, and looking back, is fit for the kingdom of God."

The Seventy Sent Out

10 After these things the Lord appointed seventy others also,[a] and sent them two by two before His face into every city and place where He Himself was about to go. [2]Then He said to them, "The harvest truly *is* great, but the laborers *are* few; therefore pray the Lord of the harvest to send out laborers into His harvest. [3]Go your way; behold, I send you out as lambs

---

9:56 [a]NU-Text omits the first sentence of this verse.   10:1 [a]NU-Text reads *seventy-two others.*

among wolves. [4]Carry neither money bag, knapsack, nor sandals; and greet no one along the road. [5]But whatever house you enter, first say, 'Peace to this house.' [6]And if a son of peace is there, your peace will rest on it; if not, it will return to you. [7]And remain in the same house, eating and drinking such things as they give, for the laborer is worthy of his wages. Do not go from house to house. [8]Whatever city you enter, and they receive you, eat such things as are set before you. [9]And heal the sick there, and say to them, 'The kingdom of God has come near to you.' [10]But whatever city you enter, and they do not receive you, go out into its streets and say, [11]'The very dust of your city which clings to us[a] we wipe off against you. Nevertheless know this, that the kingdom of God has come near you.' [12]But[a] I say to you that it will be more tolerable in that Day for Sodom than for that city.

Woe to the Impenitent Cities

[13]"Woe to you, Chorazin! Woe to you, Bethsaida! For if the mighty works which were done in you had been done in Tyre and Sidon, they would have repented long ago, sitting in sackcloth and ashes. [14]But it will be more tolerable for Tyre and Sidon at the judgment than for you. [15]And you, Capernaum, who are exalted to heaven, will be brought down to Hades.[a] [16]He who hears you hears Me, he who rejects you rejects Me, and he who rejects Me rejects Him who sent Me."

10:11 [a]NU-Text reads *our feet.*   **10:12** [a]NU-Text and M-Text omit *But.*   **10:15** [a]NU-Text reads *will you be exalted to heaven? You will be thrust down to Hades!*

The Seventy Return with Joy

[17]Then the seventy[a] returned with joy, saying, "Lord, even the demons are subject to us in Your name."

[18]And He said to them, "I saw Satan fall like lightning from heaven. [19]Behold, I give you the authority to trample on serpents and scorpions, and over all the power of the enemy, and nothing shall by any means hurt you. [20]Nevertheless do not rejoice in this, that the spirits are subject to you, but rather[a] rejoice because your names are written in heaven."

Jesus Rejoices in the Spirit

[21]In that hour Jesus rejoiced in the Spirit and said, "I thank You, Father, Lord of heaven and earth, that You have hidden these things from *the* wise and prudent and revealed them to babes. Even so, Father, for so it seemed good in Your sight. [22]All[a] things have been delivered to Me by My Father, and no one knows who the Son is except the Father, and who the Father is except the Son, and *the one* to whom the Son wills to reveal *Him.*"

[23]Then He turned to *His* disciples and said privately, "Blessed *are* the eyes which see the things you see; [24]for I tell you that many prophets and kings have desired to see what you see, and have not seen *it,* and to hear what you hear, and have not heard *it.*"

The Parable of the Good Samaritan

[25]And behold, a certain lawyer stood up and

10:17 [a]NU-Text reads *seventy-two.*   10:20 [a]NU-Text and M-Text omit *rather.*   10:22 [a]M-Text reads *And turning to the disciples He said, "All . . .*

tested Him, saying, "Teacher, what shall I do to inherit eternal life?"

26He said to him, "What is written in the law? What is your reading *of it?*"

27So he answered and said, *"'You shall love the Lord your God with all your heart, with all your soul, with all your strength, and with all your mind,'*a and *'your neighbor as yourself.'"*b

28And He said to him, "You have answered rightly; do this and you will live."

29But he, wanting to justify himself, said to Jesus, "And who is my neighbor?"

30Then Jesus answered and said: "A certain *man* went down from Jerusalem to Jericho, and fell among thieves, who stripped him of his clothing, wounded *him,* and departed, leaving *him* half dead. 31Now by chance a certain priest came down that road. And when he saw him, he passed by on the other side. 32Likewise a Levite, when he arrived at the place, came and looked, and passed by on the other side. 33But a certain Samaritan, as he journeyed, came where he was. And when he saw him, he had compassion. 34So he went to *him* and bandaged his wounds, pouring on oil and wine; and he set him on his own animal, brought him to an inn, and took care of him. 35On the next day, when he departed,a he took out two denarii, gave *them* to the innkeeper, and said to him, 'Take care of him; and whatever more you spend, when I come again, I will repay you.' 36So which of these three do you think was neighbor to him who fell among the thieves?"

37And he said, "He who showed mercy on him."

10:27 aDeuteronomy 6:5 bLeviticus 19:18   10:35 aNU-Text omits *when he departed.*

Then Jesus said to him, "Go and do likewise."

Mary and Martha Worship and Serve

38Now it happened as they went that He entered a certain village; and a certain woman named Martha welcomed Him into her house. 39And she had a sister called Mary, who also sat at Jesus'ᵃ feet and heard His word. 40But Martha was distracted with much serving, and she approached Him and said, "Lord, do You not care that my sister has left me to serve alone? Therefore tell her to help me."

41And Jesusᵃ answered and said to her, "Martha, Martha, you are worried and troubled about many things. 42But one thing is needed, and Mary has chosen that good part, which will not be taken away from her."

The Model Prayer

11 Now it came to pass, as He was praying in a certain place, when He ceased, *that* one of His disciples said to Him, "Lord, teach us to pray, as John also taught his disciples."

2So He said to them, "When you pray, say:

Our Father in heaven,ᵃ
Hallowed be Your name.
Your kingdom come.ᵇ
Your will be done
On earth as *it is* in heaven.
3Give us day by day our daily bread.
4And forgive us our sins,

10:39 ᵃNU-Text reads *the Lord's*.   10:41 ᵃNU-Text reads *the Lord*.
11:2 ᵃNU-Text omits *Our* and *in heaven*. ᵇNU-Text omits the rest of this verse.

For we also forgive everyone who is indebted
    to us.
And do not lead us into temptation,
But deliver us from the evil one.”[a]

A Friend Comes at Midnight

[5]And He said to them, “Which of you shall
have a friend, and go to him at midnight and say
to him, ‘Friend, lend me three loaves; [6]for a
friend of mine has come to me on his journey,
and I have nothing to set before him’; [7]and he
will answer from within and say, ‘Do not trouble
me; the door is now shut, and my children are
with me in bed; I cannot rise and give to you’? [8]I
say to you, though he will not rise and give to
him because he is his friend, yet because of his
persistence he will rise and give him as many as
he needs.

Keep Asking, Seeking, Knocking

[9]“So I say to you, ask, and it will be given to
you; seek, and you will find; knock, and it will
be opened to you. [10]For everyone who asks receives, and he who seeks finds, and to him who
knocks it will be opened. [11]If a son asks for
bread[a] from any father among you, will he give
him a stone? Or if *he* asks for a fish, will he give
him a serpent instead of a fish? [12]Or if he asks for
an egg, will he offer him a scorpion? [13]If you
then, being evil, know how to give good gifts to
your children, how much more will *your* heavenly Father give the Holy Spirit to those who ask
Him!”

11:4 [a]NU-Text omits *But deliver us from the evil one.*   11:11 [a]NU-
Text omits the words from *bread* through *for* in the next sentence.

A House Divided Cannot Stand

[14]And He was casting out a demon, and it was mute. So it was, when the demon had gone out, that the mute spoke; and the multitudes marveled. [15]But some of them said, "He casts out demons by Beelzebub,[a] the ruler of the demons."

[16]Others, testing *Him,* sought from Him a sign from heaven. [17]But He, knowing their thoughts, said to them: "Every kingdom divided against itself is brought to desolation, and a house *divided* against a house falls. [18]If Satan also is divided against himself, how will his kingdom stand? Because you say I cast out demons by Beelzebub. [19]And if I cast out demons by Beelzebub, by whom do your sons cast *them* out? Therefore they will be your judges. [20]But if I cast out demons with the finger of God, surely the kingdom of God has come upon you. [21]When a strong man, fully armed, guards his own palace, his goods are in peace. [22]But when a stronger than he comes upon him and overcomes him, he takes from him all his armor in which he trusted, and divides his spoils. [23]He who is not with Me is against Me, and he who does not gather with Me scatters.

An Unclean Spirit Returns

[24]"When an unclean spirit goes out of a man, he goes through dry places, seeking rest; and finding none, he says, 'I will return to my house from which I came.' [25]And when he comes, he finds *it* swept and put in order. [26]Then he goes and takes with *him* seven other spirits more wicked than himself, and they enter and dwell there; and the last *state* of that man is worse than the first."

11:15 [a]NU-Text and M-Text read *Beelzebul*.

Keeping the Word

²⁷And it happened, as He spoke these things, that a certain woman from the crowd raised her voice and said to Him, "Blessed is the womb that bore You, and *the* breasts which nursed You!"

²⁸But He said, "More than that, blessed *are* those who hear the word of God and keep it!"

Seeking a Sign

²⁹And while the crowds were thickly gathered together, He began to say, "This is an evil generation. It seeks a sign, and no sign will be given to it except the sign of Jonah the prophet.ᵃ ³⁰For as Jonah became a sign to the Ninevites, so also the Son of Man will be to this generation. ³¹The queen of the South will rise up in the judgment with the men of this generation and condemn them, for she came from the ends of the earth to hear the wisdom of Solomon; and indeed a greater than Solomon is here. ³²The men of Nineveh will rise up in the judgment with this generation and condemn it, for they repented at the preaching of Jonah; and indeed a greater than Jonah is here.

The Lamp of the Body

³³"No one, when he has lit a lamp, puts *it* in a secret place or under a basket, but on a lampstand, that those who come in may see the light. ³⁴The lamp of the body is the eye. Therefore, when your eye is good, your whole body also is full of light. But when *your eye* is bad, your body also is full of darkness. ³⁵Therefore take heed that the light which is in you is not darkness. ³⁶If then your whole body is full of light, having no part

11:29 ᵃNU-Text omits *the prophet*.

dark, *the* whole *body* will be full of light, as when the bright shining of a lamp gives you light."

Woe to the Pharisees and Lawyers

[37] And as He spoke, a certain Pharisee asked Him to dine with him. So He went in and sat down to eat. [38] When the Pharisee saw *it*, he marveled that He had not first washed before dinner.

[39] Then the Lord said to him, "Now you Pharisees make the outside of the cup and dish clean, but your inward part is full of greed and wickedness. [40] Foolish ones! Did not He who made the outside make the inside also? [41] But rather give alms of such things as you have; then indeed all things are clean to you.

[42] "But woe to you Pharisees! For you tithe mint and rue and all manner of herbs, and pass by justice and the love of God. These you ought to have done, without leaving the others undone. [43] Woe to you Pharisees! For you love the best seats in the synagogues and greetings in the marketplaces. [44] Woe to you, scribes and Pharisees, hypocrites![a] For you are like graves which are not seen, and the men who walk over *them* are not aware *of them*."

[45] Then one of the lawyers answered and said to Him, "Teacher, by saying these things You reproach us also."

[46] And He said, "Woe to you also, lawyers! For you load men with burdens hard to bear, and you yourselves do not touch the burdens with one of your fingers. [47] Woe to you! For you build the tombs of the prophets, and your fathers killed them. [48] In fact, you bear witness that you approve the deeds of your fathers; for they in-

---

11:44 [a] NU-Text omits *scribes and Pharisees, hypocrites*.

deed killed them, and you build their tombs. [49]Therefore the wisdom of God also said, 'I will send them prophets and apostles, and *some* of them they will kill and persecute,' [50]that the blood of all the prophets which was shed from the foundation of the world may be required of this generation, [51]from the blood of Abel to the blood of Zechariah who perished between the altar and the temple. Yes, I say to you, it shall be required of this generation.

[52]"Woe to you lawyers! For you have taken away the key of knowledge. You did not enter in yourselves, and those who were entering in you hindered."

[53]And as He said these things to them,[a] the scribes and the Pharisees began to assail *Him* vehemently, and to cross-examine Him about many things, [54]lying in wait for Him, and seeking to catch Him in something He might say, that they might accuse Him.[a]

Beware of Hypocrisy

12 In the meantime, when an innumerable multitude of people had gathered together, so that they trampled one another, He began to say to His disciples first *of all,* "Beware of the leaven of the Pharisees, which is hypocrisy. [2]For there is nothing covered that will not be revealed, nor hidden that will not be known. [3]Therefore whatever you have spoken in the dark will be heard in the light, and what you have spoken in the ear in inner rooms will be proclaimed on the housetops.

11:53 [a]NU-Text reads *And when He left there.*   11:54 [a]NU-Text omits *and seeking* and *that they might accuse Him.*

Jesus Teaches the Fear of God

4"And I say to you, My friends, do not be afraid of those who kill the body, and after that have no more that they can do. 5But I will show you whom you should fear: Fear Him who, after He has killed, has power to cast into hell; yes, I say to you, fear Him!

6"Are not five sparrows sold for two copper coins?[a] And not one of them is forgotten before God. 7But the very hairs of your head are all numbered. Do not fear therefore; you are of more value than many sparrows.

Confess Christ Before Men

8"Also I say to you, whoever confesses Me before men, him the Son of Man also will confess before the angels of God. 9But he who denies Me before men will be denied before the angels of God.

10"And anyone who speaks a word against the Son of Man, it will be forgiven him; but to him who blasphemes against the Holy Spirit, it will not be forgiven.

11"Now when they bring you to the synagogues and magistrates and authorities, do not worry about how or what you should answer, or what you should say. 12For the Holy Spirit will teach you in that very hour what you ought to say."

The Parable of the Rich Fool

13Then one from the crowd said to Him, "Teacher, tell my brother to divide the inheritance with me."

14But He said to him, "Man, who made Me a judge or an arbitrator over you?" 15And He said

---

12:6 [a]Greek *assarion*, a coin of very small value

to them, "Take heed and beware of covetousness,[a] for one's life does not consist in the abundance of the things he possesses."

16Then He spoke a parable to them, saying: "The ground of a certain rich man yielded plentifully. 17And he thought within himself, saying, 'What shall I do, since I have no room to store my crops?' 18So he said, 'I will do this: I will pull down my barns and build greater, and there I will store all my crops and my goods. 19And I will say to my soul, "Soul, you have many goods laid up for many years; take your ease; eat, drink, *and* be merry." ' 20But God said to him, 'Fool! This night your soul will be required of you; then whose will those things be which you have provided?'

21"So *is* he who lays up treasure for himself, and is not rich toward God."

Do Not Worry

22Then He said to His disciples, "Therefore I say to you, do not worry about your life, what you will eat; nor about the body, what you will put on. 23Life is more than food, and the body is *more* than clothing. 24Consider the ravens, for they neither sow nor reap, which have neither storehouse nor barn; and God feeds them. Of how much more value are you than the birds? 25And which of you by worrying can add one cubit to his stature? 26If you then are not able to do *the* least, why are you anxious for the rest? 27Consider the lilies, how they grow: they neither toil nor spin; and yet I say to you, even Solomon in all his glory was not arrayed like one of these. 28If then God so clothes the grass, which today is

12:15 [a]NU-Text reads *all covetousness.*

in the field and tomorrow is thrown into the oven, how much more *will He clothe* you, O *you* of little faith?

²⁹"And do not seek what you should eat or what you should drink, nor have an anxious mind. ³⁰For all these things the nations of the world seek after, and your Father knows that you need these things. ³¹But seek the kingdom of God, and all these thingsª shall be added to you.

³²"Do not fear, little flock, for it is your Father's good pleasure to give you the kingdom. ³³Sell what you have and give alms; provide yourselves money bags which do not grow old, a treasure in the heavens that does not fail, where no thief approaches nor moth destroys. ³⁴For where your treasure is, there your heart will be also.

The Faithful Servant and the Evil Servant

³⁵"Let your waist be girded and *your* lamps burning; ³⁶and you yourselves be like men who wait for their master, when he will return from the wedding, that when he comes and knocks they may open to him immediately. ³⁷Blessed *are* those servants whom the master, when he comes, will find watching. Assuredly, I say to you that he will gird himself and have them sit down *to eat,* and will come and serve them. ³⁸And if he should come in the second watch, or come in the third watch, and find *them* so, blessed are those servants. ³⁹But know this, that if the master of the house had known what hour the thief would come, he would have watched andª not allowed

---

12:31 ªNU-Text reads *His kingdom, and these things.* **12:39** ªNU-Text reads *he would not have allowed.*

his house to be broken into. [40]Therefore you also be ready, for the Son of Man is coming at an hour you do not expect."

[41]Then Peter said to Him, "Lord, do You speak this parable *only* to us, or to all *people?*"

[42]And the Lord said, "Who then is that faithful and wise steward, whom *his* master will make ruler over his household, to give *them their* portion of food in due season? [43]Blessed *is* that servant whom his master will find so doing when he comes. [44]Truly, I say to you that he will make him ruler over all that he has. [45]But if that servant says in his heart, 'My master is delaying his coming,' and begins to beat the male and female servants, and to eat and drink and be drunk, [46]the master of that servant will come on a day when he is not looking for *him*, and at an hour when he is not aware, and will cut him in two and appoint *him* his portion with the unbelievers. [47]And that servant who knew his master's will, and did not prepare *himself* or do according to his will, shall be beaten with many *stripes*. [48]But he who did not know, yet committed things deserving of stripes, shall be beaten with few. For everyone to whom much is given, from him much will be required; and to whom much has been committed, of him they will ask the more.

Christ Brings Division

[49]"I came to send fire on the earth, and how I wish it were already kindled! [50]But I have a baptism to be baptized with, and how distressed I am till it is accomplished! [51]Do *you* suppose that I came to give peace on earth? I tell you, not at all, but rather division. [52]For from now on five in

one house will be divided: three against two, and two against three. ⁵³Father will be divided against son and son against father, mother against daughter and daughter against mother, mother-in-law against her daughter-in-law and daughter-in-law against her mother-in-law."

Discern the Time

⁵⁴Then He also said to the multitudes, "Whenever you *see* a cloud rising out of the west, immediately you say, 'A shower is coming'; and so it is. ⁵⁵And when you see the south wind blow, you say, 'There will be hot weather'; and there is. ⁵⁶Hypocrites! You can discern the face of the sky and of the earth, but how *is it* you do not discern this time?

Make Peace with Your Adversary

⁵⁷"Yes, and why, even of yourselves, do you not judge what is right? ⁵⁸When you go with your adversary to the magistrate, make every effort along the way to settle with him, lest he drag you to the judge, the judge deliver you to the officer, and the officer throw you into prison. ⁵⁹I tell you, you shall not depart from there till you have paid the very last mite."

Repent or Perish

13 There were present at that season some who told Him about the Galileans whose blood Pilate had mingled with their sacrifices. ²And Jesus answered and said to them, "Do you suppose that these Galileans were worse sinners than all *other* Galileans, because they suffered such things? ³I tell you, no; but unless you repent you will all likewise perish. ⁴Or those eigh-

teen on whom the tower in Siloam fell and killed them, do you think that they were worse sinners than all *other* men who dwelt in Jerusalem? [5]I tell you, no; but unless you repent you will all likewise perish."

The Parable of the Barren Fig Tree

[6]He also spoke this parable: "A certain *man* had a fig tree planted in his vineyard, and he came seeking fruit on it and found none. [7]Then he said to the keeper of his vineyard, 'Look, for three years I have come seeking fruit on this fig tree and find none. Cut it down; why does it use up the ground?' [8]But he answered and said to him, 'Sir, let it alone this year also, until I dig around it and fertilize *it*. [9]And if it bears fruit, *well*. But if not, after that[a] you can cut it down.' "

A Spirit of Infirmity

[10]Now He was teaching in one of the synagogues on the Sabbath. [11]And behold, there was a woman who had a spirit of infirmity eighteen years, and was bent over and could in no way raise *herself* up. [12]But when Jesus saw her, He called *her* to *Him* and said to her, "Woman, you are loosed from your infirmity." [13]And He laid *His* hands on her, and immediately she was made straight, and glorified God.

[14]But the ruler of the synagogue answered with indignation, because Jesus had healed on the Sabbath; and he said to the crowd, "There are six days on which men ought to work; therefore come and be healed on them, and not on the Sabbath day."

13:9 [a]NU-Text reads *And if it bears fruit after that, well. But if not, you can cut it down.*

Why is the church full of hypocrites?

Hypocrites may show up at a church building every Sunday, but in reality there are no hypocrites in the Church. *Hypocrite* comes from the Greek word for "actor," or pretender. Hypocrisy is "the practice of professing beliefs, feelings, or virtues that one does not hold." Many people think that the "Church" is the building, and that those who sit within its confines are Christians. However, the Church is the Body of Christ, which consists only of true believers. Hypocrites are "pretenders" who sit among God's people.

I don't blame anyone for rejecting "religion" based on this hypocrisy. There are more actors in the church than there are in Hollywood. The Bible tells us that they dwell as goats among the Lord's sheep, bad fish among the good fish, tares among wheat, etc., until the day God will separate them.

It is interesting to note that the human body will reject any foreign transplant—even down to the single root of a transplanted hair. The false convert (the hypocrite) is not part of the Body of Christ. He has never truly repented, and because of his sin he is therefore rejected as part of the Body.

Jesus had harsh words of warning for religious hypocrites. In Matthew 23, He told the religious leaders that they were "fools and blind," sons of hell, full of hypocrisy and sin. He climaxed His sermon by saying, "Serpents, brood of vipers! How can you escape the condemnation of hell?" He then warned that He would say to the wicked, "Depart from Me, you cursed, into the everlasting fire prepared for the devil and his angels" (Matthew 25:41).

God knows those who love Him, and the Bible warns that He will sort out the true converts from the false on the Day of Judgment. All hypocrites—those merely pretending to be Christians—will end up in Hell.

What kind of God would order the death of children?

Let me tell you about my father. When I was young, he continually left my mom and us three kids to fend for ourselves. And he killed a helpless animal with his bare hands. You could be justified in believing that my father was a tyrant—but here's some missing information. The reason he left us each day was to earn money to provide food, clothing, and shelter for us. And he killed a helpless animal because it had been hit by a car and was in agony. He put it out of its misery, and it grieved him to do so. So, now you have a balanced view of my dad. He was a loving father and a very compassionate man.

One view of God from the Bible can paint Him to be a tyrant, but in the entirety of Scripture we see a different picture. God bestowed life on each of us. He gave you eyes to see with, ears to hear beautiful music, and taste buds to enjoy delicious food. He gave you a nose to smell the fragrance of flowers. He lavished you with His kindness. He didn't treat you according to your sins, but has shown incredible mercy to you in allowing you to live this far. On top of that, He became a person in Jesus Christ, and He demonstrated His love for us by suffering unspeakably and dying for our sins.

With that extra knowledge, it's easy for me to say, "The judgments of the Lord are true and righteous altogether." You say, "But he instigated the deaths of the Canaanites—men, women, and children!" Yes, and He did that not just with the Canaanites, but with the whole of humanity. The Judge of the universe said, "The soul who sins shall die" (Ezekiel 18:20). God proclaimed the death sentence on every man, woman, and child. But this same God of justice is rich in mercy and will grant everlasting life to every man, woman, and child who will humble themselves, repent of their sin, and trust in Jesus Christ.

¹⁵The Lord then answered him and said, "Hypocrite!ᵃ Does not each one of you on the Sabbath loose his ox or donkey from the stall, and lead *it* away to water it? ¹⁶So ought not this woman, being a daughter of Abraham, whom Satan has bound—think of it—for eighteen years, be loosed from this bond on the Sabbath?" ¹⁷And when He said these things, all His adversaries were put to shame; and all the multitude rejoiced for all the glorious things that were done by Him.

The Parable of the Mustard Seed

¹⁸Then He said, "What is the kingdom of God like? And to what shall I compare it? ¹⁹It is like a mustard seed, which a man took and put in his garden; and it grew and became a largeᵃ tree, and the birds of the air nested in its branches."

The Parable of the Leaven

²⁰And again He said, "To what shall I liken the kingdom of God? ²¹It is like leaven, which a woman took and hid in three measuresᵃ of meal till it was all leavened."

The Narrow Way

²²And He went through the cities and villages, teaching, and journeying toward Jerusalem. ²³Then one said to Him, "Lord, are there few who are saved?"

And He said to them, ²⁴"Strive to enter through the narrow gate, for many, I say to you, will seek to enter and will not be able. ²⁵When once the Master of the house has risen up and shut the door, and you begin to stand outside and knock

---

13:15 ᵃNU-Text and M-Text read *Hypocrites.*   13:19 ᵃNU-Text omits *large.*   13:21 ᵃGreek *sata,* approximately two pecks in all

at the door, saying, 'Lord, Lord, open for us,' and He will answer and say to you, 'I do not know you, where you are from.' ²⁶then you will begin to say, 'We ate and drank in Your presence, and You taught in our streets.' ²⁷But He will say, 'I tell you I do not know you, where you are from. Depart from Me, all you workers of iniquity.' ²⁸There will be weeping and gnashing of teeth, when you see Abraham and Isaac and Jacob and all the prophets in the kingdom of God, and yourselves thrust out. ²⁹They will come from the east and the west, from the north and the south, and sit down in the kingdom of God. ³⁰And indeed there are last who will be first, and there are first who will be last."

³¹On that very day[a] some Pharisees came, saying to Him, "Get out and depart from here, for Herod wants to kill You."

³²And He said to them, "Go, tell that fox, 'Behold, I cast out demons and perform cures today and tomorrow, and the third *day* I shall be perfected.' ³³Nevertheless I must journey today, tomorrow, and the *day* following; for it cannot be that a prophet should perish outside of Jerusalem.

Jesus Laments over Jerusalem

³⁴"O Jerusalem, Jerusalem, the one who kills the prophets and stones those who are sent to her! How often I wanted to gather your children together, as a hen *gathers* her brood under *her* wings, but you were not willing! ³⁵See! Your house is left to you desolate; and assuredly,[a] I say to you, you shall not see Me until *the time* comes when you say, *'Blessed is He who comes in the*

13:31 [a]NU-Text reads *In that very hour.*   13:35 [a]NU-Text and M-Text omit *assuredly.*

name of the Lord!' '[b]

A Man with Dropsy
Healed on the Sabbath

14 Now it happened, as He went into the house of one of the rulers of the Pharisees to eat bread on the Sabbath, that they watched Him closely. [2]And behold, there was a certain man before Him who had dropsy. [3]And Jesus, answering, spoke to the lawyers and Pharisees, saying, "Is it lawful to heal on the Sabbath?"[a]

[4]But they kept silent. And He took *him* and healed him, and let him go. [5]Then He answered them, saying, "Which of you, having a donkey[a] or an ox that has fallen into a pit, will not immediately pull him out on the Sabbath day?" [6]And they could not answer Him regarding these things.

Take the Lowly Place

[7]So He told a parable to those who were invited, when He noted how they chose the best places, saying to them: [8]"When you are invited by anyone to a wedding feast, do not sit down in the best place, lest one more honorable than you be invited by him; [9]and he who invited you and him come and say to you, 'Give place to this man,' and then you begin with shame to take the lowest place. [10]But when you are invited, go and sit down in the lowest place, so that when he who invited you comes he may say to you, 'Friend, go up higher.' Then you will have glory in the presence of those who sit at the table with you. [11]For whoever exalts himself will be humbled, and he

---

13:35 [b]Psalm 118:26   **14:3** [a]NU-Text adds *or not.*   **14:5** [a]NU-Text and M-Text read *son.*

who humbles himself will be exalted."

¹²Then He also said to him who invited Him, "When you give a dinner or a supper, do not ask your friends, your brothers, your relatives, nor rich neighbors, lest they also invite you back, and you be repaid. ¹³But when you give a feast, invite *the* poor, *the* maimed, *the* lame, *the* blind. ¹⁴And you will be blessed, because they cannot repay you; for you shall be repaid at the resurrection of the just."

The Parable of the Great Supper

¹⁵Now when one of those who sat at the table with Him heard these things, he said to Him, "Blessed *is* he who shall eat bread[a] in the kingdom of God!"

¹⁶Then He said to him, "A certain man gave a great supper and invited many, ¹⁷and sent his servant at supper time to say to those who were invited, 'Come, for all things are now ready.' ¹⁸But they all with one *accord* began to make excuses. The first said to him, 'I have bought a piece of ground, and I must go and see it. I ask you to have me excused.' ¹⁹And another said, 'I have bought five yoke of oxen, and I am going to test them. I ask you to have me excused.' ²⁰Still another said, 'I have married a wife, and therefore I cannot come.' ²¹So that servant came and reported these things to his master. Then the master of the house, being angry, said to his servant, 'Go out quickly into the streets and lanes of the city, and bring in here *the* poor and *the* maimed and *the* lame and *the* blind.' ²²And the servant said, 'Master, it is done as you commanded, and still there is room.' ²³Then the mas-

---

14:15 ªM-Text reads *dinner.*

ter said to the servant, 'Go out into the highways and hedges, and compel *them* to come in, that my house may be filled. [24]For I say to you that none of those men who were invited shall taste my supper.' "

Leaving All to Follow Christ

[25]Now great multitudes went with Him. And He turned and said to them, [26]"If anyone comes to Me and does not hate his father and mother, wife and children, brothers and sisters, yes, and his own life also, he cannot be My disciple. [27]And whoever does not bear his cross and come after Me cannot be My disciple. [28]For which of you, intending to build a tower, does not sit down first and count the cost, whether he has *enough* to finish *it*— [29]lest, after he has laid the foundation, and is not able to finish, all who see *it* begin to mock him, [30]saying, 'This man began to build and was not able to finish'? [31]Or what king, going to make war against another king, does not sit down first and consider whether he is able with ten thousand to meet him who comes against him with twenty thousand? [32]Or else, while the other is still a great way off, he sends a delegation and asks conditions of peace. [33]So likewise, whoever of you does not forsake all that he has cannot be My disciple.

Tasteless Salt Is Worthless

[34]"Salt *is* good; but if the salt has lost its flavor, how shall it be seasoned? [35]It is neither fit for the land nor for the dunghill, *but* men throw it out. He who has ears to hear, let him hear!"

The Parable of the Lost Sheep

15 Then all the tax collectors and the sinners drew near to Him to hear Him. [2]And the Pharisees and scribes complained, saying, "This Man receives sinners and eats with them." [3]So He spoke this parable to them, saying:

[4]"What man of you, having a hundred sheep, if he loses one of them, does not leave the ninety-nine in the wilderness, and go after the one which is lost until he finds it? [5]And when he has found *it,* he lays *it* on his shoulders, rejoicing. [6]And when he comes home, he calls together *his* friends and neighbors, saying to them, 'Rejoice with me, for I have found my sheep which was lost!' [7]I say to you that likewise there will be more joy in heaven over one sinner who repents than over ninety-nine just persons who need no repentance.

The Parable of the Lost Coin

[8]"Or what woman, having ten silver coins,[a] if she loses one coin, does not light a lamp, sweep the house, and search carefully until she finds *it*? [9]And when she has found *it,* she calls *her* friends and neighbors together, saying, 'Rejoice with me, for I have found the piece which I lost!' [10]Likewise, I say to you, there is joy in the presence of the angels of God over one sinner who repents."

The Parable of the Lost Son

[11]Then He said: "A certain man had two sons. [12]And the younger of them said to *his* father, 'Father, give me the portion of goods that falls *to me.*' So he divided to them *his* livelihood. [13]And

---

15:8 [a]Greek *drachma,* a valuable coin often worn in a ten-piece garland by married women not many days after, the younger son gathered all together, journeyed to a far country, and there wasted his possessions with prodigal living. ¹⁴But when he had spent all, there arose a severe famine in that land, and he began to be in want. ¹⁵Then he went and joined himself to a citizen of that country, and he sent him into his fields to feed swine. ¹⁶And he would gladly have filled his stomach with the pods that the swine ate, and no one gave him *anything*.

¹⁷"But when he came to himself, he said, 'How many of my father's hired servants have bread enough and to spare, and I perish with hunger! ¹⁸I will arise and go to my father, and will say to him, "Father, I have sinned against heaven and before you, ¹⁹and I am no longer worthy to be called your son. Make me like one of your hired servants." '

²⁰"And he arose and came to his father. But when he was still a great way off, his father saw him and had compassion, and ran and fell on his neck and kissed him. ²¹And the son said to him, 'Father, I have sinned against heaven and in your sight, and am no longer worthy to be called your son.'

²²"But the father said to his servants, 'Bringᵃ out the best robe and put *it* on him, and put a ring on his hand and sandals on *his* feet. ²³And bring the fatted calf here and kill *it*, and let us eat and be merry; ²⁴for this my son was dead and is alive again; he was lost and is found.' And they began to be merry.

²⁵"Now his older son was in the field. And as he came and drew near to the house, he heard music and dancing. ²⁶So he called one of the ser-

15:22 ᵃNU-Text reads *Quickly bring*.

vants and asked what these things meant. ²⁷And
he said to him, 'Your brother has come, and because he has received him safe and sound, your
father has killed the fatted calf.'

²⁸"But he was angry and would not go in.
Therefore his father came out and pleaded with
him. ²⁹So he answered and said to *his* father, 'Lo,
these many years I have been serving you; I
never transgressed your commandment at any
time; and yet you never gave me a young goat,
that I might make merry with my friends. ³⁰But
as soon as this son of yours came, who has devoured your livelihood with harlots, you killed
the fatted calf for him.'

³¹"And he said to him, 'Son, you are always
with me, and all that I have is yours. ³²It was
right that we should make merry and be glad, for
your brother was dead and is alive again, and
was lost and is found.' "

The Parable of the Unjust Steward

16 He also said to His disciples: "There was
a certain rich man who had a steward,
and an accusation was brought to him that this
man was wasting his goods. ²So he called him
and said to him, 'What is this I hear about you?
Give an account of your stewardship, for you can
no longer be steward.'

³"Then the steward said within himself,
'What shall I do? For my master is taking the
stewardship away from me. I cannot dig; I am
ashamed to beg. ⁴I have resolved what to do, that
when I am put out of the stewardship, they may
receive me into their houses.'

⁵"So he called every one of his master's
debtors to *him*, and said to the first, 'How much

do you owe my master?' [6]And he said, 'A hundred measures[a] of oil.' So he said to him, 'Take your bill, and sit down quickly and write fifty.' [7]Then he said to another, 'And how much do you owe?' So he said, 'A hundred measures[a] of wheat.' And he said to him, 'Take your bill, and write eighty.' [8]So the master commended the unjust steward because he had dealt shrewdly. For the sons of this world are more shrewd in their generation than the sons of light.

[9]"And I say to you, make friends for yourselves by unrighteous mammon, that when you fail,[a] they may receive you into an everlasting home. [10]He who *is* faithful in *what is* least is faithful also in much; and he who is unjust in *what is* least is unjust also in much. [11]Therefore if you have not been faithful in the unrighteous mammon, who will commit to your trust the true *riches?* [12]And if you have not been faithful in what is another man's, who will give you what is your own?

[13]"No servant can serve two masters; for either he will hate the one and love the other, or else he will be loyal to the one and despise the other. You cannot serve God and mammon."

The Law, the Prophets, and the Kingdom

[14]Now the Pharisees, who were lovers of money, also heard all these things, and they derided Him. [15]And He said to them, "You are those who justify yourselves before men, but God knows your hearts. For what is highly esteemed among men is an abomination in the sight of God.

16:6 [a]Greek *batos*, eight or nine gallons each (Old Testament *bath*)   16:7 [a]Greek *koros*, ten or twelve bushels each (Old Testament *kor*)   16:9 [a]NU-Text reads *it fails.*

¹⁶"The law and the prophets *were* until John. Since that time the kingdom of God has been preached, and everyone is pressing into it. ¹⁷And it is easier for heaven and earth to pass away than for one tittle of the law to fail.

¹⁸"Whoever divorces his wife and marries another commits adultery; and whoever marries her who is divorced from *her* husband commits adultery.

The Rich Man and Lazarus

¹⁹"There was a certain rich man who was clothed in purple and fine linen and fared sumptuously every day. ²⁰But there was a certain beggar named Lazarus, full of sores, who was laid at his gate, ²¹desiring to be fed with the crumbs which fell[a] from the rich man's table. Moreover the dogs came and licked his sores. ²²So it was that the beggar died, and was carried by the angels to Abraham's bosom. The rich man also died and was buried. ²³And being in torments in Hades, he lifted up his eyes and saw Abraham afar off, and Lazarus in his bosom.

²⁴"Then he cried and said, 'Father Abraham, have mercy on me, and send Lazarus that he may dip the tip of his finger in water and cool my tongue; for I am tormented in this flame.' ²⁵But Abraham said, 'Son, remember that in your lifetime you received your good things, and likewise Lazarus evil things; but now he is comforted and you are tormented. ²⁶And besides all this, between us and you there is a great gulf fixed, so that those who want to pass from here to you cannot, nor can those from there pass to us.'

²⁷"Then he said, 'I beg you therefore, father,

16:21 [a]NU-Text reads *with what fell.*

that you would send him to my father's house,
²⁸for I have five brothers, that he may testify to
them, lest they also come to this place of torment.' ²⁹Abraham said to him, 'They have Moses
and the prophets; let them hear them.' ³⁰And he
said, 'No, father Abraham; but if one goes to
them from the dead, they will repent.' ³¹But he
said to him, 'If they do not hear Moses and the
prophets, neither will they be persuaded though
one rise from the dead.' "

Jesus Warns of Offenses

17 Then He said to the disciples, "It is impossible that no offenses should come,
but woe *to him* through whom they do come! ²It
would be better for him if a millstone were hung
around his neck, and he were thrown into the
sea, than that he should offend one of these little
ones. ³Take heed to yourselves. If your brother
sins against you,ᵃ rebuke him; and if he repents,
forgive him. ⁴And if he sins against you seven
times in a day, and seven times in a day returns
to you,ᵃ saying, 'I repent,' you shall forgive him."

Faith and Duty

⁵And the apostles said to the Lord, "Increase
our faith."

⁶So the Lord said, "If you have faith as a mustard seed, you can say to this mulberry tree, 'Be
pulled up by the roots and be planted in the sea,'
and it would obey you. ⁷And which of you, having a servant plowing or tending sheep, will say
to him when he has come in from the field,
'Come at once and sit down to eat'? ⁸But will he
not rather say to him, 'Prepare something for my

17:3 ᵃNU-Text omits *against you*.   17:4 ᵃM-Text omits *to you.*

supper, and gird yourself and serve me till I have
eaten and drunk, and afterward you will eat and
drink'? ⁹Does he thank that servant because he
did the things that were commanded him? I think
not.ᵃ ¹⁰So likewise you, when you have done all
those things which you are commanded, say, 'We
are unprofitable servants. We have done what was
our duty to do.' "

Ten Lepers Cleansed

¹¹Now it happened as He went to Jerusalem
that He passed through the midst of Samaria and
Galilee. ¹²Then as He entered a certain village,
there met Him ten men who were lepers, who
stood afar off. ¹³And they lifted up *their* voices
and said, "Jesus, Master, have mercy on us!"

¹⁴So when He saw *them,* He said to them,
"Go, show yourselves to the priests." And so it
was that as they went, they were cleansed.

¹⁵And one of them, when he saw that he was
healed, returned, and with a loud voice glorified
God, ¹⁶and fell down on *his* face at His feet, giving Him thanks. And he was a Samaritan.

¹⁷So Jesus answered and said, "Were there
not ten cleansed? But where *are* the nine? ¹⁸Were
there not any found who returned to give glory
to God except this foreigner?" ¹⁹And He said to
him, "Arise, go your way. Your faith has made
you well."

The Coming of the Kingdom

²⁰Now when He was asked by the Pharisees
when the kingdom of God would come, He answered them and said, "The kingdom of God
does not come with observation; ²¹nor will they

17:9 ᵃNU-Text ends verse with *commanded*; M-Text omits *him.*

say, 'See here!' or 'See there!'ª For indeed, the kingdom of God is within you."

²²Then He said to the disciples, "The days will come when you will desire to see one of the days of the Son of Man, and you will not see *it*. ²³And they will say to you, 'Look here!' or 'Look there!'ª Do not go after *them* or follow *them*. ²⁴For as the lightning that flashes out of one *part* under heaven shines to the other *part* under heaven, so also the Son of Man will be in His day. ²⁵But first He must suffer many things and be rejected by this generation. ²⁶And as it was in the days of Noah, so it will be also in the days of the Son of Man: ²⁷They ate, they drank, they married wives, they were given in marriage, until the day that Noah entered the ark, and the flood came and destroyed them all. ²⁸Likewise as it was also in the days of Lot: They ate, they drank, they bought, they sold, they planted, they built; ²⁹but on the day that Lot went out of Sodom it rained fire and brimstone from heaven and destroyed *them* all. ³⁰Even so will it be in the day when the Son of Man is revealed.

³¹"In that day, he who is on the housetop, and his goods *are* in the house, let him not come down to take them away. And likewise the one who is in the field, let him not turn back. ³²Remember Lot's wife. ³³Whoever seeks to save his life will lose it, and whoever loses his life will preserve it. ³⁴I tell you, in that night there will be two *men* in one bed: the one will be taken and the other will be left. ³⁵Two *women* will be grinding together: the one will be taken and the other left. ³⁶Two *men* will be in the field: the one will

17:21 ªNU-Text reverses *here* and *there*. 17:23 ªNU-Text reverses *here* and *there*.

be taken and the other left."[a]

³⁷And they answered and said to Him, "Where, Lord?"

So He said to them, "Wherever the body is, there the eagles will be gathered together."

The Parable of the Persistent Widow

18 Then He spoke a parable to them, that men always ought to pray and not lose heart, ²saying: "There was in a certain city a judge who did not fear God nor regard man. ³Now there was a widow in that city; and she came to him, saying, 'Get justice for me from my adversary.' ⁴And he would not for a while; but afterward he said within himself, 'Though I do not fear God nor regard man, ⁵yet because this widow troubles me I will avenge her, lest by her continual coming she weary me.' "

⁶Then the Lord said, "Hear what the unjust judge said. ⁷And shall God not avenge His own elect who cry out day and night to Him, though He bears long with them? ⁸I tell you that He will avenge them speedily. Nevertheless, when the Son of Man comes, will He really find faith on the earth?"

The Parable of the Pharisee and the Tax Collector

⁹Also He spoke this parable to some who trusted in themselves that they were righteous, and despised others: ¹⁰"Two men went up to the temple to pray, one a Pharisee and the other a tax collector. ¹¹The Pharisee stood and prayed thus with himself, 'God, I thank You that I am not like other men—extortioners, unjust, adulterers, or

17:36 [a]NU-Text and M-Text omit verse 36.

even as this tax collector. [12]I fast twice a week; I give tithes of all that I possess.' [13]And the tax collector, standing afar off, would not so much as raise *his* eyes to heaven, but beat his breast, saying, 'God, be merciful to me a sinner!' [14]I tell you, this man went down to his house justified *rather* than the other; for everyone who exalts himself will be humbled, and he who humbles himself will be exalted."

Jesus Blesses Little Children

[15]Then they also brought infants to Him that He might touch them; but when the disciples saw *it,* they rebuked them. [16]But Jesus called them to *Him* and said, "Let the little children come to Me, and do not forbid them; for of such is the kingdom of God. [17]Assuredly, I say to you, whoever does not receive the kingdom of God as a little child will by no means enter it."

Jesus Counsels the Rich Young Ruler

[18]Now a certain ruler asked Him, saying, "Good Teacher, what shall I do to inherit eternal life?"

[19]So Jesus said to him, "Why do you call Me good? No one *is* good but One, *that is,* God. [20]You know the commandments: *'Do not commit adultery,' 'Do not murder,' 'Do not steal,' 'Do not bear false witness,' 'Honor your father and your mother.'* "[a]

[21]And he said, "All these things I have kept from my youth."

[22]So when Jesus heard these things, He said to him, "You still lack one thing. Sell all that you have and distribute to the poor, and you will have

---

18:20 [a]Exodus 20:12–16; Deuteronomy 5:16–20

treasure in heaven; and come, follow Me."

23But when he heard this, he became very sorrowful, for he was very rich.

With God All Things Are Possible

24And when Jesus saw that he became very sorrowful, He said, "How hard it is for those who have riches to enter the kingdom of God! 25For it is easier for a camel to go through the eye of a needle than for a rich man to enter the kingdom of God."

26And those who heard it said, "Who then can be saved?"

27But He said, "The things which are impossible with men are possible with God."

28Then Peter said, "See, we have left all[a] and followed You."

29So He said to them, "Assuredly, I say to you, there is no one who has left house or parents or brothers or wife or children, for the sake of the kingdom of God, 30who shall not receive many times more in this present time, and in the age to come eternal life."

Jesus a Third Time Predicts His Death and Resurrection

31Then He took the twelve aside and said to them, "Behold, we are going up to Jerusalem, and all things that are written by the prophets concerning the Son of Man will be accomplished. 32For He will be delivered to the Gentiles and will be mocked and insulted and spit upon. 33They will scourge *Him* and kill Him. And the third day He will rise again."

34But they understood none of these things;

18:28 [a]NU-Text reads *our own.*

this saying was hidden from them, and they did not know the things which were spoken.

A Blind Man Receives His Sight

[35]Then it happened, as He was coming near Jericho, that a certain blind man sat by the road begging. [36]And hearing a multitude passing by, he asked what it meant. [37]So they told him that Jesus of Nazareth was passing by. [38]And he cried out, saying, "Jesus, Son of David, have mercy on me!"

[39]Then those who went before warned him that he should be quiet; but he cried out all the more, "Son of David, have mercy on me!"

[40]So Jesus stood still and commanded him to be brought to Him. And when he had come near, He asked him, [41]saying, "What do you want Me to do for you?"

He said, "Lord, that I may receive my sight."

[42]Then Jesus said to him, "Receive your sight; your faith has made you well." [43]And immediately he received his sight, and followed Him, glorifying God. And all the people, when they saw it, gave praise to God.

Jesus Comes to Zacchaeus' House

19 Then *Jesus* entered and passed through Jericho. [2]Now behold, *there was* a man named Zacchaeus who was a chief tax collector, and he was rich. [3]And he sought to see who Jesus was, but could not because of the crowd, for he was of short stature. [4]So he ran ahead and climbed up into a sycamore tree to see Him, for He was going to pass that *way*. [5]And when Jesus came to the place, He looked up and saw him,[a]

19:5 [a]NU-Text omits *and saw him*.

and said to him, "Zacchaeus, make haste and
come down, for today I must stay at your house."
⁶So he made haste and came down, and received
Him joyfully. ⁷But when they saw *it,* they all
complained, saying, "He has gone to be a guest
with a man who is a sinner."

⁸Then Zacchaeus stood and said to the Lord,
"Look, Lord, I give half of my goods to the poor;
and if I have taken anything from anyone by false
accusation, I restore fourfold."

⁹And Jesus said to him, "Today salvation has
come to this house, because he also is a son of
Abraham; ¹⁰for the Son of Man has come to seek
and to save that which was lost."

The Parable of the Minas

¹¹Now as they heard these things, He spoke
another parable, because He was near Jerusalem
and because they thought the kingdom of God
would appear immediately. ¹²Therefore He said:
"A certain nobleman went into a far country to
receive for himself a kingdom and to return. ¹³So
he called ten of his servants, delivered to them
ten minas,ᵃ and said to them, 'Do business till I
come.' ¹⁴But his citizens hated him, and sent a
delegation after him, saying, 'We will not have
this *man* to reign over us.'

¹⁵"And so it was that when he returned, having received the kingdom, he then commanded
these servants, to whom he had given the money,
to be called to him, that he might know how
much every man had gained by trading. ¹⁶Then
came the first, saying, 'Master, your mina has
earned ten minas.' ¹⁷And he said to him, 'Well

19:13 ᵃThe *mina* (Greek *mna,* Hebrew *minah*) was worth about
three months' salary.

done, good servant; because you were faithful in a very little, have authority over ten cities.' ¹⁸And the second came, saying, 'Master, your mina has earned five minas.' ¹⁹Likewise he said to him, 'You also be over five cities.'

²⁰"Then another came, saying, 'Master, here is your mina, which I have kept put away in a handkerchief. ²¹For I feared you, because you are an austere man. You collect what you did not deposit, and reap what you did not sow.' ²²And he said to him, 'Out of your own mouth I will judge you, *you* wicked servant. You knew that I was an austere man, collecting what I did not deposit and reaping what I did not sow. ²³Why then did you not put my money in the bank, that at my coming I might have collected it with interest?'

²⁴"And he said to those who stood by, 'Take the mina from him, and give *it* to him who has ten minas.' ²⁵(But they said to him, 'Master, he has ten minas.') ²⁶'For I say to you, that to everyone who has will be given; and from him who does not have, even what he has will be taken away from him. ²⁷But bring here those enemies of mine, who did not want me to reign over them, and slay *them* before me.' "

The Triumphal Entry

²⁸When He had said this, He went on ahead, going up to Jerusalem. ²⁹And it came to pass, when He drew near to Bethphage[a] and Bethany, at the mountain called Olivet, *that* He sent two of His disciples, ³⁰saying, "Go into the village opposite *you,* where as you enter you will find a colt tied, on which no one has ever sat. Loose it and

---

19:29 [a]M-Text reads *Bethsphage.*

bring *it here.* ³¹And if anyone asks you, 'Why are you loosing *it?*' thus you shall say to him, 'Because the Lord has need of it.' "

³²So those who were sent went their way and found *it* just as He had said to them. ³³But as they were loosing the colt, the owners of it said to them, "Why are you loosing the colt?"

³⁴And they said, "The Lord has need of him." ³⁵Then they brought him to Jesus. And they threw their own clothes on the colt, and they set Jesus on him. ³⁶And as He went, *many* spread their clothes on the road.

³⁷Then, as He was now drawing near the descent of the Mount of Olives, the whole multitude of the disciples began to rejoice and praise God with a loud voice for all the mighty works they had seen, ³⁸saying:

> " 'Blessed is the King who comes in the name
> of the LORD!'[a]
> Peace in heaven and glory in the highest!"

³⁹And some of the Pharisees called to Him from the crowd, "Teacher, rebuke Your disciples."

⁴⁰But He answered and said to them, "I tell you that if these should keep silent, the stones would immediately cry out."

Jesus Weeps over Jerusalem

⁴¹Now as He drew near, He saw the city and wept over it, ⁴²saying, "If you had known, even you, especially in this your day, the things *that make* for your peace! But now they are hidden from your eyes. ⁴³For days will come upon you when your enemies will build an embankment

19:38 [a]Psalm 118:26

around you, surround you and close you in on every side, ⁴⁴and level you, and your children within you, to the ground; and they will not leave in you one stone upon another, because you did not know the time of your visitation."

Jesus Cleanses the Temple

⁴⁵Then He went into the temple and began to drive out those who bought and sold in it,^a ⁴⁶saying to them, "It is written, *'My house is*^a *a house of prayer,'*^b but you have made it a *'den of thieves.'"*^c

⁴⁷And He was teaching daily in the temple. But the chief priests, the scribes, and the leaders of the people sought to destroy Him, ⁴⁸and were unable to do anything; for all the people were very attentive to hear Him.

Jesus' Authority Questioned

20 Now it happened on one of those days, as He taught the people in the temple and preached the gospel, *that* the chief priests and the scribes, together with the elders, confronted Him ²and spoke to Him, saying, "Tell us, by what authority are You doing these things? Or who is he who gave You this authority?"

³But He answered and said to them, "I also will ask you one thing, and answer Me: ⁴The baptism of John—was it from heaven or from men?"

⁵And they reasoned among themselves, saying, "If we say, 'From heaven,' He will say, 'Why then^a did you not believe him?' ⁶But if we say,

---

19:45 ^aNU-Text reads *those who were selling.*   19:46 ^aNU-Text reads *shall be.*   ^bIsaiah 56:7   ^cJeremiah 7:11   20:5 ^aNU-Text and M-Text omit *then.*

'From men,' all the people will stone us, for they are persuaded that John was a prophet." ⁷So they answered that they did not know where *it was* from.

⁸And Jesus said to them, "Neither will I tell you by what authority I do these things."

The Parable of the Wicked Vinedressers

⁹Then He began to tell the people this parable: "A certain man planted a vineyard, leased it to vinedressers, and went into a far country for a long time. ¹⁰Now at vintage-time he sent a servant to the vinedressers, that they might give him some of the fruit of the vineyard. But the vinedressers beat him and sent *him* away empty-handed. ¹¹Again he sent another servant; and they beat him also, treated *him* shamefully, and sent *him* away empty-handed. ¹²And again he sent a third; and they wounded him also and cast *him* out.

¹³"Then the owner of the vineyard said, 'What shall I do? I will send my beloved son. Probably they will respect *him* when they see him.' ¹⁴But when the vinedressers saw him, they reasoned among themselves, saying, 'This is the heir. Come, let us kill him, that the inheritance may be ours.' ¹⁵So they cast him out of the vineyard and killed *him*. Therefore what will the owner of the vineyard do to them? ¹⁶He will come and destroy those vinedressers and give the vineyard to others."

And when they heard *it* they said, "Certainly not!"

¹⁷Then He looked at them and said, "What then is this that is written:

'The stone which the builders rejected
Has become the chief cornerstone'?ᵃ

¹⁸Whoever falls on that stone will be broken; but on whomever it falls, it will grind him to powder."

¹⁹And the chief priests and the scribes that very hour sought to lay hands on Him, but they feared the peopleᵃ—for they knew He had spoken this parable against them.

The Pharisees: Is It Lawful to Pay Taxes to Caesar?

²⁰So they watched *Him,* and sent spies who pretended to be righteous, that they might seize on His words, in order to deliver Him to the power and the authority of the governor.

²¹Then they asked Him, saying, "Teacher, we know that You say and teach rightly, and You do not show personal favoritism, but teach the way of God in truth: ²²Is it lawful for us to pay taxes to Caesar or not?"

²³But He perceived their craftiness, and said to them, "Why do you test Me?ᵃ ²⁴Show Me a denarius. Whose image and inscription does it have?"

They answered and said, "Caesar's."

²⁵And He said to them, "Render therefore to Caesar the things that are Caesar's, and to God the things that are God's."

²⁶But they could not catch Him in His words in the presence of the people. And they marveled at His answer and kept silent.

20:17 ᵃPsalm 118:22   **20:19** ᵃM-Text reads *but they were afraid.*
20:23 ᵃNU-Text omits *Why do you test Me?*

The Sadducees: What About
the Resurrection?

²⁷Then some of the Sadducees, who deny that
there is a resurrection, came to *Him* and asked
Him, ²⁸saying: "Teacher, Moses wrote to us *that* if
a man's brother dies, having a wife, and he dies
without children, his brother should take his
wife and raise up offspring for his brother.
²⁹Now there were seven brothers. And the first
took a wife, and died without children. ³⁰And
the second^a took her as wife, and he died child-
less. ³¹Then the third took her, and in like manner the seven also; and they left no children,^a
and died. ³²Last of all the woman died also.
³³Therefore, in the resurrection, whose wife does
she become? For all seven had her as wife."

³⁴Jesus answered and said to them, "The sons
of this age marry and are given in marriage. ³⁵But
those who are counted worthy to attain that age,
and the resurrection from the dead, neither
marry nor are given in marriage; ³⁶nor can they
die anymore, for they are equal to the angels and
are sons of God, being sons of the resurrection.
³⁷But even Moses showed in the *burning* bush
passage that the dead are raised, when he called
the Lord *'the God of Abraham, the God of Isaac,
and the God of Jacob.'*^a ³⁸For He is not the God
of the dead but of the living, for all live to
Him."

³⁹Then some of the scribes answered and
said, "Teacher, You have spoken well." ⁴⁰But after
that they dared not question Him anymore.

20:30 ^aNU-Text ends verse 30 here.   20:31 ^aNU-Text and M-
Text read *the seven also left no children.*   20:37 ^aExodus 3:6, 15

Jesus: How Can David Call
His Descendant Lord?

⁴¹And He said to them, "How can they say that the Christ is the Son of David? ⁴²Now David himself said in the Book of Psalms:

'The Lord said to my Lord,
"Sit at My right hand,
⁴³*Till I make Your enemies Your footstool."* ᵃ

⁴⁴Therefore David calls Him *'Lord';* how is He then his Son?"

Beware of the Scribes

⁴⁵Then, in the hearing of all the people, He said to His disciples, ⁴⁶"Beware of the scribes, who desire to go around in long robes, love greetings in the marketplaces, the best seats in the synagogues, and the best places at feasts, ⁴⁷who devour widows' houses, and for a pretense make long prayers. These will receive greater condemnation."

The Widow's Two Mites

21 And He looked up and saw the rich putting their gifts into the treasury, ²and He saw also a certain poor widow putting in two mites. ³So He said, "Truly I say to you that this poor widow has put in more than all; ⁴for all these out of their abundance have put in offerings for God,ᵃ but she out of her poverty put in all the livelihood that she had."

Jesus Predicts the
Destruction of the Temple

⁵Then, as some spoke of the temple, how it

20:43 ᵃPsalm 110:1   21:4 ᵃNU-Text omits *for God.*

was adorned with beautiful stones and donations, He said, [6]"These things which you see—the days will come in which not *one* stone shall be left upon another that shall not be thrown down."

The Signs of the Times and the End of the Age

[7]So they asked Him, saying, "Teacher, but when will these things be? And what sign *will there be* when these things are about to take place?"

[8]And He said: "Take heed that you not be deceived. For many will come in My name, saying, 'I am *He*,' and, 'The time has drawn near.' Therefore[a] do not go after them. [9]But when you hear of wars and commotions, do not be terrified; for these things must come to pass first, but the end *will* not *come* immediately."

[10]Then He said to them, "Nation will rise against nation, and kingdom against kingdom. [11]And there will be great earthquakes in various places, and famines and pestilences; and there will be fearful sights and great signs from heaven. [12]But before all these things, they will lay their hands on you and persecute *you,* delivering *you* up to the synagogues and prisons. You will be brought before kings and rulers for My name's sake. [13]But it will turn out for you as an occasion for testimony. [14]Therefore settle *it* in your hearts not to meditate beforehand on what you will answer; [15]for I will give you a mouth and wisdom which all your adversaries will not be able to contradict or resist. [16]You will be betrayed even by parents and brothers, relatives and friends; and they will put *some* of you to death. [17]And

---

21:8[a]NU-Text omits *Therefore.*

you will be hated by all for My name's sake. [18]But not a hair of your head shall be lost. [19]By your patience possess your souls.

The Destruction of Jerusalem

[20]"But when you see Jerusalem surrounded by armies, then know that its desolation is near. [21]Then let those who are in Judea flee to the mountains, let those who are in the midst of her depart, and let not those who are in the country enter her. [22]For these are the days of vengeance, that all things which are written may be fulfilled. [23]But woe to those who are pregnant and to those who are nursing babies in those days! For there will be great distress in the land and wrath upon this people. [24]And they will fall by the edge of the sword, and be led away captive into all nations. And Jerusalem will be trampled by Gentiles until the times of the Gentiles are fulfilled.

The Coming of the Son of Man

[25]"And there will be signs in the sun, in the moon, and in the stars; and on the earth distress of nations, with perplexity, the sea and the waves roaring; [26]men's hearts failing them from fear and the expectation of those things which are coming on the earth, for the powers of the heavens will be shaken. [27]Then they will see the Son of Man coming in a cloud with power and great glory. [28]Now when these things begin to happen, look up and lift up your heads, because your redemption draws near."

The Parable of the Fig Tree

[29]Then He spoke to them a parable: "Look at the fig tree, and all the trees. [30]When they are al-

ready budding, you see and know for yourselves that summer is now near. ³¹So you also, when you see these things happening, know that the kingdom of God is near. ³²Assuredly, I say to you, this generation will by no means pass away till all things take place. ³³Heaven and earth will pass away, but My words will by no means pass away.

The Importance of Watching

³⁴"But take heed to yourselves, lest your hearts be weighed down with carousing, drunkenness, and cares of this life, and that Day come on you unexpectedly. ³⁵For it will come as a snare on all those who dwell on the face of the whole earth. ³⁶Watch therefore, and pray always that you may be counted worthy[a] to escape all these things that will come to pass, and to stand before the Son of Man."

³⁷And in the daytime He was teaching in the temple, but at night He went out and stayed on the mountain called Olivet. ³⁸Then early in the morning all the people came to Him in the temple to hear Him.

The Plot to Kill Jesus

22 Now the Feast of Unleavened Bread drew near, which is called Passover. ²And the chief priests and the scribes sought how they might kill Him, for they feared the people.

³Then Satan entered Judas, surnamed Iscariot, who was numbered among the twelve. ⁴So he went his way and conferred with the chief priests and captains, how he might betray Him to them. ⁵And they were glad, and agreed to give

21:36 [a]NU-Text reads *may have strength.*

him money. ⁶So he promised and sought opportunity to betray Him to them in the absence of the multitude.

Jesus and His Disciples Prepare the Passover

⁷Then came the Day of Unleavened Bread, when the Passover must be killed. ⁸And He sent Peter and John, saying, "Go and prepare the Passover for us, that we may eat."

⁹So they said to Him, "Where do You want us to prepare?"

¹⁰And He said to them, "Behold, when you have entered the city, a man will meet you carrying a pitcher of water; follow him into the house which he enters. ¹¹Then you shall say to the master of the house, 'The Teacher says to you, "Where is the guest room where I may eat the Passover with My disciples?" ' ¹²Then he will show you a large, furnished upper room; there make ready."

¹³So they went and found it just as He had said to them, and they prepared the Passover.

Jesus Institutes the Lord's Supper

¹⁴When the hour had come, He sat down, and the twelveᵃ apostles with Him. ¹⁵Then He said to them, "With *fervent* desire I have desired to eat this Passover with you before I suffer; ¹⁶for I say to you, I will no longer eat of it until it is fulfilled in the kingdom of God."

¹⁷Then He took the cup, and gave thanks, and said, "Take this and divide *it* among yourselves; ¹⁸for I say to you,ᵃ I will not drink of the

22:14 ᵃNU-Text omits *twelve*. 22:18 ᵃNU-Text adds *from now on*.

fruit of the vine until the kingdom of God comes."

[19]And He took bread, gave thanks and broke it, and gave it to them, saying, "This is My body which is given for you; do this in remembrance of Me."

[20]Likewise He also *took* the cup after supper, saying, "This cup *is* the new covenant in My blood, which is shed for you. [21]But behold, the hand of My betrayer is with Me on the table. [22]And truly the Son of Man goes as it has been determined, but woe to that man by whom He is betrayed!"

[23]Then they began to question among themselves, which of them it was who would do this thing.

The Disciples Argue About Greatness

[24]Now there was also a dispute among them, as to which of them should be considered the greatest. [25]And He said to them, "The kings of the Gentiles exercise lordship over them, and those who exercise authority over them are called 'benefactors.' [26]But not so *among* you; on the contrary, he who is greatest among you, let him be as the younger, and he who governs as he who serves. [27]For who *is* greater, he who sits at the table, or he who serves? *Is* it not he who sits at the table? Yet I am among you as the One who serves.

[28]"But you are those who have continued with Me in My trials. [29]And I bestow upon you a kingdom, just as My Father bestowed *one* upon Me, [30]that you may eat and drink at My table in My kingdom, and sit on thrones judging the twelve tribes of Israel."

Jesus Predicts Peter's Denial

[31]And the Lord said,[a] "Simon, Simon! Indeed, Satan has asked for you, that he may sift *you* as wheat. [32]But I have prayed for you, that your faith should not fail; and when you have returned to *Me,* strengthen your brethren."

[33]But he said to Him, "Lord, I am ready to go with You, both to prison and to death."

[34]Then He said, "I tell you, Peter, the rooster shall not crow this day before you will deny three times that you know Me."

Supplies for the Road

[35]And He said to them, "When I sent you without money bag, knapsack, and sandals, did you lack anything?"

So they said, "Nothing."

[36]Then He said to them, "But now, he who has a money bag, let him take *it,* and likewise a knapsack; and he who has no sword, let him sell his garment and buy one. [37]For I say to you that this which is written must still be accomplished in Me: *'And He was numbered with the transgressors.'*[a] For the things concerning Me have an end."

[38]So they said, "Lord, look, here *are* two swords."

And He said to them, "It is enough."

The Prayer in the Garden

[39]Coming out, He went to the Mount of Olives, as He was accustomed, and His disciples also followed Him. [40]When He came to the place, He said to them, "Pray that you may not enter into temptation."

22:31 [a]NU-Text omits *And the Lord said.*   22:37 [a]Isaiah 53:12

⁴¹And He was withdrawn from them about a stone's throw, and He knelt down and prayed, ⁴²saying, "Father, if it is Your will, take this cup away from Me; nevertheless not My will, but Yours, be done." ⁴³Then an angel appeared to Him from heaven, strengthening Him. ⁴⁴And being in agony, He prayed more earnestly. Then His sweat became like great drops of blood falling down to the ground.ª

⁴⁵When He rose up from prayer, and had come to His disciples, He found them sleeping from sorrow. ⁴⁶Then He said to them, "Why do you sleep? Rise and pray, lest you enter into temptation."

Betrayal and Arrest in Gethsemane

⁴⁷And while He was still speaking, behold, a multitude; and he who was called Judas, one of the twelve, went before them and drew near to Jesus to kiss Him. ⁴⁸But Jesus said to him, "Judas, are you betraying the Son of Man with a kiss?"

⁴⁹When those around Him saw what was going to happen, they said to Him, "Lord, shall we strike with the sword?" ⁵⁰And one of them struck the servant of the high priest and cut off his right ear.

⁵¹But Jesus answered and said, "Permit even this." And He touched his ear and healed him.

⁵²Then Jesus said to the chief priests, captains of the temple, and the elders who had come to Him, "Have you come out, as against a robber, with swords and clubs? ⁵³When I was with you daily in the temple, you did not try to seize Me. But this is your hour, and the power of darkness."

22:44 ªNU-Text brackets verses 43 and 44 as not in the original text.

Peter Denies Jesus, and Weeps Bitterly

⁵⁴Having arrested Him, they led *Him* and brought Him into the high priest's house. But Peter followed at a distance. ⁵⁵Now when they had kindled a fire in the midst of the courtyard and sat down together, Peter sat among them. ⁵⁶And a certain servant girl, seeing him as he sat by the fire, looked intently at him and said, "This man was also with Him."

⁵⁷But he denied Him,ᵃ saying, "Woman, I do not know Him."

⁵⁸And after a little while another saw him and said, "You also are of them."

But Peter said, "Man, I am not!"

⁵⁹Then after about an hour had passed, another confidently affirmed, saying, "Surely this *fellow* also was with Him, for he is a Galilean."

⁶⁰But Peter said, "Man, I do not know what you are saying!"

Immediately, while he was still speaking, the roosterᵃ crowed. ⁶¹And the Lord turned and looked at Peter. Then Peter remembered the word of the Lord, how He had said to him, "Before the rooster crows,ᵃ you will deny Me three times." ⁶²So Peter went out and wept bitterly.

Jesus Mocked and Beaten

⁶³Now the men who held Jesus mocked Him and beat Him. ⁶⁴And having blindfolded Him, they struck Him on the face and asked Him,ᵃ saying, "Prophesy! Who is the one who struck You?" ⁶⁵And many other things they blasphemously spoke against Him.

22:57 ᵃNU-Text reads *denied it.* 22:60 ᵃNU-Text and M-Text read *a rooster.* 22:61 ᵃNU-Text adds *today.* 22:64 ᵃNU-Text reads *And having blindfolded Him, they asked Him.*

Jesus Faces the Sanhedrin

⁶⁶As soon as it was day, the elders of the people, both chief priests and scribes, came together and led Him into their council, saying, ⁶⁷"If You are the Christ, tell us."

But He said to them, "If I tell you, you will by no means believe. ⁶⁸And if I also ask *you*, you will by no means answer Me or let *Me* go.ᵃ ⁶⁹Hereafter the Son of Man will sit on the right hand of the power of God."

⁷⁰Then they all said, "Are You then the Son of God?"

So He said to them, "You *rightly* say that I am."

⁷¹And they said, "What further testimony do we need? For we have heard it ourselves from His own mouth."

Jesus Handed Over to Pontius Pilate

23 Then the whole multitude of them arose and led Him to Pilate. ²And they began to accuse Him, saying, "We found this *fellow* perverting theᵃ nation, and forbidding to pay taxes to Caesar, saying that He Himself is Christ, a King."

³Then Pilate asked Him, saying, "Are You the King of the Jews?"

He answered him and said, "*It is as* you say."

⁴So Pilate said to the chief priests and the crowd, "I find no fault in this Man."

⁵But they were the more fierce, saying, "He stirs up the people, teaching throughout all Judea, beginning from Galilee to this place."

22:68 ᵃNU-Text omits *also* and *Me or let Me go.* 23:2 ᵃNU-Text reads *our.*

Jesus Faces Herod

⁶When Pilate heard of Galilee,ᵃ he asked if the Man were a Galilean. ⁷And as soon as he knew that He belonged to Herod's jurisdiction, he sent Him to Herod, who was also in Jerusalem at that time. ⁸Now when Herod saw Jesus, he was exceedingly glad; for he had desired for a long *time* to see Him, because he had heard many things about Him, and he hoped to see some miracle done by Him. ⁹Then he questioned Him with many words, but He answered him nothing. ¹⁰And the chief priests and scribes stood and vehemently accused Him. ¹¹Then Herod, with his men of war, treated Him with contempt and mocked *Him,* arrayed Him in a gorgeous robe, and sent Him back to Pilate. ¹²That very day Pilate and Herod became friends with each other, for previously they had been at enmity with each other.

Taking the Place of Barabbas

¹³Then Pilate, when he had called together the chief priests, the rulers, and the people, ¹⁴said to them, "You have brought this Man to me, as one who misleads the people. And indeed, having examined *Him* in your presence, I have found no fault in this Man concerning those things of which you accuse Him; ¹⁵no, neither did Herod, for I sent you back to him;ᵃ and indeed nothing deserving of death has been done by Him. ¹⁶I will therefore chastise Him and release *Him*" ¹⁷(for it was necessary for him to release one to them at the feast).ᵃ

¹⁸And they all cried out at once, saying, "Away

23:6 ᵃNU-Text omits *of Galilee*.   23:15 ᵃNU-Text reads *for he sent Him back to us.*   23:17 ᵃNU-Text omits verse 17.

with this *Man*, and release to us Barabbas"—
[19]who had been thrown into prison for a certain
rebellion made in the city, and for murder.

[20]Pilate, therefore, wishing to release Jesus,
again called out to them. [21]But they shouted,
saying, "Crucify *Him*, crucify Him!"

[22]Then he said to them the third time, "Why,
what evil has He done? I have found no reason
for death in Him. I will therefore chastise Him
and let *Him* go."

[23]But they were insistent, demanding with
loud voices that He be crucified. And the voices
of these men and of the chief priests prevailed.[a]
[24]So Pilate gave sentence that it should be as they
requested. [25]And he released to them[a] the one
they requested, who for rebellion and murder
had been thrown into prison; but he delivered
Jesus to their will.

The King on a Cross

[26]Now as they led Him away, they laid hold of
a certain man, Simon a Cyrenian, who was coming from the country, and on him they laid the
cross that he might bear *it* after Jesus.

[27]And a great multitude of the people followed Him, and women who also mourned and
lamented Him. [28]But Jesus, turning to them,
said, "Daughters of Jerusalem, do not weep for
Me, but weep for yourselves and for your children. [29]For indeed the days are coming in which
they will say, 'Blessed *are* the barren, wombs that
never bore, and breasts which never nursed!'
[30]Then they will begin 'to say to the mountains,
"Fall on us!" and to the hills, "Cover us!" '[a] [31]For if

23:23 [a]NU-Text omits *and of the chief priests.* 23:25 [a]NU-Text
and M-Text omit *to them.* 23:30 [a]Hosea 10:8

they do these things in the green wood, what will be done in the dry?"

³²There were also two others, criminals, led with Him to be put to death. ³³And when they had come to the place called Calvary, there they crucified Him, and the criminals, one on the right hand and the other on the left. ³⁴Then Jesus said, "Father, forgive them, for they do not know what they do."[a]

And they divided His garments and cast lots. ³⁵And the people stood looking on. But even the rulers with them sneered, saying, "He saved others; let Him save Himself if He is the Christ, the chosen of God."

³⁶The soldiers also mocked Him, coming and offering Him sour wine, ³⁷and saying, "If You are the King of the Jews, save Yourself."

³⁸And an inscription also was written over Him in letters of Greek, Latin, and Hebrew:[a]

THIS IS THE KING OF THE JEWS.

³⁹Then one of the criminals who were hanged blasphemed Him, saying, "If You are the Christ,[a] save Yourself and us."

⁴⁰But the other, answering, rebuked him, saying, "Do you not even fear God, seeing you are under the same condemnation? ⁴¹And we indeed justly, for we receive the due reward of our deeds; but this Man has done nothing wrong." ⁴²Then he said to Jesus, "Lord,[a] remember me when You come into Your kingdom."

⁴³And Jesus said to him, "Assuredly, I say to you, today you will be with Me in Paradise."

23:34 [a]NU-Text brackets the first sentence as a later addition. 23:38 [a]NU-Text omits *written* and *in letters of Greek, Latin, and Hebrew.*   23:39 [a]NU-Text reads *Are You not the Christ?*   23:42 [a]NU-Text reads *And he said, "Jesus, remember me.*

Jesus Dies on the Cross

⁴⁴Now it was[a] about the sixth hour, and there was darkness over all the earth until the ninth hour. ⁴⁵Then the sun was darkened,[a] and the veil of the temple was torn in two. ⁴⁶And when Jesus had cried out with a loud voice, He said, "Father, *'into Your hands I commit My spirit.' "*[a] Having said this, He breathed His last.

⁴⁷So when the centurion saw what had happened, he glorified God, saying, "Certainly this was a righteous Man!"

⁴⁸And the whole crowd who came together to that sight, seeing what had been done, beat their breasts and returned. ⁴⁹But all His acquaintances, and the women who followed Him from Galilee, stood at a distance, watching these things.

Jesus Buried in Joseph's Tomb

⁵⁰Now behold, *there was* a man named Joseph, a council member, a good and just man. ⁵¹He had not consented to their decision and deed. *He was* from Arimathea, a city of the Jews, who himself was also waiting[a] for the kingdom of God. ⁵²This man went to Pilate and asked for the body of Jesus. ⁵³Then he took it down, wrapped it in linen, and laid it in a tomb *that was* hewn out of the rock, where no one had ever lain before. ⁵⁴That day was the Preparation, and the Sabbath drew near.

⁵⁵And the women who had come with Him from Galilee followed after, and they observed the tomb and how His body was laid. ⁵⁶Then they returned and prepared spices and fragrant oils. And they rested on the Sabbath according to the commandment.

23:44 [a]NU-Text adds *already*.   23:45 [a]NU-Text reads *obscured*.
23:46 [a]Psalm 31:5   23:51 [a]NU-Text reads *who was waiting*.

He Is Risen

24 Now on the first *day* of the week, very early in the morning, they, and certain *other women* with them,[a] came to the tomb bringing the spices which they had prepared. [2]But they found the stone rolled away from the tomb. [3]Then they went in and did not find the body of the Lord Jesus. [4]And it happened, as they were greatly[a] perplexed about this, that behold, two men stood by them in shining garments. [5]Then, as they were afraid and bowed *their* faces to the earth, they said to them, "Why do you seek the living among the dead? [6]He is not here, but is risen! Remember how He spoke to you when He was still in Galilee, [7]saying, 'The Son of Man must be delivered into the hands of sinful men, and be crucified, and the third day rise again.' "

[8]And they remembered His words. [9]Then they returned from the tomb and told all these things to the eleven and to all the rest. [10]It was Mary Magdalene, Joanna, Mary *the mother* of James, and the other *women* with them, who told these things to the apostles. [11]And their words seemed to them like idle tales, and they did not believe them. [12]But Peter arose and ran to the tomb; and stooping down, he saw the linen cloths lying[a] by themselves; and he departed, marveling to himself at what had happened.

The Road to Emmaus

[13]Now behold, two of them were traveling that same day to a village called Emmaus, which was seven miles[a] from Jerusalem. [14]And they talked together of all these things which had

24:1 [a]NU-Text omits *and certain other women with them.*   24:4 [a]NU-Text omits *greatly.*   24:12 [a]NU-Text omits *lying.*   24:13 [a]Literally *sixty stadia*

happened. ¹⁵So it was, while they conversed and reasoned, that Jesus Himself drew near and went with them. ¹⁶But their eyes were restrained, so that they did not know Him.

¹⁷And He said to them, "What kind of conversation *is* this that you have with one another as you walk and are sad?"ᵃ

¹⁸Then the one whose name was Cleopas answered and said to Him, "Are You the only stranger in Jerusalem, and have You not known the things which happened there in these days?"

¹⁹And He said to them, "What things?"

So they said to Him, "The things concerning Jesus of Nazareth, who was a Prophet mighty in deed and word before God and all the people, ²⁰and how the chief priests and our rulers delivered Him to be condemned to death, and crucified Him. ²¹But we were hoping that it was He who was going to redeem Israel. Indeed, besides all this, today is the third day since these things happened. ²²Yes, and certain women of our company, who arrived at the tomb early, astonished us. ²³When they did not find His body, they came saying that they had also seen a vision of angels who said He was alive. ²⁴And certain of those *who were* with us went to the tomb and found *it* just as the women had said; but Him they did not see."

²⁵Then He said to them, "O foolish ones, and slow of heart to believe in all that the prophets have spoken! ²⁶Ought not the Christ to have suffered these things and to enter into His glory?" ²⁷And beginning at Moses and all the Prophets, He expounded to them in all the Scriptures the

---

24:17 ᵃNU-Text reads *as you walk? And they stood still, looking sad.*

How do you know Jesus rose from the dead?

The resurrection of Jesus Christ is the cornerstone of the Christian faith. As the apostle Paul said, "If Christ is not risen, your faith is futile; you are still in your sins!" (1 Corinthians 15:17). But Christianity is not a "blind faith." God has given us "many infallible proofs" of Jesus' resurrection (Acts 1:3) and invites us to examine the evidence.

His resurrection was foretold. Jesus Himself said He would be killed and on the third day rise again. The risen Jesus spoke to two disciples on the road to Emmaus, telling them, "These are the words which I spoke to you while I was still with you, that all things must be fulfilled which were written in the Law of Moses and the Prophets and the Psalms concerning Me" (Luke 24:44). The suffering death of the Savior was foretold in numerous Old Testament prophecies, in minute details, all of which were precisely fulfilled.

Jesus died. Some skeptics have proposed the "swoon theory"—that Jesus didn't really die on the cross but instead passed out and later revived in the tomb. But He was brutally beaten, flogged with a cat-o'-nine-tails tearing His flesh, hung on a cross with thick spikes driven through His hands and feet, then—to ensure that He was dead—He was pierced in the side with a spear. The Roman soldiers were professional executioners who knew how to do a thorough job. No one in this condition could have survived, then awakened to roll away a two-ton stone and slipped by the Roman guards posted at the sealed tomb. That Jesus died and was buried is reported even by secular sources of the time.

The tomb was empty. Even Jesus' enemies did not dispute that the tomb was empty. Instead, they claimed that the body was stolen while the guards slept—even though the guards faced execution if they fell asleep on the job. It would have been impossible for the cowardly disciples, who fled upon Jesus' arrest, to overpower a squadron of professional soldiers. And why would they? They each faced persecution and death for their eyewitness testimony, fully convinced that Jesus Christ rose from the grave. What would they gain by dying for a known lie?

The Jewish leaders certainly wouldn't have stolen the body. Their goal was to stop the spread of Christianity, so having people believe in Jesus' resurrection was the furthest thing from their minds. If the body could have been found anywhere, they surely would have searched until they produced it and put this new religion to rest.

He was seen alive after the resurrection. These were not "hallucinations" or brief sightings—Jesus ate, drank, and spoke at length with His disciples. Jesus appeared at least 11 times over a 40-day period, and to *over 500* eyewitnesses! In writing of this amazing eyewitness testimony, the apostle Paul noted that "most of [them] remain to the present." With witnesses still alive for cross-examination, skeptics could have easily verified the truth of the claim.

Dr. Simon Greenleaf, a founder of Harvard Law School, was one of the greatest legal minds in this country. He concluded that the resurrection of Christ was one of the best supported events in history, according to the laws of legal evidence used in court. In fact, Greenleaf was so convinced by the overwhelming evidence, he committed his life to Christ!

Lives are radically transformed. Overnight, the fearful disciples became bold, fearless witnesses, proclaiming the resurrection of Jesus Christ. After seeing the ultimate proof of Jesus' deity, thousands of Jews abandoned centuries-old religious rituals to follow the Messiah. Truly, the Son of God has power over life and death, and He is alive to transform lives today. All who repent and trust in Him will "know Him and the power of His resurrection"—they too will encounter the risen Lord and be given eternal life.

things concerning Himself.

The Disciples' Eyes Opened

²⁸Then they drew near to the village where they were going, and He indicated that He would have gone farther. ²⁹But they constrained Him, saying, "Abide with us, for it is toward evening, and the day is far spent." And He went in to stay with them.

³⁰Now it came to pass, as He sat at the table with them, that He took bread, blessed and broke *it*, and gave it to them. ³¹Then their eyes were opened and they knew Him; and He vanished from their sight.

³²And they said to one another, "Did not our heart burn within us while He talked with us on the road, and while He opened the Scriptures to us?" ³³So they rose up that very hour and returned to Jerusalem, and found the eleven and those *who were* with them gathered together, ³⁴saying, "The Lord is risen indeed, and has appeared to Simon!" ³⁵And they told about the things *that had happened* on the road, and how He was known to them in the breaking of bread.

Jesus Appears to His Disciples

³⁶Now as they said these things, Jesus Himself stood in the midst of them, and said to them, "Peace to you." ³⁷But they were terrified and frightened, and supposed they had seen a spirit. ³⁸And He said to them, "Why are you troubled? And why do doubts arise in your hearts? ³⁹Behold My hands and My feet, that it is I Myself. Handle Me and see, for a spirit does not have flesh and bones as you see I have."

⁴⁰When He had said this, He showed them

His hands and His feet.ᵃ ⁴¹But while they still did not believe for joy, and marveled, He said to them, "Have you any food here?" ⁴²So they gave Him a piece of a broiled fish and some honeycomb.ᵃ ⁴³And He took *it* and ate in their presence.

The Scriptures Opened

⁴⁴Then He said to them, "These *are* the words which I spoke to you while I was still with you, that all things must be fulfilled which were written in the Law of Moses and *the* Prophets and *the* Psalms concerning Me." ⁴⁵And He opened their understanding, that they might comprehend the Scriptures.

⁴⁶Then He said to them, "Thus it is written, and thus it was necessary for the Christ to suffer and to riseᵃ from the dead the third day, ⁴⁷and that repentance and remission of sins should be preached in His name to all nations, beginning at Jerusalem. ⁴⁸And you are witnesses of these things. ⁴⁹Behold, I send the Promise of My Father upon you; but tarry in the city of Jerusalemᵃ until you are endued with power from on high."

The Ascension

⁵⁰And He led them out as far as Bethany, and He lifted up His hands and blessed them. ⁵¹Now it came to pass, while He blessed them, that He was parted from them and carried up into heaven. ⁵²And they worshiped Him, and returned to Jerusalem with great joy, ⁵³and were continually in the temple praising andᵃ blessing God. Amen.ᵇ

24:40 ᵃSome printed New Testaments omit this verse. It is found in nearly all Greek manuscripts.   24:42 ᵃNU-Text omits *and some honeycomb.*   24:46 ᵃNU-Text reads *written, that the Christ should suffer and rise.*   24:49 ᵃNU-Text omits *of Jerusalem.* 24:53 ᵃNU-Text omits *praising and.* ᵇNU-Text omits *Amen.*

John

The Eternal Word

1 In the beginning was the Word, and the Word was with God, and the Word was God. [2]He was in the beginning with God. [3]All things were made through Him, and without Him nothing was made that was made. [4]In Him was life, and the life was the light of men. [5]And the light shines in the darkness, and the darkness did not comprehend[a] it.

John's Witness: The True Light

[6]There was a man sent from God, whose name *was* John. [7]This man came for a witness, to bear witness of the Light, that all through him might believe. [8]He was not that Light, but *was sent* to bear witness of that Light. [9]That was the true Light which gives light to every man coming into the world.[a]

[10]He was in the world, and the world was made through Him, and the world did not know Him. [11]He came to His own,[a] and His own[b] did not receive Him. [12]But as many as received Him, to them He gave the right to become children of God, to those who believe in His name: [13]who were born, not of blood, nor of the will of the flesh, nor of the will of man, but of God.

The Word Becomes Flesh

[14]And the Word became flesh and dwelt among

1:5 [a]Or *overcome*   **1:9** [a]Or *That was the true Light which, coming into the world, gives light to every man.*   **1:11** [a]That is, His own things or domain [b]That is, His own people

us, and we beheld His glory, the glory as of the only begotten of the Father, full of grace and truth.

[15]John bore witness of Him and cried out, saying, "This was He of whom I said, 'He who comes after me is preferred before me, for He was before me.' "

[16]And[a] of His fullness we have all received, and grace for grace. [17]For the law was given through Moses, *but* grace and truth came through Jesus Christ. [18]No one has seen God at any time. The only begotten Son,[a] who is in the bosom of the Father, He has declared *Him*.

A Voice in the Wilderness

[19]Now this is the testimony of John, when the Jews sent priests and Levites from Jerusalem to ask him, "Who are you?"

[20]He confessed, and did not deny, but confessed, "I am not the Christ."

[21]And they asked him, "What then? Are you Elijah?"

He said, "I am not."

"Are you the Prophet?"

And he answered, "No."

[22]Then they said to him, "Who are you, that we may give an answer to those who sent us? What do you say about yourself?"

[23]He said: "I *am*

The voice of one crying in the wilderness:
"Make straight the way of the Lord," '[a]

as the prophet Isaiah said."

1:16 [a]NU-Text reads *For.*   **1:18** [a]NU-Text reads *only begotten God.*   **1:23** [a]Isaiah 40:3

²⁴Now those who were sent were from the Pharisees. ²⁵And they asked him, saying, "Why then do you baptize if you are not the Christ, nor Elijah, nor the Prophet?"

²⁶John answered them, saying, "I baptize with water, but there stands One among you whom you do not know. ²⁷It is He who, coming after me, is preferred before me, whose sandal strap I am not worthy to loose."

²⁸These things were done in Bethabara[a] beyond the Jordan, where John was baptizing.

The Lamb of God

²⁹The next day John saw Jesus coming toward him, and said, "Behold! The Lamb of God who takes away the sin of the world! ³⁰This is He of whom I said, 'After me comes a Man who is preferred before me, for He was before me.' ³¹I did not know Him; but that He should be revealed to Israel, therefore I came baptizing with water."

³²And John bore witness, saying, "I saw the Spirit descending from heaven like a dove, and He remained upon Him. ³³I did not know Him, but He who sent me to baptize with water said to me, 'Upon whom you see the Spirit descending, and remaining on Him, this is He who baptizes with the Holy Spirit.' ³⁴And I have seen and testified that this is the Son of God."

The First Disciples

³⁵Again, the next day John stood with two of his disciples. ³⁶And looking at Jesus as He walked, he said, "Behold the Lamb of God!"

³⁷The two disciples heard him speak, and they

1:28 [a]NU-Text and M-Text read *Bethany*.

followed Jesus. ³⁸Then Jesus turned, and seeing them following, said to them, "What do you seek?"

They said to Him, "Rabbi" (which is to say, when translated, Teacher), "where are You staying?"

³⁹He said to them, "Come and see." They came and saw where He was staying, and remained with Him that day (now it was about the tenth hour).

⁴⁰One of the two who heard John *speak*, and followed Him, was Andrew, Simon Peter's brother. ⁴¹He first found his own brother Simon, and said to him, "We have found the Messiah" (which is translated, the Christ). ⁴²And he brought him to Jesus.

Now when Jesus looked at him, He said, "You are Simon the son of Jonah.ª You shall be called Cephas" (which is translated, A Stone).

Philip and Nathanael

⁴³The following day Jesus wanted to go to Galilee, and He found Philip and said to him, "Follow Me." ⁴⁴Now Philip was from Bethsaida, the city of Andrew and Peter. ⁴⁵Philip found Nathanael and said to him, "We have found Him of whom Moses in the law, and also the prophets, wrote—Jesus of Nazareth, the son of Joseph."

⁴⁶And Nathanael said to him, "Can anything good come out of Nazareth?"

Philip said to him, "Come and see."

⁴⁷Jesus saw Nathanael coming toward Him, and said of him, "Behold, an Israelite indeed, in whom is no deceit!"

⁴⁸Nathanael said to Him, "How do You know me?"

1:42 ªNU-Text reads *John.*

Jesus answered and said to him, "Before Philip called you, when you were under the fig tree, I saw you."

[49]Nathanael answered and said to Him, "Rabbi, You are the Son of God! You are the King of Israel!"

[50]Jesus answered and said to him, "Because I said to you, 'I saw you under the fig tree,' do you believe? You will see greater things than these." [51]And He said to him, "Most assuredly, I say to you, hereafter[a] you shall see heaven open, and the angels of God ascending and descending upon the Son of Man."

Water Turned to Wine

2 On the third day there was a wedding in Cana of Galilee, and the mother of Jesus was there. [2]Now both Jesus and His disciples were invited to the wedding. [3]And when they ran out of wine, the mother of Jesus said to Him, "They have no wine."

[4]Jesus said to her, "Woman, what does your concern have to do with Me? My hour has not yet come."

[5]His mother said to the servants, "Whatever He says to you, do *it.*"

[6]Now there were set there six waterpots of stone, according to the manner of purification of the Jews, containing twenty or thirty gallons apiece. [7]Jesus said to them, "Fill the waterpots with water." And they filled them up to the brim. [8]And He said to them, "Draw *some* out now, and take *it* to the master of the feast." And they took *it.* [9]When the master of the feast had tasted the water that was made wine, and did not know

---

1:51 [a]NU-Text omits *hereafter.*

where it came from (but the servants who had drawn the water knew), the master of the feast called the bridegroom. ¹⁰And he said to him, "Every man at the beginning sets out the good wine, and when the *guests* have well drunk, then the inferior. You have kept the good wine until now!"

¹¹This beginning of signs Jesus did in Cana of Galilee, and manifested His glory; and His disciples believed in Him.

¹²After this He went down to Capernaum, He, His mother, His brothers, and His disciples; and they did not stay there many days.

Jesus Cleanses the Temple

¹³Now the Passover of the Jews was at hand, and Jesus went up to Jerusalem. ¹⁴And He found in the temple those who sold oxen and sheep and doves, and the money changers doing business. ¹⁵When He had made a whip of cords, He drove them all out of the temple, with the sheep and the oxen, and poured out the changers' money and overturned the tables. ¹⁶And He said to those who sold doves, "Take these things away! Do not make My Father's house a house of merchandise!" ¹⁷Then His disciples remembered that it was written, *"Zeal for Your house has eaten[a] Me up."[b]*

¹⁸So the Jews answered and said to Him, "What sign do You show to us, since You do these things?"

¹⁹Jesus answered and said to them, "Destroy this temple, and in three days I will raise it up."

²⁰Then the Jews said, "It has taken forty-six years to build this temple, and will You raise it

---

2:17 [a]NU-Text and M-Text read *will eat.* [b]Psalm 69:9

up in three days?"

²¹But He was speaking of the temple of His body. ²²Therefore, when He had risen from the dead, His disciples remembered that He had said this to them;[a] and they believed the Scripture and the word which Jesus had said.

The Discerner of Hearts

²³Now when He was in Jerusalem at the Passover, during the feast, many believed in His name when they saw the signs which He did. ²⁴But Jesus did not commit Himself to them, because He knew all *men,* ²⁵and had no need that anyone should testify of man, for He knew what was in man.

The New Birth

3 There was a man of the Pharisees named Nicodemus, a ruler of the Jews. ²This man came to Jesus by night and said to Him, "Rabbi, we know that You are a teacher come from God; for no one can do these signs that You do unless God is with him."

³Jesus answered and said to him, "Most assuredly, I say to you, unless one is born again, he cannot see the kingdom of God."

⁴Nicodemus said to Him, "How can a man be born when he is old? Can he enter a second time into his mother's womb and be born?"

⁵Jesus answered, "Most assuredly, I say to you, unless one is born of water and the Spirit, he cannot enter the kingdom of God. ⁶That which is born of the flesh is flesh, and that which is born of the Spirit is spirit. ⁷Do not marvel that I said to you, 'You must be born again.' ⁸The wind

2:22 [a]NU-Text and M-Text omit *to them.*

blows where it wishes, and you hear the sound of it, but cannot tell where it comes from and where it goes. So is everyone who is born of the Spirit."

[9]Nicodemus answered and said to Him, "How can these things be?"

[10]Jesus answered and said to him, "Are you the teacher of Israel, and do not know these things? [11]Most assuredly, I say to you, We speak what We know and testify what We have seen, and you do not receive Our witness. [12]If I have told you earthly things and you do not believe, how will you believe if I tell you heavenly things? [13]No one has ascended to heaven but He who came down from heaven, *that is,* the Son of Man who is in heaven.[a] [14]And as Moses lifted up the serpent in the wilderness, even so must the Son of Man be lifted up, [15]that whoever believes in Him should not perish but[a] have eternal life. [16]For God so loved the world that He gave His only begotten Son, that whoever believes in Him should not perish but have everlasting life. [17]For God did not send His Son into the world to condemn the world, but that the world through Him might be saved.

[18]"He who believes in Him is not condemned; but he who does not believe is condemned already, because he has not believed in the name of the only begotten Son of God. [19]And this is the condemnation, that the light has come into the world, and men loved darkness rather than light, because their deeds were evil. [20]For everyone practicing evil hates the light and does not come to the light, lest his deeds should be

---

3:13 [a]NU-Text omits *who is in heaven.*   3:15 [a]NU-Text omits *not perish but.*

exposed. ²¹But he who does the truth comes to the light, that his deeds may be clearly seen, that they have been done in God."

John the Baptist Exalts Christ

²²After these things Jesus and His disciples came into the land of Judea, and there He remained with them and baptized. ²³Now John also was baptizing in Aenon near Salim, because there was much water there. And they came and were baptized. ²⁴For John had not yet been thrown into prison.

²⁵Then there arose a dispute between *some* of John's disciples and the Jews about purification. ²⁶And they came to John and said to him, "Rabbi, He who was with you beyond the Jordan, to whom you have testified—behold, He is baptizing, and all are coming to Him!"

²⁷John answered and said, "A man can receive nothing unless it has been given to him from heaven. ²⁸You yourselves bear me witness, that I said, 'I am not the Christ,' but, 'I have been sent before Him.' ²⁹He who has the bride is the bridegroom; but the friend of the bridegroom, who stands and hears him, rejoices greatly because of the bridegroom's voice. Therefore this joy of mine is fulfilled. ³⁰He must increase, but I *must* decrease. ³¹He who comes from above is above all; he who is of the earth is earthly and speaks of the earth. He who comes from heaven is above all. ³²And what He has seen and heard, that He testifies; and no one receives His testimony. ³³He who has received His testimony has certified that God is true. ³⁴For He whom God has sent speaks the words of God, for God does not give the Spirit by measure. ³⁵The Father loves

the Son, and has given all things into His hand.
³⁶He who believes in the Son has everlasting life; and he who does not believe the Son shall not see life, but the wrath of God abides on him."

A Samaritan Woman Meets Her Messiah

4 Therefore, when the Lord knew that the Pharisees had heard that Jesus made and baptized more disciples than John ²(though Jesus Himself did not baptize, but His disciples), ³He left Judea and departed again to Galilee. ⁴But He needed to go through Samaria.

⁵So He came to a city of Samaria which is called Sychar, near the plot of ground that Jacob gave to his son Joseph. ⁶Now Jacob's well was there. Jesus therefore, being wearied from His journey, sat thus by the well. It was about the sixth hour.

⁷A woman of Samaria came to draw water. Jesus said to her, "Give Me a drink." ⁸For His disciples had gone away into the city to buy food.

⁹Then the woman of Samaria said to Him, "How is it that You, being a Jew, ask a drink from me, a Samaritan woman?" For Jews have no dealings with Samaritans.

¹⁰Jesus answered and said to her, "If you knew the gift of God, and who it is who says to you, 'Give Me a drink,' you would have asked Him, and He would have given you living water."

¹¹The woman said to Him, "Sir, You have nothing to draw with, and the well is deep. Where then do You get that living water? ¹²Are You greater than our father Jacob, who gave us the well, and drank from it himself, as well as his sons and his livestock?"

¹³Jesus answered and said to her, "Whoever drinks of this water will thirst again, ¹⁴but whoever drinks of the water that I shall give him will never thirst. But the water that I shall give him will become in him a fountain of water springing up into everlasting life."

¹⁵The woman said to Him, "Sir, give me this water, that I may not thirst, nor come here to draw."

¹⁶Jesus said to her, "Go, call your husband, and come here."

¹⁷The woman answered and said, "I have no husband."

Jesus said to her, "You have well said, 'I have no husband,' ¹⁸for you have had five husbands, and the one whom you now have is not your husband; in that you spoke truly."

¹⁹The woman said to Him, "Sir, I perceive that You are a prophet. ²⁰Our fathers worshiped on this mountain, and you *Jews* say that in Jerusalem is the place where one ought to worship."

²¹Jesus said to her, "Woman, believe Me, the hour is coming when you will neither on this mountain, nor in Jerusalem, worship the Father. ²²You worship what you do not know; we know what we worship, for salvation is of the Jews. ²³But the hour is coming, and now is, when the true worshipers will worship the Father in spirit and truth; for the Father is seeking such to worship Him. ²⁴God *is* Spirit, and those who worship Him must worship in spirit and truth."

²⁵The woman said to Him, "I know that Messiah is coming" (who is called Christ). "When He comes, He will tell us all things."

²⁶Jesus said to her, "I who speak to you am *He*."

The Whitened Harvest

²⁷And at this *point* His disciples came, and they marveled that He talked with a woman; yet no one said, "What do You seek?" or, "Why are You talking with her?"

²⁸The woman then left her waterpot, went her way into the city, and said to the men, ²⁹"Come, see a Man who told me all things that I ever did. Could this be the Christ?" ³⁰Then they went out of the city and came to Him.

³¹In the meantime His disciples urged Him, saying, "Rabbi, eat."

³²But He said to them, "I have food to eat of which you do not know."

³³Therefore the disciples said to one another, "Has anyone brought Him *anything* to eat?"

³⁴Jesus said to them, "My food is to do the will of Him who sent Me, and to finish His work. ³⁵Do you not say, 'There are still four months and *then* comes the harvest'? Behold, I say to you, lift up your eyes and look at the fields, for they are already white for harvest! ³⁶And he who reaps receives wages, and gathers fruit for eternal life, that both he who sows and he who reaps may rejoice together. ³⁷For in this the saying is true: 'One sows and another reaps.' ³⁸I sent you to reap that for which you have not labored; others have labored, and you have entered into their labors."

The Savior of the World

³⁹And many of the Samaritans of that city believed in Him because of the word of the woman who testified, "He told me all that I *ever* did." ⁴⁰So when the Samaritans had come to Him, they urged Him to stay with them; and He stayed

there two days. [41]And many more believed because of His own word.

[42]Then they said to the woman, "Now we believe, not because of what you said, for we ourselves have heard *Him* and we know that this is indeed the Christ,[a] the Savior of the world."

Welcome at Galilee

[43]Now after the two days He departed from there and went to Galilee. [44]For Jesus Himself testified that a prophet has no honor in his own country. [45]So when He came to Galilee, the Galileans received Him, having seen all the things He did in Jerusalem at the feast; for they also had gone to the feast.

A Nobleman's Son Healed

[46]So Jesus came again to Cana of Galilee where He had made the water wine. And there was a certain nobleman whose son was sick at Capernaum. [47]When he heard that Jesus had come out of Judea into Galilee, he went to Him and implored Him to come down and heal his son, for he was at the point of death. [48]Then Jesus said to him, "Unless you *people* see signs and wonders, you will by no means believe."

[49]The nobleman said to Him, "Sir, come down before my child dies!"

[50]Jesus said to him, "Go your way; your son lives." So the man believed the word that Jesus spoke to him, and he went his way. [51]And as he was now going down, his servants met him and told *him*, saying, "Your son lives!"

[52]Then he inquired of them the hour when he got better. And they said to him, "Yesterday at the

---

4:42 [a]NU-Text omits *the Christ.*

seventh hour the fever left him." ⁵³So the father knew that *it was* at the same hour in which Jesus said to him, "Your son lives." And he himself believed, and his whole household.

⁵⁴This again *is* the second sign Jesus did when He had come out of Judea into Galilee.

A Man Healed at the Pool of Bethesda

5 After this there was a feast of the Jews, and Jesus went up to Jerusalem. ²Now there is in Jerusalem by the Sheep *Gate* a pool, which is called in Hebrew, Bethesda,ᵃ having five porches. ³In these lay a great multitude of sick people, blind, lame, paralyzed, waiting for the moving of the water. ⁴For an angel went down at a certain time into the pool and stirred up the water; then whoever stepped in first, after the stirring of the water, was made well of whatever disease he had.ᵃ ⁵Now a certain man was there who had an infirmity thirty-eight years. ⁶When Jesus saw him lying there, and knew that he already had been *in that condition* a long time, He said to him, "Do you want to be made well?"

⁷The sick man answered Him, "Sir, I have no man to put me into the pool when the water is stirred up; but while I am coming, another steps down before me."

⁸Jesus said to him, "Rise, take up your bed and walk." ⁹And immediately the man was made well, took up his bed, and walked.

And that day was the Sabbath. ¹⁰The Jews therefore said to him who was cured, "It is the Sabbath; it is not lawful for you to carry your bed."

5:2 ᵃNU-Text reads *Bethzatha.*   5:4 ᵃNU-Text omits *waiting for the moving of the water* at the end of verse 3, and all of verse 4.

¹¹He answered them, "He who made me well said to me, 'Take up your bed and walk.' "

¹²Then they asked him, "Who is the Man who said to you, 'Take up your bed and walk'?" ¹³But the one who was healed did not know who it was, for Jesus had withdrawn, a multitude being in *that* place. ¹⁴Afterward Jesus found him in the temple, and said to him, "See, you have been made well. Sin no more, lest a worse thing come upon you."

¹⁵The man departed and told the Jews that it was Jesus who had made him well.

Honor the Father and the Son

¹⁶For this reason the Jews persecuted Jesus, and sought to kill Him,[a] because He had done these things on the Sabbath. ¹⁷But Jesus answered them, "My Father has been working until now, and I have been working."

¹⁸Therefore the Jews sought all the more to kill Him, because He not only broke the Sabbath, but also said that God was His Father, making Himself equal with God. ¹⁹Then Jesus answered and said to them, "Most assuredly, I say to you, the Son can do nothing of Himself, but what He sees the Father do; for whatever He does, the Son also does in like manner. ²⁰For the Father loves the Son, and shows Him all things that He Himself does; and He will show Him greater works than these, that you may marvel. ²¹For as the Father raises the dead and gives life to *them,* even so the Son gives life to whom He will. ²²For the Father judges no one, but has committed all judgment to the Son, ²³that all should honor the Son just as they honor the Father. He who does not

5:16 [a]NU-Text omits *and sought to kill Him.*

honor the Son does not honor the Father who
sent Him.

Life and Judgment Are
Through the Son

²⁴"Most assuredly, I say to you, he who hears
My word and believes in Him who sent Me has
everlasting life, and shall not come into judgment, but has passed from death into life. ²⁵Most
assuredly, I say to you, the hour is coming, and
now is, when the dead will hear the voice of the
Son of God; and those who hear will live. ²⁶For
as the Father has life in Himself, so He has
granted the Son to have life in Himself, ²⁷and has
given Him authority to execute judgment also,
because He is the Son of Man. ²⁸Do not marvel
at this; for the hour is coming in which all who
are in the graves will hear His voice ²⁹and come
forth—those who have done good, to the resurrection of life, and those who have done evil, to
the resurrection of condemnation. ³⁰I can of Myself do nothing. As I hear, I judge; and My judgment is righteous, because I do not seek My own
will but the will of the Father who sent Me.

The Fourfold Witness

³¹"If I bear witness of Myself, My witness is
not true. ³²There is another who bears witness of
Me, and I know that the witness which He witnesses of Me is true. ³³You have sent to John, and
he has borne witness to the truth. ³⁴Yet I do not
receive testimony from man, but I say these
things that you may be saved. ³⁵He was the
burning and shining lamp, and you were willing
for a time to rejoice in his light. ³⁶But I have a
greater witness than John's; for the works which

the Father has given Me to finish—the very works that I do—bear witness of Me, that the Father has sent Me. [37]And the Father Himself, who sent Me, has testified of Me. You have neither heard His voice at any time, nor seen His form. [38]But you do not have His word abiding in you, because whom He sent, Him you do not believe. [39]You search the Scriptures, for in them you think you have eternal life; and these are they which testify of Me. [40]But you are not willing to come to Me that you may have life.

[41]"I do not receive honor from men. [42]But I know you, that you do not have the love of God in you. [43]I have come in My Father's name, and you do not receive Me; if another comes in his own name, him you will receive. [44]How can you believe, who receive honor from one another, and do not seek the honor that *comes* from the only God? [45]Do not think that I shall accuse you to the Father; there is *one* who accuses you—Moses, in whom you trust. [46]For if you believed Moses, you would believe Me; for he wrote about Me. [47]But if you do not believe his writings, how will you believe My words?"

Feeding the Five Thousand

6 After these things Jesus went over the Sea of Galilee, which is *the Sea* of Tiberias. [2]Then a great multitude followed Him, because they saw His signs which He performed on those who were diseased. [3]And Jesus went up on the mountain, and there He sat with His disciples.

[4]Now the Passover, a feast of the Jews, was near. [5]Then Jesus lifted up *His* eyes, and seeing a great multitude coming toward Him, He said to Philip, "Where shall we buy bread, that these may

eat?" [6]But this He said to test him, for He Himself knew what He would do.

[7]Philip answered Him, "Two hundred denarii worth of bread is not sufficient for them, that every one of them may have a little."

[8]One of His disciples, Andrew, Simon Peter's brother, said to Him, [9]"There is a lad here who has five barley loaves and two small fish, but what are they among so many?"

[10]Then Jesus said, "Make the people sit down." Now there was much grass in the place. So the men sat down, in number about five thousand. [11]And Jesus took the loaves, and when He had given thanks He distributed *them* to the disciples, and the disciples[a] to those sitting down; and likewise of the fish, as much as they wanted. [12]So when they were filled, He said to His disciples, "Gather up the fragments that remain, so that nothing is lost." [13]Therefore they gathered *them* up, and filled twelve baskets with the fragments of the five barley loaves which were left over by those who had eaten. [14]Then those men, when they had seen the sign that Jesus did, said, "This is truly the Prophet who is to come into the world."

Jesus Walks on the Sea

[15]Therefore when Jesus perceived that they were about to come and take Him by force to make Him king, He departed again to the mountain by Himself alone.

[16]Now when evening came, His disciples went down to the sea, [17]got into the boat, and went over the sea toward Capernaum. And it was already dark, and Jesus had not come to them.

6:11 [a]NU-Text omits *to the disciples, and the disciples.*

¹⁸Then the sea arose because a great wind was blowing. ¹⁹So when they had rowed about three or four miles,^a they saw Jesus walking on the sea and drawing near the boat; and they were afraid. ²⁰But He said to them, "It is I; do not be afraid." ²¹Then they willingly received Him into the boat, and immediately the boat was at the land where they were going.

The Bread from Heaven

²²On the following day, when the people who were standing on the other side of the sea saw that there was no other boat there, except that one which His disciples had entered,^a and that Jesus had not entered the boat with His disciples, but His disciples had gone away alone— ²³however, other boats came from Tiberias, near the place where they ate bread after the Lord had given thanks— ²⁴when the people therefore saw that Jesus was not there, nor His disciples, they also got into boats and came to Capernaum, seeking Jesus. ²⁵And when they found Him on the other side of the sea, they said to Him, "Rabbi, when did You come here?"

²⁶Jesus answered them and said, "Most assuredly, I say to you, you seek Me, not because you saw the signs, but because you ate of the loaves and were filled. ²⁷Do not labor for the food which perishes, but for the food which endures to everlasting life, which the Son of Man will give you, because God the Father has set His seal on Him."

²⁸Then they said to Him, "What shall we do, that we may work the works of God?"

6:19 ^aLiterally *twenty-five or thirty stadia*   6:22 ^aNU-Text omits *that* and *which His disciples had entered*.

²⁹Jesus answered and said to them, "This is the work of God, that you believe in Him whom He sent."

³⁰Therefore they said to Him, "What sign will You perform then, that we may see it and believe You? What work will You do? ³¹Our fathers ate the manna in the desert; as it is written, *'He gave them bread from heaven to eat.' "*[a]

³²Then Jesus said to them, "Most assuredly, I say to you, Moses did not give you the bread from heaven, but My Father gives you the true bread from heaven. ³³For the bread of God is He who comes down from heaven and gives life to the world."

³⁴Then they said to Him, "Lord, give us this bread always."

³⁵And Jesus said to them, "I am the bread of life. He who comes to Me shall never hunger, and he who believes in Me shall never thirst. ³⁶But I said to you that you have seen Me and yet do not believe. ³⁷All that the Father gives Me will come to Me, and the one who comes to Me I will by no means cast out. ³⁸For I have come down from heaven, not to do My own will, but the will of Him who sent Me. ³⁹This is the will of the Father who sent Me, that of all He has given Me I should lose nothing, but should raise it up at the last day. ⁴⁰And this is the will of Him who sent Me, that everyone who sees the Son and believes in Him may have everlasting life; and I will raise him up at the last day."

Rejected by His Own

⁴¹The Jews then complained about Him, be-

6:31 ᵃExodus 16:4; Nehemiah 9:15; Psalm 78:24

cause He said, "I am the bread which came down from heaven." [42]And they said, "Is not this Jesus, the son of Joseph, whose father and mother we know? How is it then that He says, 'I have come down from heaven'?"

[43]Jesus therefore answered and said to them, "Do not murmur among yourselves. [44]No one can come to Me unless the Father who sent Me draws him; and I will raise him up at the last day. [45]It is written in the prophets, *'And they shall all be taught by God.'*[a] Therefore everyone who has heard and learned[b] from the Father comes to Me. [46]Not that anyone has seen the Father, except He who is from God; He has seen the Father. [47]Most assuredly, I say to you, he who believes in Me[a] has everlasting life. [48]I am the bread of life. [49]Your fathers ate the manna in the wilderness, and are dead. [50]This is the bread which comes down from heaven, that one may eat of it and not die. [51]I am the living bread which came down from heaven. If anyone eats of this bread, he will live forever; and the bread that I shall give is My flesh, which I shall give for the life of the world."

[52]The Jews therefore quarreled among themselves, saying, "How can this Man give us *His* flesh to eat?"

[53]Then Jesus said to them, "Most assuredly, I say to you, unless you eat the flesh of the Son of Man and drink His blood, you have no life in you. [54]Whoever eats My flesh and drinks My blood has eternal life, and I will raise him up at the last day. [55]For My flesh is food indeed,[a] and My blood is drink indeed. [56]He who eats My

---

6:45 [a]Isaiah 54:13 [b]M-Text reads *hears and has learned.* 6:47 [a]NU-Text omits *in Me.* 6:55 [a]NU-Text reads *true food* and *true drink.*

flesh and drinks My blood abides in Me, and I in him. [57]As the living Father sent Me, and I live because of the Father, so he who feeds on Me will live because of Me. [58]This is the bread which came down from heaven—not as your fathers ate the manna, and are dead. He who eats this bread will live forever."

[59]These things He said in the synagogue as He taught in Capernaum.

Many Disciples Turn Away

[60]Therefore many of His disciples, when they heard *this,* said, "This is a hard saying; who can understand it?"

[61]When Jesus knew in Himself that His disciples complained about this, He said to them, "Does this offend you? [62]*What* then if you should see the Son of Man ascend where He was before? [63]It is the Spirit who gives life; the flesh profits nothing. The words that I speak to you are spirit, and *they* are life. [64]But there are some of you who do not believe." For Jesus knew from the beginning who they were who did not believe, and who would betray Him. [65]And He said, "Therefore I have said to you that no one can come to Me unless it has been granted to him by My Father."

[66]From that *time* many of His disciples went back and walked with Him no more. [67]Then Jesus said to the twelve, "Do you also want to go away?"

[68]But Simon Peter answered Him, "Lord, to whom shall we go? You have the words of eternal life. [69]Also we have come to believe and know that You are the Christ, the Son of the living God."[a]

6:69 [a]NU-Text reads *You are the Holy One of God.*

How do you know Jesus is God?

Most people have no idea that the entire Bible is about one person—Jesus of Nazareth. It speaks of Him from the book of Genesis to the book of Revelation. It tells us that He created all things, including the eyes you are using to see these words, the lungs that are breathing in the oxygen He created, to feed the brain that He made so you can process them (see John 1:1–3).

Of course, His name hasn't always been Jesus of Nazareth. The Bible tells us that He is God—eternally preexistent before the "incarnation." He is "the image of the invisible God" (Colossians 1:15). The reason He created a body for Himself and became a man was to suffer and die for the sin of the world.

Consider how the New Testament exalts Jesus of Nazareth. It calls Him "Lord" an incredible 618 times. He is the One to whom all humanity will one day bow the knee. He is called the "Christ" 543 times, and at times He is referred to as Christ Jesus. This is because "Christ" ("Messiah," or anointed One) is a title rather than a name. In the same way, we say the title "President" before the name of the person in that position.

Jesus is called "Son of Man" 84 times, because He truly was a man who had the ability to feel pain, experience thirst, and know the torment of fear. He is called "Son of God" 37 times, because He was truly God is human form, manifesting His authority over His creation by walking on water, stilling storms, healing disease, and conquering death.

That Jesus performed miracles is undeniable, attested to by even His enemies. The miracles prove that He has power over nature, over humanity, and over death itself.

There has never been anyone like Jesus of Nazareth. Listen to what Philip Schaff said of Him: "This

Jesus of Nazareth, without money and arms, conquered more millions than Alexander, Caesar, Mohammed, and Napoleon; without science and learning, He shed more light on things human and divine than all philosophers and scholars combined; without the eloquence of schools, He spoke such words of life as were never spoken before or since, and produced effects which lie beyond the reach of orator or poet; without writing a single line, He set more pens in motion, and furnished themes for more sermons, orations, discussions, learned volumes, works of art, and songs of praise than the whole army of great men of ancient and modern times."

Some believe it's intolerant to say that Jesus is the only way to God. But *Jesus* is the One who said that He is the only way to the Father. In John 14:6 He said, "I am the way, the truth, and the life. No one comes to the Father except through Me." In one sweeping statement, Jesus discards all other religions as a means of finding forgiveness of sins. This agrees with other Scriptures: "Nor is there salvation in any other, for there is no other name under heaven given among men by which we must be saved" (Acts 4:12), and "For there is one God and one Mediator between God and men, the Man Christ Jesus" (1 Timothy 2:5).

Take the time to open the New Testament and read about Jesus of Nazareth—who He was, and what He did for you. You have nothing to lose and everything to gain. If in this life you refuse to humble yourself and bow the knee to Him as Savior so that your sins can be forgiven, you will bow the knee to Him as Lord on Judgment Day so that justice will be done. That will be a fearful thing . . . with terrible eternal consequences.

But if you turn from your sin and place your trust in Him, He promises to reveal Himself to you so you can *know* that He is real, that He's alive, and that He is God.

⁷⁰Jesus answered them, "Did I not choose you, the twelve, and one of you is a devil?" ⁷¹He spoke of Judas Iscariot, *the son* of Simon, for it was he who would betray Him, being one of the twelve.

Jesus' Brothers Disbelieve

7 After these things Jesus walked in Galilee; for He did not want to walk in Judea, because the Jews[a] sought to kill Him. ²Now the Jews' Feast of Tabernacles was at hand. ³His brothers therefore said to Him, "Depart from here and go into Judea, that Your disciples also may see the works that You are doing. ⁴For no one does anything in secret while he himself seeks to be known openly. If You do these things, show Yourself to the world." ⁵For even His brothers did not believe in Him.

⁶Then Jesus said to them, "My time has not yet come, but your time is always ready. ⁷The world cannot hate you, but it hates Me because I testify of it that its works are evil. ⁸You go up to this feast. I am not yet[a] going up to this feast, for My time has not yet fully come." ⁹When He had said these things to them, He remained in Galilee.

The Heavenly Scholar

¹⁰But when His brothers had gone up, then He also went up to the feast, not openly, but as it were in secret. ¹¹Then the Jews sought Him at the feast, and said, "Where is He?" ¹²And there was much complaining among the people concerning Him. Some said, "He is good"; others said, "No, on the contrary, He deceives the people." ¹³However, no one spoke openly of Him for fear

7:1 ᵃThat is, the ruling authorities   7:8 ᵃNU-Text omits *yet*.

of the Jews.

¹⁴Now about the middle of the feast Jesus went up into the temple and taught. ¹⁵And the Jews marveled, saying, "How does this Man know letters, having never studied?"

¹⁶Jesus[a] answered them and said, "My doctrine is not Mine, but His who sent Me. ¹⁷If anyone wills to do His will, he shall know concerning the doctrine, whether it is from God or *whether* I speak on My own *authority*. ¹⁸He who speaks from himself seeks his own glory; but He who seeks the glory of the One who sent Him is true, and no unrighteousness is in Him. ¹⁹Did not Moses give you the law, yet none of you keeps the law? Why do you seek to kill Me?"

²⁰The people answered and said, "You have a demon. Who is seeking to kill You?"

²¹Jesus answered and said to them, "I did one work, and you all marvel. ²²Moses therefore gave you circumcision (not that it is from Moses, but from the fathers), and you circumcise a man on the Sabbath. ²³If a man receives circumcision on the Sabbath, so that the law of Moses should not be broken, are you angry with Me because I made a man completely well on the Sabbath? ²⁴Do not judge according to appearance, but judge with righteous judgment."

Could This Be the Christ?

²⁵Now some of them from Jerusalem said, "Is this not He whom they seek to kill? ²⁶But look! He speaks boldly, and they say nothing to Him. Do the rulers know indeed that this is truly[a] the Christ? ²⁷However, we know where this Man is

---

7:16 [a]NU-Text and M-Text read *So Jesus.*   7:26 [a]NU-Text omits *truly.*

from; but when the Christ comes, no one knows where He is from."

28Then Jesus cried out, as He taught in the temple, saying, "You both know Me, and you know where I am from; and I have not come of Myself, but He who sent Me is true, whom you do not know. 29But[a] I know Him, for I am from Him, and He sent Me."

30Therefore they sought to take Him; but no one laid a hand on Him, because His hour had not yet come. 31And many of the people believed in Him, and said, "When the Christ comes, will He do more signs than these which this *Man* has done?"

Jesus and the Religious Leaders

32The Pharisees heard the crowd murmuring these things concerning Him, and the Pharisees and the chief priests sent officers to take Him. 33Then Jesus said to them,[a] "I shall be with you a little while longer, and *then* I go to Him who sent Me. 34You will seek Me and not find *Me,* and where I am you cannot come."

35Then the Jews said among themselves, "Where does He intend to go that we shall not find Him? Does He intend to go to the Dispersion among the Greeks and teach the Greeks? 36What is this thing that He said, 'You will seek Me and not find Me, and where I am you cannot come'?"

The Promise of the Holy Spirit

37On the last day, that great *day* of the feast, Jesus stood and cried out, saying, "If anyone thirsts, let him come to Me and drink. 38He who

---

7:29 [a]NU-Text and M-Text omit *But.*   7:33 [a]NU-Text and M-Text omit *to them.*

believes in Me, as the Scripture has said, out of his heart will flow rivers of living water." [39]But this He spoke concerning the Spirit, whom those believing[a] in Him would receive; for the Holy[b] Spirit was not yet *given*, because Jesus was not yet glorified.

Who Is He?

[40]Therefore many[a] from the crowd, when they heard this saying, said, "Truly this is the Prophet." [41]Others said, "This is the Christ."

But some said, "Will the Christ come out of Galilee? [42]Has not the Scripture said that the Christ comes from the seed of David and from the town of Bethlehem, where David was?" [43]So there was a division among the people because of Him. [44]Now some of them wanted to take Him, but no one laid hands on Him.

Rejected by the Authorities

[45]Then the officers came to the chief priests and Pharisees, who said to them, "Why have you not brought Him?"

[46]The officers answered, "No man ever spoke like this Man!"

[47]Then the Pharisees answered them, "Are you also deceived? [48]Have any of the rulers or the Pharisees believed in Him? [49]But this crowd that does not know the law is accursed."

[50]Nicodemus (he who came to Jesus by night,[a] being one of them) said to them, [51]"Does our law judge a man before it hears him and knows what he is doing?"

[52]They answered and said to him, "Are you

7:39 [a]NU-Text reads *who believed.* [b]NU-Text omits Holy.   7:40 [a]NU-Text reads *some.*   7:50 [a]NU-Text reads *before.*

also from Galilee? Search and look, for no
prophet has arisen[a] out of Galilee."

An Adulteress Faces the
Light of the World

[53]And everyone went to his *own* house.[a]

8   But Jesus went to the Mount of Olives.
[2]Now early[a] in the morning He came
again into the temple, and all the people came
to Him; and He sat down and taught them.
[3]Then the scribes and Pharisees brought to Him
a woman caught in adultery. And when they had
set her in the midst, [4]they said to Him, "Teacher,
this woman was caught[a] in adultery, in the very
act. [5]Now Moses, in the law, commanded[a] us that
such should be stoned.[b] But what do You say?"[c]
[6]This they said, testing Him, that they might
have *something* of which to accuse Him. But
Jesus stooped down and wrote on the ground
with *His* finger, as though He did not hear.[a]

[7]So when they continued asking Him, He
raised Himself up[a] and said to them, "He who is
without sin among you, let him throw a stone at
her first." [8]And again He stooped down and
wrote on the ground. [9]Then those who heard *it*,
being convicted by *their* conscience,[a] went out
one by one, beginning with the oldest *even* to the
last. And Jesus was left alone, and the woman
standing in the midst. [10]When Jesus had raised

7:52 [a]NU-Text reads *is to rise.*   7:53 [a]The words *And everyone*
through *sin no more* (8:11) are bracketed by NU-Text as not original. They are present in over 900 manuscripts.   8:2 [a]M-Text
reads *very early.*   8:4 [a]M-Text reads *we found this woman.*   8:5
[a]M-Text reads *in our law Moses commanded.* [b]NU-Text and M-
Text read *to stone such.* [c]M-Text adds *about her.*   8:6 [a]NU-Text
and M-Text omit *as though He did not hear.*   8:7 [a]M-Text reads
He looked up.   8:9 [a]NU-Text and M-Text omit *being convicted by
their conscience.*

Himself up and saw no one but the woman, He said to her,[a] "Woman, where are those accusers of yours?[b] Has no one condemned you?"

[11]She said, "No one, Lord."

And Jesus said to her, "Neither do I condemn you; go and[a] sin no more."

[12]Then Jesus spoke to them again, saying, "I am the light of the world. He who follows Me shall not walk in darkness, but have the light of life."

Jesus Defends His Self-Witness

[13]The Pharisees therefore said to Him, "You bear witness of Yourself; Your witness is not true."

[14]Jesus answered and said to them, "Even if I bear witness of Myself, My witness is true, for I know where I came from and where I am going; but you do not know where I come from and where I am going. [15]You judge according to the flesh; I judge no one. [16]And yet if I do judge, My judgment is true; for I am not alone, but I *am* with the Father who sent Me. [17]It is also written in your law that the testimony of two men is true. [18]I am One who bears witness of Myself, and the Father who sent Me bears witness of Me."

[19]Then they said to Him, "Where is Your Father?"

Jesus answered, "You know neither Me nor My Father. If you had known Me, you would have known My Father also."

[20]These words Jesus spoke in the treasury, as He taught in the temple; and no one laid hands

---

8:10 [a]NU-Text omits *and saw no one but the woman;* M-Text reads *He saw her and said.* [b]NU-Text and M-Text omit *of yours.* **8:11** [a]NU-Text and M-Text add *from now on.*

on Him, for His hour had not yet come.

Jesus Predicts His Departure

[21]Then Jesus said to them again, "I am going away, and you will seek Me, and will die in your sin. Where I go you cannot come."

[22]So the Jews said, "Will He kill Himself, because He says, 'Where I go you cannot come'?"

[23]And He said to them, "You are from beneath; I am from above. You are of this world; I am not of this world. [24]Therefore I said to you that you will die in your sins; for if you do not believe that I am *He,* you will die in your sins."

[25]Then they said to Him, "Who are You?"

And Jesus said to them, "Just what I have been saying to you from the beginning. [26]I have many things to say and to judge concerning you, but He who sent Me is true; and I speak to the world those things which I heard from Him."

[27]They did not understand that He spoke to them of the Father.

[28]Then Jesus said to them, "When you lift up the Son of Man, then you will know that I am *He,* and *that* I do nothing of Myself; but as My Father taught Me, I speak these things. [29]And He who sent Me is with Me. The Father has not left Me alone, for I always do those things that please Him." [30]As He spoke these words, many believed in Him.

The Truth Shall Make You Free

[31]Then Jesus said to those Jews who believed Him, "If you abide in My word, you are My disciples indeed. [32]And you shall know the truth, and the truth shall make you free."

[33]They answered Him, "We are Abraham's de-

scendants, and have never been in bondage to anyone. How *can* You say, 'You will be made free'?"

³⁴Jesus answered them, "Most assuredly, I say to you, whoever commits sin is a slave of sin. ³⁵And a slave does not abide in the house forever, *but* a son abides forever. ³⁶Therefore if the Son makes you free, you shall be free indeed.

Abraham's Seed and Satan's

³⁷"I know that you are Abraham's descendants, but you seek to kill Me, because My word has no place in you. ³⁸I speak what I have seen with My Father, and you do what you have seen with* your father."

³⁹They answered and said to Him, "Abraham is our father."

Jesus said to them, "If you were Abraham's children, you would do the works of Abraham. ⁴⁰But now you seek to kill Me, a Man who has told you the truth which I heard from God. Abraham did not do this. ⁴¹You do the deeds of your father."

Then they said to Him, "We were not born of fornication; we have one Father—God."

⁴²Jesus said to them, "If God were your Father, you would love Me, for I proceeded forth and came from God; nor have I come of Myself, but He sent Me. ⁴³Why do you not understand My speech? Because you are not able to listen to My word. ⁴⁴You are of *your* father the devil, and the desires of your father you want to do. He was a murderer from the beginning, and does not stand in the truth, because there is no truth in him. When he speaks a lie, he speaks from his own *resources,* for he is a liar and the father of it.

8:38 ªNU-Text reads *heard from.*

⁴⁵But because I tell the truth, you do not believe Me. ⁴⁶Which of you convicts Me of sin? And if I tell the truth, why do you not believe Me? ⁴⁷He who is of God hears God's words; therefore you do not hear, because you are not of God."

Before Abraham Was, I AM

⁴⁸Then the Jews answered and said to Him, "Do we not say rightly that You are a Samaritan and have a demon?"

⁴⁹Jesus answered, "I do not have a demon; but I honor My Father, and you dishonor Me. ⁵⁰And I do not seek My *own* glory; there is One who seeks and judges. ⁵¹Most assuredly, I say to you, if anyone keeps My word he shall never see death."

⁵²Then the Jews said to Him, "Now we know that You have a demon! Abraham is dead, and the prophets; and You say, 'If anyone keeps My word he shall never taste death.' ⁵³Are You greater than our father Abraham, who is dead? And the prophets are dead. Who do You make Yourself out to be?"

⁵⁴Jesus answered, "If I honor Myself, My honor is nothing. It is My Father who honors Me, of whom you say that He is your[a] God. ⁵⁵Yet you have not known Him, but I know Him. And if I say, 'I do not know Him,' I shall be a liar like you; but I do know Him and keep His word. ⁵⁶Your father Abraham rejoiced to see My day, and he saw *it* and was glad."

⁵⁷Then the Jews said to Him, "You are not yet fifty years old, and have You seen Abraham?"

⁵⁸Jesus said to them, "Most assuredly, I say to you, before Abraham was, I AM."

8:54 [a]NU-Text and M-Text read *our.*

⁵⁹Then they took up stones to throw at Him; but Jesus hid Himself and went out of the temple,ᵃ going through the midst of them, and so passed by.

A Man Born Blind Receives Sight

9 Now as *Jesus* passed by, He saw a man who was blind from birth. ²And His disciples asked Him, saying, "Rabbi, who sinned, this man or his parents, that he was born blind?"

³Jesus answered, "Neither this man nor his parents sinned, but that the works of God should be revealed in him. ⁴Iᵃ must work the works of Him who sent Me while it is day; *the* night is coming when no one can work. ⁵As long as I am in the world, I am the light of the world."

⁶When He had said these things, He spat on the ground and made clay with the saliva; and He anointed the eyes of the blind man with the clay. ⁷And He said to him, "Go, wash in the pool of Siloam" (which is translated, Sent). So he went and washed, and came back seeing.

⁸Therefore the neighbors and those who previously had seen that he was blindᵃ said, "Is not this he who sat and begged?"

⁹Some said, "This is he." Others *said,* "He is like him."ᵃ

He said, "I am *he.*"

¹⁰Therefore they said to him, "How were your eyes opened?"

¹¹He answered and said, "A Man called Jesus made clay and anointed my eyes and said to me, 'Go to the pool ofᵃ Siloam and wash.' So I went

8:59 ᵃNU-Text omits the rest of this verse.   9:4 ᵃNU-Text reads We.   9:8 ᵃNU-Text reads *a beggar.*   9:9 ᵃNU-Text reads *"No, but he is like him."*   9:11 ᵃNU-Text omits *the pool of.*

and washed, and I received sight."

¹²Then they said to him, "Where is He?"

He said, "I do not know."

The Pharisees Excommunicate the Healed Man

¹³They brought him who formerly was blind to the Pharisees. ¹⁴Now it was a Sabbath when Jesus made the clay and opened his eyes. ¹⁵Then the Pharisees also asked him again how he had received his sight. He said to them, "He put clay on my eyes, and I washed, and I see."

¹⁶Therefore some of the Pharisees said, "This Man is not from God, because He does not keep the Sabbath."

Others said, "How can a man who is a sinner do such signs?" And there was a division among them.

¹⁷They said to the blind man again, "What do you say about Him because He opened your eyes?"

He said, "He is a prophet."

¹⁸But the Jews did not believe concerning him, that he had been blind and received his sight, until they called the parents of him who had received his sight. ¹⁹And they asked them, saying, "Is this your son, who you say was born blind? How then does he now see?"

²⁰His parents answered them and said, "We know that this is our son, and that he was born blind; ²¹but by what means he now sees we do not know, or who opened his eyes we do not know. He is of age; ask him. He will speak for himself." ²²His parents said these *things* because they feared the Jews, for the Jews had agreed already that if anyone confessed *that* He *was* Christ, he would be put out of the synagogue.

²³Therefore his parents said, "He is of age; ask him."

²⁴So they again called the man who was blind, and said to him, "Give God the glory! We know that this Man is a sinner."

²⁵He answered and said, "Whether He is a sinner *or not* I do not know. One thing I know: that though I was blind, now I see."

²⁶Then they said to him again, "What did He do to you? How did He open your eyes?"

²⁷He answered them, "I told you already, and you did not listen. Why do you want to hear *it* again? Do you also want to become His disciples?"

²⁸Then they reviled him and said, "You are His disciple, but we are Moses' disciples. ²⁹We know that God spoke to Moses; *as for* this *fellow,* we do not know where He is from."

³⁰The man answered and said to them, "Why, this is a marvelous thing, that you do not know where He is from; yet He has opened my eyes! ³¹Now we know that God does not hear sinners; but if anyone is a worshiper of God and does His will, He hears him. ³²Since the world began it has been unheard of that anyone opened the eyes of one who was born blind. ³³If this Man were not from God, He could do nothing."

³⁴They answered and said to him, "You were completely born in sins, and are you teaching us?" And they cast him out.

True Vision and True Blindness

³⁵Jesus heard that they had cast him out; and when He had found him, He said to him, "Do you believe in the Son of God?"ᵃ

9:35 ᵃNU-Text reads *Son of Man.*

³⁶He answered and said, "Who is He, Lord, that I may believe in Him?"

³⁷And Jesus said to him, "You have both seen Him and it is He who is talking with you."

³⁸Then he said, "Lord, I believe!" And he worshiped Him.

³⁹And Jesus said, "For judgment I have come into this world, that those who do not see may see, and that those who see may be made blind."

⁴⁰Then *some* of the Pharisees who were with Him heard these words, and said to Him, "Are we blind also?"

⁴¹Jesus said to them, "If you were blind, you would have no sin; but now you say, 'We see.' Therefore your sin remains.

Jesus the True Shepherd

10 "Most assuredly, I say to you, he who does not enter the sheepfold by the door, but climbs up some other way, the same is a thief and a robber. ²But he who enters by the door is the shepherd of the sheep. ³To him the doorkeeper opens, and the sheep hear his voice; and he calls his own sheep by name and leads them out. ⁴And when he brings out his own sheep, he goes before them; and the sheep follow him, for they know his voice. ⁵Yet they will by no means follow a stranger, but will flee from him, for they do not know the voice of strangers." ⁶Jesus used this illustration, but they did not understand the things which He spoke to them.

Jesus the Good Shepherd

⁷Then Jesus said to them again, "Most assuredly, I say to you, I am the door of the sheep.

[8]All who *ever* came before Me[a] are thieves and robbers, but the sheep did not hear them. [9]I am the door. If anyone enters by Me, he will be saved, and will go in and out and find pasture. [10]The thief does not come except to steal, and to kill, and to destroy. I have come that they may have life, and that they may have *it* more abundantly.

[11]"I am the good shepherd. The good shepherd gives His life for the sheep. [12]But a hireling, *he who is* not the shepherd, one who does not own the sheep, sees the wolf coming and leaves the sheep and flees; and the wolf catches the sheep and scatters them. [13]The hireling flees because he is a hireling and does not care about the sheep. [14]I am the good shepherd; and I know My *sheep,* and am known by My own. [15]As the Father knows Me, even so I know the Father; and I lay down My life for the sheep. [16]And other sheep I have which are not of this fold; them also I must bring, and they will hear My voice; and there will be one flock *and* one shepherd.

[17]"Therefore My Father loves Me, because I lay down My life that I may take it again. [18]No one takes it from Me, but I lay it down of Myself. I have power to lay it down, and I have power to take it again. This command I have received from My Father."

[19]Therefore there was a division again among the Jews because of these sayings. [20]And many of them said, "He has a demon and is mad. Why do you listen to Him?"

[21]Others said, "These are not the words of one who has a demon. Can a demon open the eyes of the blind?"

10:8 [a]M-Text omits *before Me.*

The Shepherd Knows His Sheep

²²Now it was the Feast of Dedication in Jerusalem, and it was winter. ²³And Jesus walked in the temple, in Solomon's porch. ²⁴Then the Jews surrounded Him and said to Him, "How long do You keep us in doubt? If You are the Christ, tell us plainly."

²⁵Jesus answered them, "I told you, and you do not believe. The works that I do in My Father's name, they bear witness of Me. ²⁶But you do not believe, because you are not of My sheep, as I said to you.[a] ²⁷My sheep hear My voice, and I know them, and they follow Me. ²⁸And I give them eternal life, and they shall never perish; neither shall anyone snatch them out of My hand. ²⁹My Father, who has given *them* to Me, is greater than all; and no one is able to snatch *them* out of My Father's hand. ³⁰I and My Father are one."

Renewed Efforts to Stone Jesus

³¹Then the Jews took up stones again to stone Him. ³²Jesus answered them, "Many good works I have shown you from My Father. For which of those works do you stone Me?"

³³The Jews answered Him, saying, "For a good work we do not stone You, but for blasphemy, and because You, being a Man, make Yourself God."

³⁴Jesus answered them, "Is it not written in your law, *'I said, "You are gods"* '?[a] ³⁵If He called them gods, to whom the word of God came (and the Scripture cannot be broken), ³⁶do you say of Him whom the Father sanctified and sent into the world, 'You are blaspheming,' because I said, 'I am the Son of God'? ³⁷If I do not do the works of My Father, do not believe Me; ³⁸but if I do,

10:26 [a]NU-Text omits *as I said to you.*   10:34 [a]Psalm 82:6

though you do not believe Me, believe the works, that you may know and believe[a] that the Father is in Me, and I in Him." ³⁹Therefore they sought again to seize Him, but He escaped out of their hand.

The Believers Beyond Jordan

⁴⁰And He went away again beyond the Jordan to the place where John was baptizing at first, and there He stayed. ⁴¹Then many came to Him and said, "John performed no sign, but all the things that John spoke about this Man were true." ⁴²And many believed in Him there.

The Death of Lazarus

11 Now a certain *man* was sick, Lazarus of Bethany, the town of Mary and her sister Martha. ²It was *that* Mary who anointed the Lord with fragrant oil and wiped His feet with her hair, whose brother Lazarus was sick. ³Therefore the sisters sent to Him, saying, "Lord, behold, he whom You love is sick."

⁴When Jesus heard *that*, He said, "This sickness is not unto death, but for the glory of God, that the Son of God may be glorified through it."

⁵Now Jesus loved Martha and her sister and Lazarus. ⁶So, when He heard that he was sick, He stayed two more days in the place where He was. ⁷Then after this He said to *the* disciples, "Let us go to Judea again."

⁸*The* disciples said to Him, "Rabbi, lately the Jews sought to stone You, and are You going there again?"

⁹Jesus answered, "Are there not twelve hours in the day? If anyone walks in the day, he does

---

10:38 [a]NU-Text reads *understand.*

not stumble, because he sees the light of this world. [10]But if one walks in the night, he stumbles, because the light is not in him." [11]These things He said, and after that He said to them, "Our friend Lazarus sleeps, but I go that I may wake him up."

[12]Then His disciples said, "Lord, if he sleeps he will get well." [13]However, Jesus spoke of his death, but they thought that He was speaking about taking rest in sleep.

[14]Then Jesus said to them plainly, "Lazarus is dead. [15]And I am glad for your sakes that I was not there, that you may believe. Nevertheless let us go to him."

[16]Then Thomas, who is called the Twin, said to his fellow disciples, "Let us also go, that we may die with Him."

I Am the Resurrection and the Life

[17]So when Jesus came, He found that he had already been in the tomb four days. [18]Now Bethany was near Jerusalem, about two miles[a] away. [19]And many of the Jews had joined the women around Martha and Mary, to comfort them concerning their brother.

[20]Now Martha, as soon as she heard that Jesus was coming, went and met Him, but Mary was sitting in the house. [21]Now Martha said to Jesus, "Lord, if You had been here, my brother would not have died. [22]But even now I know that whatever You ask of God, God will give You."

[23]Jesus said to her, "Your brother will rise again."

[24]Martha said to Him, "I know that he will rise again in the resurrection at the last day."

11:18 [a]Literally *fifteen stadia*

²⁵Jesus said to her, "I am the resurrection and the life. He who believes in Me, though he may die, he shall live. ²⁶And whoever lives and believes in Me shall never die. Do you believe this?"

²⁷She said to Him, "Yes, Lord, I believe that You are the Christ, the Son of God, who is to come into the world."

Jesus and Death, the Last Enemy

²⁸And when she had said these things, she went her way and secretly called Mary her sister, saying, "The Teacher has come and is calling for you." ²⁹As soon as she heard *that,* she arose quickly and came to Him. ³⁰Now Jesus had not yet come into the town, but was[a] in the place where Martha met Him. ³¹Then the Jews who were with her in the house, and comforting her, when they saw that Mary rose up quickly and went out, followed her, saying, "She is going to the tomb to weep there."[a]

³²Then, when Mary came where Jesus was, and saw Him, she fell down at His feet, saying to Him, "Lord, if You had been here, my brother would not have died."

³³Therefore, when Jesus saw her weeping, and the Jews who came with her weeping, He groaned in the spirit and was troubled. ³⁴And He said, "Where have you laid him?"

They said to Him, "Lord, come and see."

³⁵Jesus wept. ³⁶Then the Jews said, "See how He loved him!"

³⁷And some of them said, "Could not this Man, who opened the eyes of the blind, also have kept this man from dying?"

11:30 [a]NU-Text adds *still.*   11:31 [a]NU-Text reads *supposing that she was going to the tomb to weep there.*

Lazarus Raised from the Dead

³⁸Then Jesus, again groaning in Himself, came to the tomb. It was a cave, and a stone lay against it. ³⁹Jesus said, "Take away the stone."

Martha, the sister of him who was dead, said to Him, "Lord, by this time there is a stench, for he has been *dead* four days."

⁴⁰Jesus said to her, "Did I not say to you that if you would believe you would see the glory of God?" ⁴¹Then they took away the stone *from the place* where the dead man was lying.[a] And Jesus lifted up *His* eyes and said, "Father, I thank You that You have heard Me. ⁴²And I know that You always hear Me, but because of the people who are standing by I said *this,* that they may believe that You sent Me." ⁴³Now when He had said these things, He cried with a loud voice, "Lazarus, come forth!" ⁴⁴And he who had died came out bound hand and foot with graveclothes, and his face was wrapped with a cloth. Jesus said to them, "Loose him, and let him go."

The Plot to Kill Jesus

⁴⁵Then many of the Jews who had come to Mary, and had seen the things Jesus did, believed in Him. ⁴⁶But some of them went away to the Pharisees and told them the things Jesus did. ⁴⁷Then the chief priests and the Pharisees gathered a council and said, "What shall we do? For this Man works many signs. ⁴⁸If we let Him alone like this, everyone will believe in Him, and the Romans will come and take away both our place and nation."

⁴⁹And one of them, Caiaphas, being high priest

11:41 ªNU-Text omits *from the place where the dead man was lying.*

that year, said to them, "You know nothing at all,
⁵⁰nor do you consider that it is expedient for us^a
that one man should die for the people, and not
that the whole nation should perish." ⁵¹Now this
he did not say on his own *authority;* but being
high priest that year he prophesied that Jesus
would die for the nation, ⁵²and not for that nation only, but also that He would gather together
in one the children of God who were scattered
abroad.

⁵³Then, from that day on, they plotted to put
Him to death. ⁵⁴Therefore Jesus no longer walked
openly among the Jews, but went from there into
the country near the wilderness, to a city called
Ephraim, and there remained with His disciples.

⁵⁵And the Passover of the Jews was near, and
many went from the country up to Jerusalem before the Passover, to purify themselves. ⁵⁶Then
they sought Jesus, and spoke among themselves
as they stood in the temple, "What do you think
—that He will not come to the feast?" ⁵⁷Now
both the chief priests and the Pharisees had given
a command, that if anyone knew where He was,
he should report *it,* that they might seize Him.

The Anointing at Bethany

12Then, six days before the Passover, Jesus
came to Bethany, where Lazarus was who
had been dead,^a whom He had raised from the
dead. ²There they made Him a supper; and
Martha served, but Lazarus was one of those who
sat at the table with Him. ³Then Mary took a
pound of very costly oil of spikenard, anointed
the feet of Jesus, and wiped His feet with her

11:50 ^aNU-Text reads *you.*   **12:1** ^aNU-Text omits *who had been dead.*

hair. And the house was filled with the fragrance of the oil.

[4]But one of His disciples, Judas Iscariot, Simon's *son*, who would betray Him, said, [5]"Why was this fragrant oil not sold for three hundred denarii[a] and given to the poor?" [6]This he said, not that he cared for the poor, but because he was a thief, and had the money box; and he used to take what was put in it.

[7]But Jesus said, "Let her alone; she has kept[a] this for the day of My burial. [8]For the poor you have with you always, but Me you do not have always."

The Plot to Kill Lazarus

[9]Now a great many of the Jews knew that He was there; and they came, not for Jesus' sake only, but that they might also see Lazarus, whom He had raised from the dead. [10]But the chief priests plotted to put Lazarus to death also, [11]because on account of him many of the Jews went away and believed in Jesus.

The Triumphal Entry

[12]The next day a great multitude that had come to the feast, when they heard that Jesus was coming to Jerusalem, [13]took branches of palm trees and went out to meet Him, and cried out:

"Hosanna!
'Blessed is He who comes in the name of the
    LORD!'[a]
The King of Israel!"

12:5 [a]About one year's wages for a worker   12:7 [a]NU-Text reads *that she may keep.*   12:13 [a]Psalm 118:26

¹⁴Then Jesus, when He had found a young donkey, sat on it; as it is written:

¹⁵"Fear not, daughter of Zion;
    Behold, your King is coming,
    Sitting on a donkey's colt."ᵃ

¹⁶His disciples did not understand these things at first; but when Jesus was glorified, then they remembered that these things were written about Him and *that* they had done these things to Him.

¹⁷Therefore the people, who were with Him when He called Lazarus out of his tomb and raised him from the dead, bore witness. ¹⁸For this reason the people also met Him, because they heard that He had done this sign. ¹⁹The Pharisees therefore said among themselves, "You see that you are accomplishing nothing. Look, the world has gone after Him!"

The Fruitful Grain of Wheat

²⁰Now there were certain Greeks among those who came up to worship at the feast. ²¹Then they came to Philip, who was from Bethsaida of Galilee, and asked him, saying, "Sir, we wish to see Jesus."

²²Philip came and told Andrew, and in turn Andrew and Philip told Jesus.

²³But Jesus answered them, saying, "The hour has come that the Son of Man should be glorified. ²⁴Most assuredly, I say to you, unless a grain of wheat falls into the ground and dies, it remains alone; but if it dies, it produces much grain. ²⁵He who loves his life will lose it, and he

12:15 ᵃZechariah 9:9

who hates his life in this world will keep it for eternal life. ²⁶If anyone serves Me, let him follow Me; and where I am, there My servant will be also. If anyone serves Me, him *My* Father will honor.

Jesus Predicts His Death on the Cross

²⁷"Now My soul is troubled, and what shall I say? 'Father, save Me from this hour'? But for this purpose I came to this hour. ²⁸Father, glorify Your name."

Then a voice came from heaven, *saying,* "I have both glorified *it* and will glorify *it* again."

²⁹Therefore the people who stood by and heard *it* said that it had thundered. Others said, "An angel has spoken to Him."

³⁰Jesus answered and said, "This voice did not come because of Me, but for your sake. ³¹Now is the judgment of this world; now the ruler of this world will be cast out. ³²And I, if I am lifted up from the earth, will draw all *peoples* to Myself." ³³This He said, signifying by what death He would die.

³⁴The people answered Him, "We have heard from the law that the Christ remains forever; and how *can* You say, 'The Son of Man must be lifted up'? Who is this Son of Man?"

³⁵Then Jesus said to them, "A little while longer the light is with you. Walk while you have the light, lest darkness overtake you; he who walks in darkness does not know where he is going. ³⁶While you have the light, believe in the light, that you may become sons of light." These things Jesus spoke, and departed, and was hidden from them.

Who Has Believed Our Report?

[37]But although He had done so many signs before them, they did not believe in Him, [38]that the word of Isaiah the prophet might be fulfilled, which he spoke:

> "Lord, who has believed our report?
>   And to whom has the arm of the LORD been
>   revealed?"[a]

[39]Therefore they could not believe, because Isaiah said again:

> [40]"He has blinded their eyes and hardened their
>   hearts,
>   Lest they should see with their eyes,
>   Lest they should understand with their hearts
>   and turn,
>   So that I should heal them."[a]

[41]These things Isaiah said when[a] he saw His glory and spoke of Him.

Walk in the Light

[42]Nevertheless even among the rulers many believed in Him, but because of the Pharisees they did not confess *Him,* lest they should be put out of the synagogue; [43]for they loved the praise of men more than the praise of God.

[44]Then Jesus cried out and said, "He who believes in Me, believes not in Me but in Him who sent Me. [45]And he who sees Me sees Him who sent Me. [46]I have come *as* a light into the world, that whoever believes in Me should not abide in

---

12:38 [a]Isaiah 53:1   12:40 [a]Isaiah 6:10   12:41 [a]NU-Text reads *because.*

How can you know you are "saved"?

A two-year-old boy was once staring at a heater, fascinated by its bright orange glow. His father saw him and warned, "Don't touch that heater, son. It may look pretty, but it's hot." The little boy believed him, and moved away from the heater.

Some time later, after his father had left the room, the boy thought, "I wonder if it really is hot?" He then reached out to touch it to see for himself. The second his flesh burned, he stopped *believing* it was hot; he now *knew* it was hot! He had moved out of the realm of *belief* into the realm of *experience*.

Most Christians believed in God's existence before their conversion. However, when they obeyed the Word of God, turned from their sins, and placed their trust in Jesus, they stopped merely believing. The moment they reached out and touched the heater bar of God's mercy, they moved out of *belief* into the realm of *experience*. This change is so radical, Jesus referred to it as being "born again" (see John 3:1–5).

The Bible says that those who don't know God are spiritually dead (see Ephesians 2:1; 4:18). We are born with physical life, but not spiritual life. We are like corpses walking around, but by repenting and placing our faith in Jesus Christ, we receive His very life. There is a radical difference between a corpse and a living, breathing human, just as there is when sinners pass from spiritual death to life. The apostle Paul said if you are "in Christ," you are a brand new creation (see 2 Corinthians 5:17).

Becoming a Christian isn't a change of mind. It's not an adherence to religious belief or dogma. It's a complete rebirth. It's not a wax and polish, a tune-up, or a new paint job. It's a brand new car. That's what astounds me about Christianity. A true convert experiences the power of the invisible God giving him a brand new heart with new desires.

Those who now have God's Spirit living in them will love what He loves and desire to do His will; they will have a hunger for His Word, a love for other believers, and a burden for the lost. The Holy Spirit also confirms in their spirit that they are now children of God (see Romans 8:16). Those who believe on the name of the Son of God can *know* that they have eternal life (see 1 John 5:12,13). A Christian is not someone who has a "belief," but someone who has a relationship with the living God. They come to know the God of the universe experientially.

At the risk of being redundant, I don't "believe" that He exists. I know Him. Personally. I have a living relationship with the Creator. I talk to Him through prayer, and He guides me though His Word and by His Holy Spirit. I have known the Lord since April 25, 1972, at 1:30 in the morning.

I not only know Him, but I love Him with all of my heart, soul, mind, and strength. He is my life. He's my joy, my Creator, my Savior, my Lord and my God.

Suppose two experts—a heater manufacturer and a skin specialist—walked into the room just after that child had burned his hand on the heater. Both assured the boy that he couldn't possibly have been burned. But all the experts, theories, and arguments in the world will not dissuade that boy, because of his experience. Those who have been transformed by God's power need never fear scientific or other arguments, because the man with an experience is not at the mercy of a man with an argument. "For our gospel did not come to you in word only, but also in power, and in the Holy Spirit and in much assurance . . ." (1 Thessalonians 1:5).

My earnest hope and prayer would be that you would soften your sinful heart, and repent and trust Jesus Christ, so that you too can testify to this unchanging truth: "This is eternal life, that they may *know* You, the only true God, and Jesus Christ whom You have sent" (John 17:3).

darkness. [47]And if anyone hears My words and does not believe,[a] I do not judge him; for I did not come to judge the world but to save the world. [48]He who rejects Me, and does not receive My words, has that which judges him—the word that I have spoken will judge him in the last day. [49]For I have not spoken on My own *authority*; but the Father who sent Me gave Me a command, what I should say and what I should speak. [50]And I know that His command is everlasting life. Therefore, whatever I speak, just as the Father has told Me, so I speak."

Jesus Washes the Disciples' Feet

13 Now before the Feast of the Passover, when Jesus knew that His hour had come that He should depart from this world to the Father, having loved His own who were in the world, He loved them to the end.

[2]And supper being ended,[a] the devil having already put it into the heart of Judas Iscariot, Simon's *son*, to betray Him, [3]Jesus, knowing that the Father had given all things into His hands, and that He had come from God and was going to God, [4]rose from supper and laid aside His garments, took a towel and girded Himself. [5]After that, He poured water into a basin and began to wash the disciples' feet, and to wipe *them* with the towel with which He was girded. [6]Then He came to Simon Peter. And *Peter* said to Him, "Lord, are You washing my feet?"

[7]Jesus answered and said to him, "What I am doing you do not understand now, but you will know after this."

12:47 [a]NU-Text reads *keep them*.   13:2 [a]NU-Text reads *And during supper.*

⁸Peter said to Him, "You shall never wash my feet!"

Jesus answered him, "If I do not wash you, you have no part with Me."

⁹Simon Peter said to Him, "Lord, not my feet only, but also *my* hands and *my* head!"

¹⁰Jesus said to him, "He who is bathed needs only to wash *his* feet, but is completely clean; and you are clean, but not all of you." ¹¹For He knew who would betray Him; therefore He said, "You are not all clean."

¹²So when He had washed their feet, taken His garments, and sat down again, He said to them, "Do you know what I have done to you? ¹³You call Me Teacher and Lord, and you say well, for *so* I am. ¹⁴If I then, *your* Lord and Teacher, have washed your feet, you also ought to wash one another's feet. ¹⁵For I have given you an example, that you should do as I have done to you. ¹⁶Most assuredly, I say to you, a servant is not greater than his master; nor is he who is sent greater than he who sent him. ¹⁷If you know these things, blessed are you if you do them.

Jesus Identifies His Betrayer

¹⁸"I do not speak concerning all of you. I know whom I have chosen; but that the Scripture may be fulfilled, '*He who eats bread with Me*ᵃ *has lifted up his heel against Me.*'ᵇ ¹⁹Now I tell you before it comes, that when it does come to pass, you may believe that I am He. ²⁰Most assuredly, I say to you, he who receives whomever I send receives Me; and he who receives Me receives Him who sent Me."

²¹When Jesus had said these things, He was

13:18 ᵃNU-Text reads *My bread.* ᵇPsalm 41:9

troubled in spirit, and testified and said, "Most assuredly, I say to you, one of you will betray Me." [22]Then the disciples looked at one another, perplexed about whom He spoke.

[23]Now there was leaning on Jesus' bosom one of His disciples, whom Jesus loved. [24]Simon Peter therefore motioned to him to ask who it was of whom He spoke.

[25]Then, leaning back[a] on Jesus' breast, he said to Him, "Lord, who is it?"

[26]Jesus answered, "It is he to whom I shall give a piece of bread when I have dipped *it*." And having dipped the bread, He gave *it* to Judas Iscariot, *the son* of Simon. [27]Now after the piece of bread, Satan entered him. Then Jesus said to him, "What you do, do quickly." [28]But no one at the table knew for what reason He said this to him. [29]For some thought, because Judas had the money box, that Jesus had said to him, "Buy *those things* we need for the feast," or that he should give something to the poor.

[30]Having received the piece of bread, he then went out immediately. And it was night.

The New Commandment

[31]So, when he had gone out, Jesus said, "Now the Son of Man is glorified, and God is glorified in Him. [32]If God is glorified in Him, God will also glorify Him in Himself, and glorify Him immediately. [33]Little children, I shall be with you a little while longer. You will seek Me; and as I said to the Jews, 'Where I am going, you cannot come,' so now I say to you. [34]A new commandment I give to you, that you love one another; as

---

13:25 [a]NU-Text and M-Text add *thus.*

I have loved you, that you also love one another. ³⁵By this all will know that you are My disciples, if you have love for one another."

Jesus Predicts Peter's Denial

³⁶Simon Peter said to Him, "Lord, where are You going?"

Jesus answered him, "Where I am going you cannot follow Me now, but you shall follow Me afterward."

³⁷Peter said to Him, "Lord, why can I not follow You now? I will lay down my life for Your sake."

³⁸Jesus answered him, "Will you lay down your life for My sake? Most assuredly, I say to you, the rooster shall not crow till you have denied Me three times.

The Way, the Truth, and the Life

14 "Let not your heart be troubled; you believe in God, believe also in Me. ²In My Father's house are many mansions;ᵃ if *it were* not so, I would have told you. I go to prepare a place for you.ᵇ ³And if I go and prepare a place for you, I will come again and receive you to Myself; that where I am, *there* you may be also. ⁴And where I go you know, and the way you know." ⁵Thomas said to Him, "Lord, we do not know where You are going, and how can we know the way?" ⁶Jesus said to him, "I am the way, the truth, and the life. No one comes to the Father except through Me.

14:2 ᵃLiterally *dwellings* ᵇNU-Text adds a word which would cause the text to read either *if it were not so, would I have told you that I go to prepare a place for you?* or *if it were not so I would have told you; for I go to prepare a place for you.*

The Father Revealed

[7] "If you had known Me, you would have known My Father also; and from now on you know Him and have seen Him."

[8] Philip said to Him, "Lord, show us the Father, and it is sufficient for us."

[9] Jesus said to him, "Have I been with you so long, and yet you have not known Me, Philip? He who has seen Me has seen the Father; so how can you say, 'Show us the Father'? [10] Do you not believe that I am in the Father, and the Father in Me? The words that I speak to you I do not speak on My own *authority;* but the Father who dwells in Me does the works. [11] Believe Me that I *am* in the Father and the Father in Me, or else believe Me for the sake of the works themselves.

The Answered Prayer

[12] "Most assuredly, I say to you, he who believes in Me, the works that I do he will do also; and greater *works* than these he will do, because I go to My Father. [13] And whatever you ask in My name, that I will do, that the Father may be glorified in the Son. [14] If you ask[a] anything in My name, I will do *it.*

Jesus Promises Another Helper

[15] "If you love Me, keep[a] My commandments. [16] And I will pray the Father, and He will give you another Helper, that He may abide with you forever— [17] the Spirit of truth, whom the world cannot receive, because it neither sees Him nor knows Him; but you know Him, for He dwells with you and will be in you. [18] I will not leave you orphans; I will come to you.

14:14 [a] NU-Text adds *Me.*   14:15 [a] NU-Text reads *you will keep.*

Indwelling of the Father and the Son

[19]"A little while longer and the world will see Me no more, but you will see Me. Because I live, you will live also. [20]At that day you will know that I *am* in My Father, and you in Me, and I in you. [21]He who has My commandments and keeps them, it is he who loves Me. And he who loves Me will be loved by My Father, and I will love him and manifest Myself to him."

[22]Judas (not Iscariot) said to Him, "Lord, how is it that You will manifest Yourself to us, and not to the world?"

[23]Jesus answered and said to him, "If anyone loves Me, he will keep My word; and My Father will love him, and We will come to him and make Our home with him. [24]He who does not love Me does not keep My words; and the word which you hear is not Mine but the Father's who sent Me.

The Gift of His Peace

[25]"These things I have spoken to you while being present with you. [26]But the Helper, the Holy Spirit, whom the Father will send in My name, He will teach you all things, and bring to your remembrance all things that I said to you. [27]Peace I leave with you, My peace I give to you; not as the world gives do I give to you. Let not your heart be troubled, neither let it be afraid. [28]You have heard Me say to you, 'I am going away and coming *back* to you.' If you loved Me, you would rejoice because I said,[a] 'I am going to the Father,' for My Father is greater than I.

[29]"And now I have told you before it comes, that when it does come to pass, you may believe.

14:28 [a]NU-Text omits *I said.*

³⁰I will no longer talk much with you, for the ruler of this world is coming, and he has nothing in Me. ³¹But that the world may know that I love the Father, and as the Father gave Me commandment, so I do. Arise, let us go from here.

The True Vine

15 "I am the true vine, and My Father is the vinedresser. ²Every branch in Me that does not bear fruit He takes away;ᵃ and every *branch* that bears fruit He prunes, that it may bear more fruit. ³You are already clean because of the word which I have spoken to you. ⁴Abide in Me, and I in you. As the branch cannot bear fruit of itself, unless it abides in the vine, neither can you, unless you abide in Me.

⁵"I am the vine, you *are* the branches. He who abides in Me, and I in him, bears much fruit; for without Me you can do nothing. ⁶If anyone does not abide in Me, he is cast out as a branch and is withered; and they gather them and throw *them* into the fire, and they are burned. ⁷If you abide in Me, and My words abide in you, you willᵃ ask what you desire, and it shall be done for you. ⁸By this My Father is glorified, that you bear much fruit; so you will be My disciples.

Love and Joy Perfected

⁹"As the Father loved Me, I also have loved you; abide in My love. ¹⁰If you keep My commandments, you will abide in My love, just as I have kept My Father's commandments and abide in His love.

¹¹"These things I have spoken to you, that My

15:2 ᵃOr *lifts up*   **15:7** ᵃNU-Text omits *you will*.

joy may remain in you, and *that* your joy may be full. ¹²This is My commandment, that you love one another as I have loved you. ¹³Greater love has no one than this, than to lay down one's life for his friends. ¹⁴You are My friends if you do whatever I command you. ¹⁵No longer do I call you servants, for a servant does not know what his master is doing; but I have called you friends, for all things that I heard from My Father I have made known to you. ¹⁶You did not choose Me, but I chose you and appointed you that you should go and bear fruit, and *that* your fruit should remain, that whatever you ask the Father in My name He may give you. ¹⁷These things I command you, that you love one another.

The World's Hatred

¹⁸"If the world hates you, you know that it hated Me before *it hated* you. ¹⁹If you were of the world, the world would love its own. Yet because you are not of the world, but I chose you out of the world, therefore the world hates you. ²⁰Remember the word that I said to you, 'A servant is not greater than his master.' If they persecuted Me, they will also persecute you. If they kept My word, they will keep yours also. ²¹But all these things they will do to you for My name's sake, because they do not know Him who sent Me. ²²If I had not come and spoken to them, they would have no sin, but now they have no excuse for their sin. ²³He who hates Me hates My Father also. ²⁴If I had not done among them the works which no one else did, they would have no sin; but now they have seen and also hated both Me and My Father. ²⁵But *this happened* that the word might be fulfilled which is written in their law,

'They hated Me without a cause.'[a]

The Coming Rejection

[26]"But when the Helper comes, whom I shall send to you from the Father, the Spirit of truth who proceeds from the Father, He will testify of Me. [27]And you also will bear witness, because you have been with Me from the beginning.

16 "These things I have spoken to you, that you should not be made to stumble. [2]They will put you out of the synagogues; yes, the time is coming that whoever kills you will think that he offers God service. [3]And these things they will do to you[a] because they have not known the Father nor Me. [4]But these things I have told you, that when the[a] time comes, you may remember that I told you of them.

"And these things I did not say to you at the beginning, because I was with you.

The Work of the Holy Spirit

[5]"But now I go away to Him who sent Me, and none of you asks Me, 'Where are You going?' [6]But because I have said these things to you, sorrow has filled your heart. [7]Nevertheless I tell you the truth. It is to your advantage that I go away; for if I do not go away, the Helper will not come to you; but if I depart, I will send Him to you. [8]And when He has come, He will convict the world of sin, and of righteousness, and of judgment: [9]of sin, because they do not believe in Me; [10]of righteousness, because I go to My Father and you see Me no more; [11]of judgment, because the

---

15:25 [a]Psalm 69:4   16:3 [a]NU-Text and M-Text omit *to you.*
16:4 [a]NU-Text reads *their.*

ruler of this world is judged.

¹²"I still have many things to say to you, but you cannot bear *them* now. ¹³However, when He, the Spirit of truth, has come, He will guide you into all truth; for He will not speak on His own *authority,* but whatever He hears He will speak; and He will tell you things to come. ¹⁴He will glorify Me, for He will take of what is Mine and declare *it* to you. ¹⁵All things that the Father has are Mine. Therefore I said that He will take of Mine and declare *it* to you.ª

Sorrow Will Turn to Joy

¹⁶"A little while, and you will not see Me; and again a little while, and you will see Me, because I go to the Father."

¹⁷Then *some* of His disciples said among themselves, "What is this that He says to us, 'A little while, and you will not see Me; and again a little while, and you will see Me'; and, 'because I go to the Father'?" ¹⁸They said therefore, "What is this that He says, 'A little while'? We do not know what He is saying."

¹⁹Now Jesus knew that they desired to ask Him, and He said to them, "Are you inquiring among yourselves about what I said, 'A little while, and you will not see Me; and again a little while, and you will see Me'? ²⁰Most assuredly, I say to you that you will weep and lament, but the world will rejoice; and you will be sorrowful, but your sorrow will be turned into joy. ²¹A woman, when she is in labor, has sorrow because her hour has come; but as soon as she has given birth to the child, she no longer remembers the an-

---

16:15 ªNU-Text and M-Text read *He takes of Mine and will declare it to you.*

guish, for joy that a human being has been born into the world. ²²Therefore you now have sorrow; but I will see you again and your heart will rejoice, and your joy no one will take from you.

²³"And in that day you will ask Me nothing. Most assuredly, I say to you, whatever you ask the Father in My name He will give you. ²⁴Until now you have asked nothing in My name. Ask, and you will receive, that your joy may be full.

Jesus Christ Has Overcome the World

²⁵"These things I have spoken to you in figurative language; but the time is coming when I will no longer speak to you in figurative language, but I will tell you plainly about the Father. ²⁶In that day you will ask in My name, and I do not say to you that I shall pray the Father for you; ²⁷for the Father Himself loves you, because you have loved Me, and have believed that I came forth from God. ²⁸I came forth from the Father and have come into the world. Again, I leave the world and go to the Father."

²⁹His disciples said to Him, "See, now You are speaking plainly, and using no figure of speech! ³⁰Now we are sure that You know all things, and have no need that anyone should question You. By this we believe that You came forth from God."

³¹Jesus answered them, "Do you now believe? ³²Indeed the hour is coming, yes, has now come, that you will be scattered, each to his own, and will leave Me alone. And yet I am not alone, because the Father is with Me. ³³These things I have spoken to you, that in Me you may have peace. In the world you willᵃ have tribulation; but be of

---

16:33 ᵃNU-Text and M-Text omit will.

good cheer, I have overcome the world."

Jesus Prays for Himself

17 Jesus spoke these words, lifted up His eyes to heaven, and said: "Father, the hour has come. Glorify Your Son, that Your Son also may glorify You, ²as You have given Him authority over all flesh, that He should[a] give eternal life to as many as You have given Him. ³And this is eternal life, that they may know You, the only true God, and Jesus Christ whom You have sent. ⁴I have glorified You on the earth. I have finished the work which You have given Me to do. ⁵And now, O Father, glorify Me together with Yourself, with the glory which I had with You before the world was.

Jesus Prays for His Disciples

⁶"I have manifested Your name to the men whom You have given Me out of the world. They were Yours, You gave them to Me, and they have kept Your word. ⁷Now they have known that all things which You have given Me are from You. ⁸For I have given to them the words which You have given Me; and they have received *them,* and have known surely that I came forth from You; and they have believed that You sent Me.

⁹"I pray for them. I do not pray for the world but for those whom You have given Me, for they are Yours. ¹⁰And all Mine are Yours, and Yours are Mine, and I am glorified in them. ¹¹Now I am no longer in the world, but these are in the world, and I come to You. Holy Father, keep through Your name those whom You have given Me,[a] that they may be one as We *are.* ¹²While I

17:2 [a]M-Text reads *shall.*   17:11 [a]NU-Text and M-Text read *keep them through Your name which You have given Me.*

was with them in the world,[a] I kept them in Your name. Those whom You gave Me I have kept;[b] and none of them is lost except the son of perdition, that the Scripture might be fulfilled. [13]But now I come to You, and these things I speak in the world, that they may have My joy fulfilled in themselves. [14]I have given them Your word; and the world has hated them because they are not of the world, just as I am not of the world. [15]I do not pray that You should take them out of the world, but that You should keep them from the evil one. [16]They are not of the world, just as I am not of the world. [17]Sanctify them by Your truth. Your word is truth. [18]As You sent Me into the world, I also have sent them into the world. [19]And for their sakes I sanctify Myself, that they also may be sanctified by the truth.

Jesus Prays for All Believers

[20]"I do not pray for these alone, but also for those who will[a] believe in Me through their word; [21]that they all may be one, as You, Father, *are* in Me, and I in You; that they also may be one in Us, that the world may believe that You sent Me. [22]And the glory which You gave Me I have given them, that they may be one just as We are one: [23]I in them, and You in Me; that they may be made perfect in one, and that the world may know that You have sent Me, and have loved them as You have loved Me.

[24]"Father, I desire that they also whom You gave Me may be with Me where I am, that they may behold My glory which You have given Me;

17:12 [a]NU-Text omits *in the world.* [b]NU-Text reads *in Your name which You gave Me. And I guarded them;* (or *it;*).   **17:20** [a]NU-Text and M-Text omit *will.*

for You loved Me before the foundation of the world. ²⁵O righteous Father! The world has not known You, but I have known You; and these have known that You sent Me. ²⁶And I have declared to them Your name, and will declare *it,* that the love with which You loved Me may be in them, and I in them."

Betrayal and Arrest in Gethsemane

18 When Jesus had spoken these words, He went out with His disciples over the Brook Kidron, where there was a garden, which He and His disciples entered. ²And Judas, who betrayed Him, also knew the place; for Jesus often met there with His disciples. ³Then Judas, having received a detachment *of troops,* and officers from the chief priests and Pharisees, came there with lanterns, torches, and weapons. ⁴Jesus therefore, knowing all things that would come upon Him, went forward and said to them, "Whom are you seeking?"

⁵They answered Him, "Jesus of Nazareth."

Jesus said to them, "I am *He.*" And Judas, who betrayed Him, also stood with them. ⁶Now when He said to them, "I am *He,*" they drew back and fell to the ground.

⁷Then He asked them again, "Whom are you seeking?"

And they said, "Jesus of Nazareth."

⁸Jesus answered, "I have told you that I am *He.* Therefore, if you seek Me, let these go their way," ⁹that the saying might be fulfilled which He spoke, "Of those whom You gave Me I have lost none."

¹⁰Then Simon Peter, having a sword, drew it and struck the high priest's servant, and cut off

his right ear. The servant's name was Malchus.

¹¹So Jesus said to Peter, "Put your sword into the sheath. Shall I not drink the cup which My Father has given Me?"

Before the High Priest

¹²Then the detachment *of troops* and the captain and the officers of the Jews arrested Jesus and bound Him. ¹³And they led Him away to Annas first, for he was the father-in-law of Caiaphas who was high priest that year. ¹⁴Now it was Caiaphas who advised the Jews that it was expedient that one man should die for the people.

Peter Denies Jesus

¹⁵And Simon Peter followed Jesus, and so *did* another[a] disciple. Now that disciple was known to the high priest, and went with Jesus into the courtyard of the high priest. ¹⁶But Peter stood at the door outside. Then the other disciple, who was known to the high priest, went out and spoke to her who kept the door, and brought Peter in. ¹⁷Then the servant girl who kept the door said to Peter, "You are not also *one* of this Man's disciples, are you?"

He said, "I am not."

¹⁸Now the servants and officers who had made a fire of coals stood there, for it was cold, and they warmed themselves. And Peter stood with them and warmed himself.

Jesus Questioned by the High Priest

¹⁹The high priest then asked Jesus about His disciples and His doctrine.

²⁰Jesus answered him, "I spoke openly to the

18:15 [a]M-Text reads *the other.*

world. I always taught in synagogues and in the temple, where the Jews always meet,[a] and in secret I have said nothing. [21]Why do you ask Me? Ask those who have heard Me what I said to them. Indeed they know what I said."

[22]And when He had said these things, one of the officers who stood by struck Jesus with the palm of his hand, saying, "Do You answer the high priest like that?"

[23]Jesus answered him, "If I have spoken evil, bear witness of the evil; but if well, why do you strike Me?"

[24]Then Annas sent Him bound to Caiaphas the high priest.

Peter Denies Twice More

[25]Now Simon Peter stood and warmed himself. Therefore they said to him, "You are not also *one* of His disciples, are you?"

He denied *it* and said, "I am not!"

[26]One of the servants of the high priest, a relative *of him* whose ear Peter cut off, said, "Did I not see you in the garden with Him?" [27]Peter then denied again; and immediately a rooster crowed.

In Pilate's Court

[28]Then they led Jesus from Caiaphas to the Praetorium, and it was early morning. But they themselves did not go into the Praetorium, lest they should be defiled, but that they might eat the Passover. [29]Pilate then went out to them and said, "What accusation do you bring against this Man?"

[30]They answered and said to him, "If He were not an evildoer, we would not have delivered Him

18:20 [a]NU-Text reads *where all the Jews meet.*

up to you."

³¹Then Pilate said to them, "You take Him and judge Him according to your law."

Therefore the Jews said to him, "It is not lawful for us to put anyone to death," ³²that the saying of Jesus might be fulfilled which He spoke, signifying by what death He would die.

³³Then Pilate entered the Praetorium again, called Jesus, and said to Him, "Are You the King of the Jews?"

³⁴Jesus answered him, "Are you speaking for yourself about this, or did others tell you this concerning Me?"

³⁵Pilate answered, "Am I a Jew? Your own nation and the chief priests have delivered You to me. What have You done?"

³⁶Jesus answered, "My kingdom is not of this world. If My kingdom were of this world, My servants would fight, so that I should not be delivered to the Jews; but now My kingdom is not from here."

³⁷Pilate therefore said to Him, "Are You a king then?"

Jesus answered, "You say *rightly* that I am a king. For this cause I was born, and for this cause I have come into the world, that I should bear witness to the truth. Everyone who is of the truth hears My voice."

³⁸Pilate said to Him, "What is truth?" And when he had said this, he went out again to the Jews, and said to them, "I find no fault in Him at all.

Taking the Place of Barabbas

³⁹"But you have a custom that I should release someone to you at the Passover. Do you therefore

want me to release to you the King of the Jews?"

⁴⁰Then they all cried again, saying, "Not this Man, but Barabbas!" Now Barabbas was a robber.

The Soldiers Mock Jesus

19 So then Pilate took Jesus and scourged *Him.* ²And the soldiers twisted a crown of thorns and put *it* on His head, and they put on Him a purple robe. ³Then they said,ᵃ "Hail, King of the Jews!" And they struck Him with their hands.

⁴Pilate then went out again, and said to them, "Behold, I am bringing Him out to you, that you may know that I find no fault in Him."

Pilate's Decision

⁵Then Jesus came out, wearing the crown of thorns and the purple robe. And *Pilate* said to them, "Behold the Man!"

⁶Therefore, when the chief priests and officers saw Him, they cried out, saying, "Crucify *Him,* crucify *Him!* "

Pilate said to them, "You take Him and crucify *Him,* for I find no fault in Him."

⁷The Jews answered him, "We have a law, and according to ourᵃ law He ought to die, because He made Himself the Son of God."

⁸Therefore, when Pilate heard that saying, he was the more afraid, ⁹and went again into the Praetorium, and said to Jesus, "Where are You from?" But Jesus gave him no answer.

¹⁰Then Pilate said to Him, "Are You not speaking to me? Do You not know that I have power to crucify You, and power to release You?"

19:3 ᵃNU-Text reads *And they came up to Him and said.*   19:7 ᵃNU-Text reads *the law.*

¹¹Jesus answered, "You could have no power at all against Me unless it had been given you from above. Therefore the one who delivered Me to you has the greater sin."

¹²From then on Pilate sought to release Him, but the Jews cried out, saying, "If you let this Man go, you are not Caesar's friend. Whoever makes himself a king speaks against Caesar."

¹³When Pilate therefore heard that saying, he brought Jesus out and sat down in the judgment seat in a place that is called *The* Pavement, but in Hebrew, Gabbatha. ¹⁴Now it was the Preparation Day of the Passover, and about the sixth hour. And he said to the Jews, "Behold your King!"

¹⁵But they cried out, "Away with *Him,* away with *Him!* Crucify Him!"

Pilate said to them, "Shall I crucify your King?"

The chief priests answered, "We have no king but Caesar!"

¹⁶Then he delivered Him to them to be crucified. Then they took Jesus and led *Him* away.[a]

The King on a Cross

¹⁷And He, bearing His cross, went out to a place called *the Place* of a Skull, which is called in Hebrew, Golgotha, ¹⁸where they crucified Him, and two others with Him, one on either side, and Jesus in the center. ¹⁹Now Pilate wrote a title and put *it* on the cross. And the writing was:

JESUS OF NAZARETH,
THE KING OF THE JEWS.

²⁰Then many of the Jews read this title, for the place where Jesus was crucified was near the

19:16 [a]NU-Text omits *and led Him away.*

city; and it was written in Hebrew, Greek, *and* Latin.

²¹Therefore the chief priests of the Jews said to Pilate, "Do not write, 'The King of the Jews,' but, 'He said, "I am the King of the Jews." ' "

²²Pilate answered, "What I have written, I have written."

²³Then the soldiers, when they had crucified Jesus, took His garments and made four parts, to each soldier a part, and also the tunic. Now the tunic was without seam, woven from the top in one piece. ²⁴They said therefore among themselves, "Let us not tear it, but cast lots for it, whose it shall be," that the Scripture might be fulfilled which says:

*"They divided My garments among them,
And for My clothing they cast lots."*[a]

Therefore the soldiers did these things.

Behold Your Mother

²⁵Now there stood by the cross of Jesus His mother, and His mother's sister, Mary the *wife* of Clopas, and Mary Magdalene. ²⁶When Jesus therefore saw His mother, and the disciple whom He loved standing by, He said to His mother, "Woman, behold your son!" ²⁷Then He said to the disciple, "Behold your mother!" And from that hour that disciple took her to his own *home*.

It Is Finished

²⁸After this, Jesus, knowing[a] that all things were now accomplished, that the Scripture might be fulfilled, said, "I thirst!" ²⁹Now a vessel full of

---

19:24 [a]Psalm 22:18   19:28 [a]M-Text reads *seeing*.

sour wine was sitting there; and they filled a
sponge with sour wine, put *it* on hyssop, and put
it to His mouth. ³⁰So when Jesus had received
the sour wine, He said, "It is finished!" And bowing His head, He gave up His spirit.

Jesus' Side Is Pierced

³¹Therefore, because it was the Preparation
Day, that the bodies should not remain on the
cross on the Sabbath (for that Sabbath was a high
day), the Jews asked Pilate that their legs might
be broken, and *that* they might be taken away.
³²Then the soldiers came and broke the legs of
the first and of the other who was crucified with
Him. ³³But when they came to Jesus and saw
that He was already dead, they did not break His
legs. ³⁴But one of the soldiers pierced His side
with a spear, and immediately blood and water
came out. ³⁵And he who has seen has testified,
and his testimony is true; and he knows that he
is telling the truth, so that you may believe. ³⁶For
these things were done that the Scripture should
be fulfilled, *"Not one of His bones shall be broken."*ᵃ ³⁷And again another Scripture says, *"They
shall look on Him whom they pierced."*ᵃ

Jesus Buried in Joseph's Tomb

³⁸After this, Joseph of Arimathea, being a disciple of Jesus, but secretly, for fear of the Jews,
asked Pilate that he might take away the body of
Jesus; and Pilate gave *him* permission. So he
came and took the body of Jesus. ³⁹And Nicodemus, who at first came to Jesus by night, also
came, bringing a mixture of myrrh and aloes,

19:36 ᵃExodus 12:46; Numbers 9:12; Psalm 34:20   19:37
ᵃZechariah 12:10

about a hundred pounds. ⁴⁰Then they took the body of Jesus, and bound it in strips of linen with the spices, as the custom of the Jews is to bury. ⁴¹Now in the place where He was crucified there was a garden, and in the garden a new tomb in which no one had yet been laid. ⁴²So there they laid Jesus, because of the Jews' Preparation Day, for the tomb was nearby.

The Empty Tomb

20 Now the first *day* of the week Mary Magdalene went to the tomb early, while it was still dark, and saw *that* the stone had been taken away from the tomb. ²Then she ran and came to Simon Peter, and to the other disciple, whom Jesus loved, and said to them, "They have taken away the Lord out of the tomb, and we do not know where they have laid Him."

³Peter therefore went out, and the other disciple, and were going to the tomb. ⁴So they both ran together, and the other disciple outran Peter and came to the tomb first. ⁵And he, stooping down and looking in, saw the linen cloths lying *there;* yet he did not go in. ⁶Then Simon Peter came, following him, and went into the tomb; and he saw the linen cloths lying *there,* ⁷and the handkerchief that had been around His head, not lying with the linen cloths, but folded together in a place by itself. ⁸Then the other disciple, who came to the tomb first, went in also; and he saw and believed. ⁹For as yet they did not know the Scripture, that He must rise again from the dead. ¹⁰Then the disciples went away again to their own homes.

Mary Magdalene Sees
the Risen Lord

[11]But Mary stood outside by the tomb weeping, and as she wept she stooped down *and looked* into the tomb. [12]And she saw two angels in white sitting, one at the head and the other at the feet, where the body of Jesus had lain. [13]Then they said to her, "Woman, why are you weeping?"

She said to them, "Because they have taken away my Lord, and I do not know where they have laid Him."

[14]Now when she had said this, she turned around and saw Jesus standing *there,* and did not know that it was Jesus. [15]Jesus said to her, "Woman, why are you weeping? Whom are you seeking?"

She, supposing Him to be the gardener, said to Him, "Sir, if You have carried Him away, tell me where You have laid Him, and I will take Him away."

[16]Jesus said to her, "Mary!"

She turned and said to Him,[a] "Rabboni!" (which is to say, Teacher).

[17]Jesus said to her, "Do not cling to Me, for I have not yet ascended to My Father; but go to My brethren and say to them, 'I am ascending to My Father and your Father, and *to* My God and your God.' "

[18]Mary Magdalene came and told the disciples that she had seen the Lord,[a] and *that* He had spoken these things to her.

20:16 [a]NU-Text adds *in Hebrew.*   20:18 [a]NU-Text reads *disciples,* *"I have seen the Lord,"* . . .

The Apostles Commissioned

[19]Then, the same day at evening, being the first *day* of the week, when the doors were shut where the disciples were assembled,[a] for fear of the Jews, Jesus came and stood in the midst, and said to them, "Peace *be* with you." [20]When He had said this, He showed them *His* hands and His side. Then the disciples were glad when they saw the Lord.

[21]So Jesus said to them again, "Peace to you! As the Father has sent Me, I also send you." [22]And when He had said this, He breathed on *them,* and said to them, "Receive the Holy Spirit. [23]If you forgive the sins of any, they are forgiven them; if you retain the *sins* of any, they are retained."

Seeing and Believing

[24]Now Thomas, called the Twin, one of the twelve, was not with them when Jesus came. [25]The other disciples therefore said to him, "We have seen the Lord."

So he said to them, "Unless I see in His hands the print of the nails, and put my finger into the print of the nails, and put my hand into His side, I will not believe."

[26]And after eight days His disciples were again inside, and Thomas with them. Jesus came, the doors being shut, and stood in the midst, and said, "Peace to you!" [27]Then He said to Thomas, "Reach your finger here, and look at My hands; and reach your hand *here,* and put *it* into My side. Do not be unbelieving, but believing."

[28]And Thomas answered and said to Him, "My Lord and my God!"

20:19 [a]NU-Text omits *assembled.*

²⁹Jesus said to him, "Thomas,ᵃ because you have seen Me, you have believed. Blessed *are* those who have not seen and *yet* have believed."

That You May Believe

³⁰And truly Jesus did many other signs in the presence of His disciples, which are not written in this book; ³¹but these are written that you may believe that Jesus is the Christ, the Son of God, and that believing you may have life in His name.

Breakfast by the Sea

21 After these things Jesus showed Himself again to the disciples at the Sea of Tiberias, and in this way He showed *Himself:* ²Simon Peter, Thomas called the Twin, Nathanael of Cana in Galilee, the *sons* of Zebedee, and two others of His disciples were together. ³Simon Peter said to them, "I am going fishing."

They said to him, "We are going with you also." They went out and immediatelyᵃ got into the boat, and that night they caught nothing. ⁴But when the morning had now come, Jesus stood on the shore; yet the disciples did not know that it was Jesus. ⁵Then Jesus said to them, "Children, have you any food?"

They answered Him, "No."

⁶And He said to them, "Cast the net on the right side of the boat, and you will find *some.*" So they cast, and now they were not able to draw it in because of the multitude of fish.

⁷Therefore that disciple whom Jesus loved said to Peter, "It is the Lord!" Now when Simon

---

20:29 ᵃNU-Text and M-Text omit *Thomas.*   21:3 ᵃNU-Text omits *immediately.*

Peter heard that it was the Lord, he put on *his* outer garment (for he had removed it), and plunged into the sea. ⁸But the other disciples came in the little boat (for they were not far from land, but about two hundred cubits), dragging the net with fish. ⁹Then, as soon as they had come to land, they saw a fire of coals there, and fish laid on it, and bread. ¹⁰Jesus said to them, "Bring some of the fish which you have just caught."

¹¹Simon Peter went up and dragged the net to land, full of large fish, one hundred and fifty-three; and although there were so many, the net was not broken. ¹²Jesus said to them, "Come *and* eat breakfast." Yet none of the disciples dared ask Him, "Who are You?"—knowing that it was the Lord. ¹³Jesus then came and took the bread and gave it to them, and likewise the fish.

¹⁴This *is* now the third time Jesus showed Himself to His disciples after He was raised from the dead.

Jesus Restores Peter

¹⁵So when they had eaten breakfast, Jesus said to Simon Peter, "Simon, *son* of Jonah,ᵃ do you love Me more than these?"

He said to Him, "Yes, Lord; You know that I love You."

He said to him, "Feed My lambs."

¹⁶He said to him again a second time, "Simon, *son* of Jonah,ᵃ do you love Me?"

He said to Him, "Yes, Lord; You know that I love You."

He said to him, "Tend My sheep."

¹⁷He said to him the third time, "Simon, *son of*

21:15 ᵃNU-Text reads *John.*   21:16 ᵃNU-Text reads *John.*

Jonah,[a] do you love Me?" Peter was grieved because He said to him the third time, "Do you love Me?"

And he said to Him, "Lord, You know all things; You know that I love You."

Jesus said to him, "Feed My sheep. [18]Most assuredly, I say to you, when you were younger, you girded yourself and walked where you wished; but when you are old, you will stretch out your hands, and another will gird you and carry *you* where you do not wish." [19]This He spoke, signifying by what death he would glorify God. And when He had spoken this, He said to him, "Follow Me."

The Beloved Disciple and His Book

[20]Then Peter, turning around, saw the disciple whom Jesus loved following, who also had leaned on His breast at the supper, and said, "Lord, who is the one who betrays You?" [21]Peter, seeing him, said to Jesus, "But Lord, what *about* this man?"

[22]Jesus said to him, "If I will that he remain till I come, what is *that* to you? You follow Me."

[23]Then this saying went out among the brethren that this disciple would not die. Yet Jesus did not say to him that he would not die, but, "If I will that he remain till I come, what is *that* to you?"

[24]This is the disciple who testifies of these things, and wrote these things; and we know that his testimony is true.

[25]And there are also many other things that Jesus did, which if they were written one by one, I suppose that even the world itself could not contain the books that would be written. Amen.

21:17 [a]NU-Text reads *John.*

APPENDICES

Save Yourself Some Pain

Helpful principles for new Christians

It is my sincere hope that you have made peace with God through trusting in Jesus Christ. Becoming a Christian is the most incredible event that will ever take place in your life. If you have obeyed the gospel, by turning from your sins and placing your trust in Jesus Christ alone for your salvation, *you have found everlasting life!* (See John 3:16; Romans 6:23; 10:9–13; 1 John 5:11–13.) Be assured, God will never leave you nor forsake you. He has brought you this far and He will complete the wonderful work He has begun in you. He knows your every thought, your every care, and your deepest concerns.

Let's look at some of those possible concerns. First, and of primary concern, do you have "assurance" of your salvation? The Bible says to "be even more diligent to make your call and election sure" (2 Peter 1:10), so let's go through a short "checklist" to confirm that you are truly saved:

- Are you aware that God became flesh in the person of Jesus Christ (1 Timothy 3:16), and that He died for the sins of the world?

- Did you come to the Savior because you knew that you had sinned against God?

- Are you convinced that Jesus suffered and died on the cross for your sins, and that He rose again on the third day?

- Did you truly repent (turn from your sin) and put your faith (trust) in Jesus?

God acquits us from the Courtroom of Eternal Justice on the grounds that Jesus Christ paid our fine. We are "justified" (made right with God) by His suffering death. The resurrection of Jesus Christ was

351

God's seal of approval signifying that His precious blood was sufficient to pay the fine. If we repent and trust in Jesus, God will grant us mercy. However, if you're not sure of your salvation, read Psalm 51 and make it your own prayer.

Following are several important principles that can save you a great deal of pain.

1. Feeding on the Word: Daily Nutrition

A healthy baby has a healthy appetite. If you have truly been "born" of the Spirit of God, you will have a healthy appetite. The Bible says, "As newborn babes, desire the pure milk of the word, that you may grow thereby" (1 Peter 2:2). So feed yourself daily without fail. The more you eat, the quicker you will grow, and the less bruising you will have. Speed up the process and save yourself some pain—vow to read God's Word every day, without fail. Job said, "I have treasured the words of His mouth more than my necessary food" (Job 23:12). Be like Job, and put your Bible *before* your belly. Say to yourself, "No Bible, no breakfast. No read, no feed." If you do that, God promises that you will be like a fruitful, strong, and healthy tree (see Psalm 1).

Each day, find somewhere quiet and thoroughly soak your soul in the Word of God. There may be times when you read through its pages with great enthusiasm, and other times when it seems dry and even boring. But food profits your body whether you enjoy it or not. As a child, you no doubt ate desserts with great enthusiasm. Perhaps vegetables weren't so exciting. If you were a normal child, you probably had to be encouraged to eat them at first. Then, as you matured in life, you learned to discipline yourself to eat vegetables. This is because they nourish and strengthen you, even though they may not bring pleasure to your taste buds.

2. Faith: Elevators Can Let You Down

When a young man once said to me, "Ray, I find it hard to believe some of the things in the Bible," I smiled and asked, "What's your name?" When he said, "Paul," I casually answered, "I don't believe you." He looked at me questioningly. I repeated, "What's your name?" Again he said, "Paul," and again I answered, "I don't believe you." Then I asked, "Where do you live?" When he told me, I said, "I don't believe that either." His reaction, understandably, was anger. I said, "You look a little upset. Do you know why? You're upset because I didn't believe what you told me. If you tell me that your name is Paul, and I say, 'I don't believe you,' it means that I think you are a liar. You are trying to deceive me by telling me your name is Paul, when it's not."

Then I told him that if he, a mere man, felt insulted by my lack of faith in his word, how much more does he insult Almighty God by refusing to believe His Word. In doing so, he was saying that God isn't worth trusting—that He is a liar and a deceiver. The Bible says, "He who does not believe God has made Him a liar" (1 John 5:10). It also says, "Beware, brethren, lest there be in any of you an evil heart of unbelief . . ." (Hebrews 3:12). Martin Luther said, "What greater insult . . . can there be to God, than not to believe His promises."

I have heard people say, "But I just find it hard to have faith in God," not realizing the implications of their words. These are the same people who often accept the daily weather forecast, believe the newspapers, and trust their lives to a pilot they have never seen whenever they board a plane. We exercise faith every day. We rely on our car's brakes. We trust history books, medical books, and elevators. Yet planes can crash. History books can be wrong. Elevators can let us down. How much more then should we trust the sure and true promises of Almighty God. He will never let us down . . . if we trust Him.

Cynics often argue, "You can't trust the Bible—it's full of mistakes." It is. The first mistake was when man rejected God, and the Scriptures show men and women making the same tragic mistake again and again. It's also full of what *seem* to be contradictions. For example, the Scriptures tell us that "with God nothing will be impossible" (Luke 1:37); there is nothing Almighty God cannot do. Yet we are also told that it is "impossible for God to lie" (Hebrews 6:18). So there *is* something God cannot do! Isn't that an obvious "mistake" in the Bible? The answer to this dilemma is found in the lowly worm.

Do you know that it would be impossible for me to eat worms? I once saw a man on TV butter his toast, then pour on a can of live, fat, wriggling, blood-filled worms. He carefully took a knife and fork, cut into his moving meal, and ate it. It made me feel sick. It was disgusting. The thought of chewing cold, live worms is so repulsive, so distasteful, I can candidly say that it would be *impossible* for me to eat them, even though I have seen it done. It is so abhorrent, I draw on the strength of the word "impossible" to substantiate my claim.

Lying, deception, bearing false witness, etc., is so repulsive to God, so disgusting to Him, so against His holy character, that the Scriptures draw on the strength of the word "impossible" to substantiate the claim. He cannot, could not, and would not lie.

That means in a world where we are continually let down, we can totally rely on, trust in, and count on His promises. They are sure, certain, indisputable, true, trustworthy, reliable, faithful, unfailing, dependable, steadfast, and an anchor for the soul. In other words, you can truly believe them, and because of that, you can throw yourself blindfolded and without reserve into His mighty hands. He will never, *ever* let you down. Do you believe that?

3. Evangelism: Our Most Sobering Task

Late in December 1996, a large family gathered in Los Angeles for a joyous Christmas. There were so many gathered that night, five of the children slept in the converted garage, kept warm during the night by an electric heater placed near the door.

During the early hours of the morning, the heater suddenly burst into flames, blocking the doorway. In seconds the room became a blazing inferno. A frantic 911 call revealed the unspeakable terror as one of the children could be heard screaming, *"I'm on fire!"* The distraught father rushed into the flames to try to save his beloved children, receiving burns to 50 percent of his body. Tragically, all five children burned to death. They died because steel bars on the windows had thwarted their escape. There was only one door, and it was blocked by the flames.

Imagine you are back in time, just minutes before the heater burst into flames. You peer through the darkness at the peaceful sight of five sleeping youngsters, knowing that at any moment the room will erupt into an inferno and burn the flesh of horrified children. *Can you in good conscience walk away?* No! You *must* awaken them, and warn them to run from that death trap!

The world sleeps peacefully in the darkness of ignorance. There is only one Door by which they may escape death. The steel bars of sin prevent their salvation, and at the same time call for the flames of eternal justice. What a fearful thing Judgment Day will be! The fires of the wrath of Almighty God will burn for eternity. The Church has been entrusted with the task of awakening the lost before it's too late. We cannot turn our backs and walk away in complacency. Think of how the father *ran* into the flames. His love knew no bounds. Our devotion to the sober task God has given us will be in direct proportion to our love for the lost. There are only a few laborers who run headlong into the flames to warn them to flee (Luke 10:2). *Please* be one of them. We really have no choice. The apostle Paul said, "Woe is me if I do not preach the gospel!" (1 Corinthians 9:16).

If you and I ignore a drowning child and let him die when we had the ability to save him, we are guilty of the crime of "depraved indifference." God forbid that any Christian should be guilty of that crime when it comes to those around us who are perishing. We have an obligation to reach out to them. The "Prince of Preachers," Charles Spurgeon, said, "Have you no wish for others to be saved? Then you are not saved yourself. Be sure of that." A Christian *cannot* be apathetic about the salvation of the world. The love of God in him will motivate him to seek and save that which is lost.

You probably have a limited amount of time after your conversion to impact your unsaved friends and family with the gospel. After the initial shock of your conversion, they will put you in a neat little ribbon-tied box and keep you at arm's length. So it's important that you take advantage of the short time you have while you still have their ears.

Here's some advice that may save you a great deal of grief. As a new Christian, I did almost irreparable damage by acting like a wild bull in a crystal show-room. I bullied my mom, my dad, and many of my friends into making a "decision for Christ." I was sincere, zealous, loving, kind, and stupid. I didn't understand that salvation doesn't come through making a "decision," but through *repentance*, and that repentance is God-given (2 Timothy 2:25). The Bible teaches that no one can come to the Son unless the Father "draws" him (John 6:44). If you are able to get a "decision" but the person has no conviction of sin, you will almost certainly end up with a still-born on your hands.

In my "zeal without knowledge" I actually inoculated the very ones I was so desperately trying to reach. There is nothing more important to you than the salvation of your loved ones, and you don't want to blow it. If you do, you may find that you don't have a second chance. Fervently pray for them, asking God for their salvation. Let them *see* your faith. Let them *feel* your kindness, your genuine love, and your gentleness. Buy gifts for no reason. Do chores when you are not asked to. Go the extra mile. Put yourself in their position. You know that you have found everlasting life—*death has lost its sting!* Your joy is unspeakable. But as far as they are concerned, you've been brainwashed and have become part of a weird sect. So your loving actions will speak more loudly than ten thousand eloquent sermons.

For this reason you should avoid verbal confrontation until you have knowledge that will guide your zeal. Pray for wisdom and for sensitivity to God's timing. You may have only one shot, so make it count. Keep your cool. If you don't, you may end up with a lifetime of regret. *Believe* me. It is better to hear a loved one or a close friend say, "Tell me about your faith in Jesus Christ," rather than you saying, "Sit down. I want to talk to you." Continue to persevere in prayer for them, that God would open their eyes to the truth.

Remember also that you have the sobering responsibility of speaking to other people's loved ones. Perhaps another Christian has prayed earnestly that God would use a faithful witness to speak to his beloved mom or dad, and *you* are that answer to prayer. You are the true and faithful witness God wants to use. We should share our faith with others *whenever* we can. The Bible says that we should proclaim the message and "be ready in season and out of season" (2 Timothy 4:2).

Keep the fate of the ungodly before your eyes. Too many of us settle down on a padded pew and become introverted. Our friends are confined solely to those *within* the Church, when Jesus was the "friend of sinners." So take the time to deliberately befriend the lost for the sake of their salvation. Remember that each and every person who dies in his sins has an appointment with the Judge of the Universe. Hell opens wide its terrible jaws. There is no more sobering task than to be entrusted with the gospel of salvation—working with God for the eternal well-being of dying humanity.

Have the same attitude as the apostle Paul, who pleaded for prayer for his own personal witness. He said, "[Pray] for me, that utterance may be given to me, that I may open my mouth boldly to make known the mystery of the gospel, for which I am an ambassador in chains; that in it I may speak boldly, as I ought to speak" (Ephesians 6:19,20).

4. Prayer: "Wait for a Minute"

God always answers prayer. Sometimes He says yes; sometimes He says no; and sometimes He says, "Wait for a minute." And since God is outside the dimension of time, to Him a thousand years is no different than a day (see 2 Peter 3:8)—which could mean a ten-year wait for us. So ask in faith, but rest in peace-filled patience.

Surveys show that over 90 percent of Americans pray daily. No doubt they pray for health, wealth, happiness, etc. They also pray when Grandma gets sick, so when Grandma doesn't get better (or dies), many end up disillusioned or bitter. This is because they don't understand what the Bible says about prayer. It teaches, among other things, that our sin will keep God from even hearing our prayers (Psalm 66:18), and that if we pray with doubt, we will not get an answer (James 1:6,7). Here's how to be heard:

- Pray with faith (Hebrews 11:6).

- Pray with clean hands and a pure heart (Psalm 24:3,4).

- Pray genuine heartfelt prayers, rather than vain repetitions (Matthew 6:7).

- Make sure you are praying to the God revealed in the Holy Scriptures (Exodus 20:3–6).

How do you "pray with faith"? Someone once said to me, "Ray, you're a man of great faith in God," thinking that they were paying me a compliment. But they weren't—the compliment was to God. For example, if I said, "I'm a man of great faith in my doctor," it's actually the doctor I'm complimenting. If I have great faith in him, it means that I see him as being a man of integrity, a man of great ability—that he is trustworthy. I give "glory" to the man through my faith in him. The Bible says that Abraham "did not waver at the promise of God through unbelief, but was strengthened in faith, giving glory to God, and being fully convinced that what He had promised He was also able to perform" (Romans 4:20,21). Abraham was a man of great faith in God. Remember, that is not a compliment to Abraham. He merely caught a glimpse of God's incredible ability, His impeccable integrity, and His wonderful faithfulness to keep every promise He makes. Abraham's faith gave "glory" to a faithful God.

As far as God is concerned, if you belong to Jesus, you are a VIP. You can boldly come before the throne of grace (Hebrews 4:16). You have access to the King because *you are the son or daughter of the King*. When you were a child, did you have to grovel to get your needs met by your parents? I hope not.

So don't pray, "Oh, God, I *hope* you will supply my needs." Instead say something like, "Father, thank You that You keep every promise You make. Your Word says that you will supply *all* my needs according to Your riches in glory in Christ Jesus [Philippians

4:19]. Therefore, I thank You that You will do this thing for my family. I ask this in the wonderful name of Jesus. Amen." See how Jesus prayed in John 11:42.

The great missionary Hudson Taylor said, "The prayer power has never been tried to its full capacity. If we want to see Divine power wrought in the place of weakness, failure, and disappointment, let us answer God's standing challenge, "Call to Me, and I will answer you, and show you great and mighty things, which you do not know" (Jeremiah 33:3).

How do you get "clean hands and a pure heart"?

Simply by confessing your sins to God, through Jesus Christ, whose blood cleanses us from all our sin (see 1 John 1:7–9). God promises not only to forgive your every sin, but to *forget* them (Hebrews 8:12). He will count it as though you had never sinned in the first place. He will make you pure in His sight—sinless. He will even "purge" your conscience, so you will no longer have a sense of guilt that you sinned. That's why you need to soak yourself in Holy Scripture; read the letters to the churches and see the wonderful things God has done for us through the cross of Calvary. If you don't bother to read the "will," you won't have any idea what has been given to you.

How do you pray "genuine heartfelt prayers"?

Simply by keeping yourself in the love of God. If the love of God is in you, you will never pray hypocritical or selfish prayers. Just talk to your heavenly Father as candidly and intimately as a young child, nestled on Daddy's lap, would talk to his earthly father. How would you feel if every day your child pulled out a pre-written statement to dryly recite to you, rather than pouring out the events and emotions of that day? God wants to hear from your heart. And when your prayer life is pleasing to God, He will reward you openly (see Matthew 6:6).

How do you know you're praying to "the God revealed in Scripture"? Study the Bible. Don't accept the image of God portrayed by the world, even though it appeals to the natural mind. A gentle, kind, Santa Claus figure, dispensing good things with no sense of justice or truth, appeals to guilty sinners. Look to the thundering and lightning of Mount Sinai. Gaze at Jesus on the cross of Calvary—hanging in unspeakable agony because of the justice of a holy God. Such thoughts tend to banish idolatry.

5. Warfare: Praise the Lord and Pass the Ammunition

When you became a Christian, you stepped right into the heat of an age-old battle. You now have a three-fold enemy: the world, the flesh, and the devil. Let's look at these three resistant enemies.

Our first enemy is the world, which refers to the sinful, rebellious, world system. The world loves the darkness and hates the light (John 3:20), and is governed by the "prince of the power of the air" (Ephesians 2:2). The Bible says that the Christian has escaped the corruption that is in the world through lust.

"Lust" is unlawful desire, and is the life's blood of the world—whether it be lust for sexual sin, for power, for money, for material things. Lust is a monster that will never be gratified, so don't feed it. It will grow bigger and bigger until it weighs heavy upon your back, and will be the death of you (James 1:15).

There is nothing wrong with sex, power, money, or material things, but when desire for these becomes predominant, it becomes idolatry (Colossians 3:5). We are told, "Do not love the world or the things in the world. If anyone loves the world, the love of the Father is not in him," and, "Whoever therefore wants to be a friend of the world makes himself an enemy of God" (1 John 2:15; James 4:4).

The second enemy is the devil, who is the "god of this age" (2 Corinthians 4:4). He was your spiritual father before you joined the family of God (John 8:44; Ephesians 2:2). Jesus called the devil a thief who came to steal, kill, and destroy (John 10:10). The way to overcome him and his demons is to make sure you are outfitted with the spiritual armor of God listed in Ephesians 6:10–18. Become intimately familiar with it. Sleep in it. Never take it off. Bind the sword to your hand so you never lose its grip. The reason for this brings us to the third enemy.

The third enemy is what the Bible calls the "flesh." This is your sinful nature. The domain for the battle is your mind. *If you have a mind to*, you will be attracted to the world and all its sin. The mind is the control panel for the eyes and the ears, the center of your appetites. All sin begins in the "heart" (Proverbs 4:23; Matthew 15:19). We think of sin before we commit it. James 1:15 warns that lust brings forth sin, and sin when it's conceived brings forth death. Every day of life, we have a choice. To sin or not to sin—that is the question. The answer is to have the fear of God. If you don't fear God, you will sin to your sinful heart's delight.

Did you know that God kills people? He killed a man for what he did sexually (Genesis 38:9,10), killed another man for being greedy (Luke 12:15–21), and killed a husband and wife for telling one lie (Acts 5:1–10). Knowledge of God's goodness—His righteous judgments against evil—should put the fear of God in us and help us not to indulge in sin.

If we know that the eyes of the Lord are in every place beholding the evil and the good, and that He will bring every work to judgment, we will live accordingly. Such weighty thoughts are valuable, for "by the fear of the LORD one departs from evil" (Proverbs 16:6). Jesus said, "My friends, do not be afraid of those who kill the body, and after that have no more that they can do. But I will show you whom you should fear: Fear Him who, after He has killed, has power to cast into hell; yes, I say to you, fear Him!" (Luke 12:4,5).

6. Fellowship: Flutter By Butterfly

One evidence that you have been truly saved is that you will have a love for other Christians (1 John 3:14). You will want to fellowship with them. The old saying that "birds of a feather flock together" is true of Christians. You gather together for the breaking of bread (communion), for teaching from the Word, and for fellowship. You share the same inspirations, illuminations, inclinations, temptations, motivations, and perspirations—you are working together for the same thing: the furtherance of the kingdom of God on earth. This is why you attend church—not because you have to, but because you want to.

Pray about where you should fellowship. Make sure the place you select as your church home calls sin what it is—sin. Do they believe the promises of God? Are they loving? Does the pastor treat his wife with respect? Is he a man of the Word? Does he have a humble heart and a gentle spirit? Listen closely to his teaching. It should glorify God, magnify Jesus, and edify the believer.

Don't become a "spiritual butterfly." If you are flitting from church to church, how will your pastor know what type of food you are digesting? The Bible says that your shepherd is accountable to God for you (Hebrews 13:17), so make yourself known to your pastor. Pray for him regularly. Pray also for his wife, his family, and the church leaders. Being a pastor is no easy task. Most people don't realize how long it takes to prepare a fresh sermon each week. They don't appreciate the time spent in prayer and in the study of the Word. If the pastor repeats a joke or a story, remember, he's human. So give him a great deal of grace and double honor. Never murmur about him. If you don't like something he has said, pray about it, then leave the issue with God. If that doesn't satisfy you, leave the church, rather than divide it through murmuring and complaining. God hates those who cause division among believers (Proverbs 6:16–19).

7. Thanksgiving: Do the Right Thing

For the Christian, every day should be Thanksgiving Day. We should be thankful even in the midst of problems. The apostle Paul said, "I am exceedingly joyful in all our tribulation" (2 Corinthians 7:4). He knew that God was working all things together for his good, even his trials (Romans 8:28).

Problems *will* come your way. God will see to it personally that you grow as a Christian. He will allow storms in your life, in order to send your roots deep into the soil of His Word. We also pray more in the midst of problems. It's been well said that you will see more from your knees than on your tiptoes.

A man once watched a butterfly struggling to get out of its cocoon. In an effort to help it, he took a razor blade and carefully slit the edge of the cocoon. The butterfly escaped from its problem... but immediately died. It is God's way to have the butterfly struggle. It is the struggle that causes its tiny heart to beat fast, sending the life's blood into its wings.

Trials have their purpose. They are a cocoon in which we often find ourselves. They make us struggle—they bring us to our knees. It is there that the life's blood of faith in God helps us spread our wings.

Faith and thanksgiving are close friends. If you have faith in God, you will be thankful because you know His loving hand is upon you, even though you are in a lion's den. That will give you a deep sense of joy—the barometer of the depth of faith you have in God. Let me give you an example. Imagine if I said I'd give you one million dollars if you sent me an email.

Of course, you don't believe I would do that. But imagine if you did, and that you knew 1,000 people who had sent me an email, and every one received their million dollars—no strings attached. More than that, you actually called me, and I assured you personally that I would keep my word. If you believed me, wouldn't you have joy? If you didn't believe me —no joy. The amount of joy you have would be a barometer of how much you believed my promise.

We have so much for which to be thankful. God has given us "exceedingly great and precious promises" that are "more to be desired than gold." Do yourself a big favor: believe those promises, thank God continually for them, and "let your joy be full."

8. Water Baptism: Sprinkle or Immerse?

The Bible says, "Repent, and let every one of you be baptized in the name of Jesus Christ for the remission of sins" (Acts 2:38). There is no question about whether you should be baptized. The questions are, how, when, and by whom?

It would seem clear from Scripture that those who were baptized were fully immersed in water. Here's one reason why: "John also was baptizing in Aenon near Salim, because there was much water there" (John 3:23). If John were merely sprinkling believers, he would have needed only a cupful of water. Baptism by immersion pictures our death to sin, our burial, and our resurrection to new life in Christ (see Romans 6:4, Colossians 2:12).

The Philippian jailer and his family were baptized at midnight, the same hour they believed (Acts 16:30–33). The Ethiopian eunuch was baptized as soon as he believed (Acts 8:35–37), as was Paul (Acts 9:17,18). Baptism is a step of obedience, and God blesses our obedience. So what are you waiting for?

Who should baptize you? It is clear from Scripture that other believers had the privilege, but check with your pastor; he may want the honor himself.

9. Tithing: The Final Frontier

It has been said that the wallet is the "final frontier." It is the final area to be conquered—the last thing that we surrender to God. Jesus spoke much about money. He said that we cannot serve both God and money (Matthew 6:24). Either money is our source of joy, our great love, our sense of security, the supplier of our needs . . . or God is.

When you open your purse or wallet, give generously and regularly to your local church. A guide to how much you should give can be found in the Old Testament "tithe": 10 percent of your income. Whatever amount you give, make sure you give *something* to the work of God (see Malachi 3:8–11). Give because you want to, not because you have to. God loves a cheerful giver (2 Corinthians 9:6,7), so learn to hold your money with a loose hand.

10. Troubleshooting: Cults, Atheists, Skeptics

If you know the Lord, nothing will shake your faith. It is true that the man with an experience is not at the mercy of a man with an argument. If you are converted and the Holy Spirit "testifies" that you are a child of God (Romans 8:16), you will never be shaken by a skeptic.

When cults tell you that to be saved you must call God by a certain name, worship on a certain day, or be baptized by an elder of their church, don't panic. Merely go back to the Instruction Manual. The Bible has all the answers, and searching them out will make you grow. If you feel intimidated by atheists—if you think they are "intellectuals"—read my book *God Doesn't Believe in Atheists*. It will reveal that they are the opposite. It will also show you how to *prove* God's existence, and also prove that the "atheist" doesn't exist. (See also *How to Know God Exists: Scientific Proof of God*.)

Finally, the way to prevent sports injuries and pain is to keep yourself fit. Exercise. The apostle Paul kept fit through exercise. He said, "Herein do I exercise myself, to always have a conscience void of offense toward God, and toward men" (Acts 24:16, KJV). Do the same. Listen to the voice of your conscience. It's your friend, not your enemy. Remember the words of Solomon: "Fear God and keep His commandments, for this is man's all. For God will bring every work into judgment, including every secret thing, whether good or evil" (Ecclesiastes 12:13,14).

Keep the Day of Judgment before your eyes. On that Day, you will be glad that you cultivated a tender conscience. I hope these principles have been helpful and that they will some day save you some pain.

Seek and Save the Lost the Way Jesus Did

Biblical principles for Christians

As a Christian, there is no greater joy than to do God's will—seeking to save what is lost. With no greater example than Jesus, we encourage you to follow in the footsteps of the Master, and discover what Charles Spurgeon called "our ablest auxiliary"—our most powerful weapon in the battle for souls! By following these principles, you will learn to share your faith simply, effectively, biblically...the way Jesus did.

The Key to Reaching the Lost

Have you ever thought, "There must be a key to reaching the lost"? There is, and the Bible actually calls it "the key." Its purpose is to bring us to Christ, to unlock the Door of the Savior (John 10:9).

Throughout history the Church used it to unlock the doors of revival. The problem is that it was lost around the turn of the twentieth century, and much of the Church today doesn't even know it exists.

Jesus used it. So did Paul (Romans 3:19,20), Timothy (1 Timothy 1:8–11), and James (James 2:10). Stephen used it when he preached (Acts 7:53). Peter found that it opened the door to release 3,000 imprisoned souls on the Day of Pentecost. Jesus said the lawyers had "taken away" the key, and even refused to use it to let people enter into the kingdom of God.

Satan has tried to prejudice the modern Church against the key. He hates it because of what it does. To find out what this key is, let's look at what God's Word says on the subject.

In Acts 28:23 the Bible tells us that Paul sought to persuade his hearers "concerning Jesus from both the Law of Moses and the Prophets." Here we have two effective means of persuading the unsaved "concerning Jesus."

The first is fulfilled prophecy, which *proves* the inspiration of Scripture. Any skeptic who reads the prophetic words of Isaiah, Ezekiel, Joel, etc., or the words of Jesus in Matthew 24 cannot but be challenged that this is no ordinary book.

The other means by which Paul persuaded sinners concerning Jesus was "the Law of Moses." The Bible tells us that the Law is good if it is used legitimately (1 Timothy 1:8), for the purpose for which it was intended. It was given by God as a tutor to lead us to Christ (Galatians 3:24). Paul said he "would not have known sin except through the law" (Romans 7:7). First John 3:4 tells us sin is the breaking of the law. The moral Law of God (the Ten Commandments) is the "key of knowledge" that Jesus spoke of in Luke 11:52. He was addressing experts in the Law—those who should have been teaching God's Law so sinners would have the "knowledge of sin" (Romans 3:20) and thus recognize their need for the Savior.

Prophecy speaks to the *intellect* of the sinner, while the Law speaks to the *conscience*. One produces *faith* in the Word of God; the other brings *knowledge* of sin in the heart of the sinner. It is the Law that is the God-given "key" to unlock the Door of salvation. Charles Spurgeon said, "I do not believe that any man can preach the gospel who does not preach the Law. The Law is the needle, and you cannot draw the silken thread of the gospel through a man's heart unless you first send the needle of the Law to make way for it."

The "Good" News

If I were to approach you and tell you that someone you don't know just paid a $25,000 speeding ticket on your behalf, it wouldn't be "good" news to you. It would be foolishness—you would say "I don't *have* a $25,000 speeding ticket"—and it would be offensive because I would be insinuating that you've broken the law when you don't think you have.

However, suppose I were to tell you this: "On the way here today, the law clocked you going 55 mph through an area set aside for a blind children's convention, and there were ten clear warning signs stating that 15 mph was the limit but you went straight through at 55 mph. What you did was extremely dangerous. The law was about to take its course when someone you don't know stepped in and paid your fine for you. You are very fortunate." Can you see how telling you what you've done wrong *first* actually makes the good news make sense?

In the same way, when we approach an unbeliever and tell him that Jesus died on the cross for his sins, it will be foolishness to him and offensive. It's foolishness because it won't make sense. The Bible says that "the message of the cross is foolishness to those who are perishing" (1 Corinthians 1:18). And it's offensive because I'm insinuating he's a sinner when he doesn't think he is. As far as he's concerned, there are many people much worse than him.

It would make sense, however, if we were to first bring instruction to him through the Ten Commandments and allow the Divine Law to serve the purpose for which it was intended—to convert the soul (Psalm 19:7). When the sinner sees precisely what he's done wrong—that he has offended God by violating His Law—then he becomes "convicted by the law as a transgressor" (James 2:9). The good news of Christ's sacrifice to pay his fine will not be foolishness, it will not be offensive, it will be "the power of God to salvation" (Romans 1:16).

To see the biblical use of the Law, let's look to the Master Evangelist and follow in His footsteps.

Personal Witnessing—What *Did* Jesus Do?

First, to share our faith effectively, we must show that we care by being friendly. Greet people at the park, gas station, or grocery store with a simple, "Hi, how are you?" or "Good morning! Nice day, isn't it?" If the person responds warmly, we may then ask, "Do you live around here?" and develop a conversation.

In talking with the woman at the well, Jesus began in the natural realm (everyday things). You may want to do the same by talking about sports or the weather, then perhaps using something in the news to transition to spiritual things. Another simple way to swing to the spiritual is to offer a gospel tract and ask, "Did you get one of these?" When the person takes it, say, "It's a gospel tract. Do you have a Christian background?"

By using the following "WDJD" outline, you can then confidently lead any witnessing encounter. You'll know exactly where you are in a conversation and exactly where it is going. You can say goodbye to your fears! Let's follow the way of the Master given in Luke 18:18–23. Jesus first addressed the man's understanding of good.

W: "Would you consider yourself to be a good person?"

People are not offended by this question, because you are asking about their favorite subject—themselves. Almost everyone will respond, "Yes, I'm a good person" (see Proverbs 20:6). This reveals their pride and self-righteousness. At this point you are ready to use the moral Law to point to *God's* standard of goodness to humble them . . . the way Jesus did.

D: "Do you think you have kept the Ten Commandments?"

With the rich, young ruler, Jesus used the Law to bring "the knowledge of sin" (Romans 3:20). We can do the same by asking this question. Most people think they have, so follow with, "Let's take a look at a few and see. How many lies do you think you have told in your life?" Most will say, "So many, I've lost count."

The Scriptures tell us that the "work of the law is written on their hearts" and "their consciences testify in support of this" (Romans 2:15). The word "conscience" means "with knowledge" (*con* is "with"; *science* is "knowledge"). So every time people lie, steal, blaspheme, etc., they know that it's wrong. Have confidence that the conscience will do its work and affirm the truth of each Commandment.

Some will admit to lying; others will say they have told only "white lies." Ask, "What does that make you?" They will hesitate to say, but get them to admit, "A liar." Continue going through the Commandments. Ask, "Have you ever stolen something, even if it's small?" Ask, "What does that make you?" and press them to say, "A thief." Say, "Jesus said, 'Whoever looks at a woman to lust for her has already committed adultery with her in his heart.' Have you ever looked at someone with lust?"

Then ask, "Have you ever used God's name in vain?" Gently explain, "So instead of using a four-letter filth word to express disgust, you've taken the name of the One who gave you life and everything that is precious to you, and you have dragged it through the mud. That's called 'blasphemy,' and God promises that He will not hold anyone blameless who takes His name in vain."

At this point, the individual may grow quiet, indicating his "mouth may be shut" by the Law (Romans 3:19). Ask his name and say, "John, *by your own admission*, you're a lying thief, a blasphemer, and an adulterer at heart, and we've only looked at four of the Ten Commandments."

J—Judgment: "If God judges you by the Ten Commandments on the Day of Judgment, will you be innocent or guilty?"

If he says he will be innocent, say, "You just told me

that you broke God's Law. Think about it. Will you be innocent or guilty?" It's very important that you get an admission of guilt before asking the next question.

D—Destiny: "Will you go to Heaven or Hell?"
People won't be offended because you are simply asking a question, rather than telling them where they're going. From there the conversation may go one of three ways:

1. **He may confidently say, "I don't believe in Hell."** Gently respond, "That doesn't matter. You still have to face God on Judgment Day whether you believe in it or not. If I step onto the freeway when a massive truck is heading for me and I say, 'I don't believe in trucks,' my lack of belief isn't going to change reality."

2. **He may admit he's guilty, but say he'll go to Heaven.** He may think God is "good" and will therefore overlook sin in his case. Point out that if a judge has a guilty murderer standing before him, if he's a good judge, he can't just let him go. He must ensure that the guilty man is punished. If God is good, He must (by nature) punish murderers, rapists, thieves, liars, adulterers, and all who live in rebellion to the inner light that God has given to every man.

3. **He may admit that he is guilty and therefore going to Hell.** Ask if that concerns him. Speak about how much he values his eyes and how much more therefore he should value the salvation of his soul.

If the person has been humbled by the Law and admits he's concerned, he is ready for grace. You now have the privilege of sharing the cross with him, encouraging him to repent and place his faith in the Savior. If he's willing to confess and forsake his sins, encourage him pray and ask God to forgive him.

Then pray for him. Point him to the truth of the Bible, instructing him to read it daily and obey what he reads, and get into a Bible-believing church.

The Gospel: Why Not Preach That Jesus Gives Happiness, Peace, and Joy?

To better understand the importance of biblical evangelism, carefully consider the following illustration.

Two men are seated on a plane. The first is given a parachute and told to put it on as it would improve his flight. He's skeptical at first, since he can't see how wearing a parachute on a plane could possibly improve his flight. He decides to experiment and see if the claims are true. As he puts it on, he notices the weight of it on his shoulders and finds he has difficulty in sitting upright. However, he was told that the parachute would improve his flight, so he decides to give it a little time.

As he waits he notices that other passengers are laughing at him for wearing a parachute on a plane. He begins to feel humiliated. As they point and laugh at him, he can stand it no longer. He slinks in his seat, unstraps the parachute and throws it to the floor. Disillusionment and bitterness fill his heart, because as far as he's concerned he was told an outright lie.

The second man is given a parachute, but listen to what he is told. He's instructed to put it on because at any moment he'll be jumping 25,000 feet out of the plane. He gratefully puts the parachute on. He doesn't notice the weight of it on his shoulders, nor that he can't sit upright. His mind is consumed with the thought of what would happen to him if he jumped without the parachute.

Let's now analyze the motive and the result of each passenger's experience. The first man's motive for putting on the parachute was solely to improve his flight. The result of his experience was that he was humiliated by the passengers, disillusioned, and somewhat embittered against those who gave him the parachute. As far as he's concerned, it will be a long time before anyone gets one of those things on his back again. The second man put the parachute on solely to escape the jump to come. And because of his knowledge of what would happen to him if he jumped without it, he has a deep-rooted joy and peace in his heart knowing that he's saved from sure death. This knowledge gives him the ability to withstand the mockery of the other passengers. His attitude toward those who gave him the parachute is one of heartfelt gratitude.

Now listen to what the modern gospel says: "Accept Jesus Christ as your Lord and Savior. He'll give you love, joy, peace, fulfillment, and lasting happiness." In other words, Jesus will improve your flight. The sinner responds, and in an experimental fashion puts on the Savior to see if the claims are true. Then when the promised temptation, tribulation, and persecution come (the other "passengers" mock him), he takes off the Lord Jesus Christ; he's offended for the Word's sake; he's disillusioned and somewhat embittered...and quite rightly so. He was promised love, joy, peace, and fulfillment, and all he got were trials and humiliation. His bitterness is directed toward those who gave him the "good news." His latter end becomes worse than the first, and he's another inoculated and bitter "backslider."

Instead of preaching that Jesus improves the flight, we should be warning sinners that they have to jump out of the plane. That it's appointed for man to die once and then face judgment (Hebrews 9:27). When a sinner understands the horrific consequences of breaking the Law of God, he will flee to the Savior, solely to escape the wrath that's to come. If we are true and faithful witnesses, that's what we'll be preaching—that there is wrath to come, that God "commands all men everywhere to repent, because

He has appointed a day on which He will judge the world in righteousness" (Acts 17:30,31).

The issue isn't one of happiness, but of righteousness. It doesn't matter how happy a sinner is, or how much he is enjoying the pleasures of sin for a season; without the righteousness of Christ, he will perish on the day of wrath. Proverbs 11:4 says, "Riches do not profit in the day of wrath, but righteousness delivers from death." Peace and joy are legitimate fruits of salvation, but it's not legitimate to use these fruits as a drawing card *for* salvation. If we do so, the sinner will respond with an impure motive, lacking repentance.

However, if we have put on the Lord Jesus Christ for the right motive, we have "all joy and peace in believing" (Romans 15:13) because we know that the righteousness of Christ is going to deliver us on the day of wrath. When tribulation strikes, when the flight gets bumpy, we won't get angry at God, and we won't lose our joy and peace. We didn't come to Christ for a better lifestyle, but to flee from the wrath to come. If anything, tribulation drives the true believer closer to the Savior. Sadly, we have multitudes of professing Christians who lose their joy and peace when the flight gets bumpy. Why? They are the product of a man-centered gospel. They came lacking repentance, without which they cannot be saved.

Is Repentance Necessary for Salvation?

It is true that numerous Bible verses speak of the promise of salvation with no mention of repentance. These verses merely say to "believe" on Jesus Christ and you shall be saved (Acts 16:31; Romans 10:9). However, the Bible makes it clear that God is holy and man is sinful, and that sin makes a separation between the two (Isaiah 59:1,2). Without repentance from sin, wicked men cannot have fellowship with a holy God. We are *dead* in our trespasses and sins

(Ephesians 2:1) and until we forsake them through repentance, we cannot be made alive in Christ. The Scriptures speak of "repentance to life" (Acts 11:18). We turn *from* sin *to* the Savior. This is why Paul preached "repentance toward God and faith toward our Lord Jesus Christ" (Acts 20:21).

The first public word Jesus preached was "repent" (Matthew 4:17). John the Baptist began his ministry the same way (Matthew 3:2). Jesus told His hearers that without repentance, they would perish (Luke 13:3). If belief is all that is necessary for salvation, then the logical conclusion is that one need never repent. However, the Bible tells us that a false convert "believes" and yet is not saved (Luke 8:13); he remains a "worker of iniquity." Look at the warning of Scripture: "If we say that we have fellowship with Him, and walk in darkness, we lie and do not practice the truth" (1 John 1:6). The Scriptures also say, "He who covers his sins will not prosper, but whoever confesses and forsakes them will have mercy" (Proverbs 28:13). Jesus said that there was joy in heaven over one sinner who "repents" (Luke 15:10). If there is no repentance, there is no joy because there is no salvation.

As Peter preached on the Day of Pentecost, he commanded his hearers to repent "for the remission of sins" (Acts 2:38). Without repentance, there is no remission of sins; we are still under God's wrath. Peter further said, "Repent . . . and be converted, that your sins may be blotted out" (Acts 3:19). We cannot be "converted" unless we repent. God Himself "commands *all* men *everywhere* [leaving no exceptions] to repent" (Acts 17:30). Peter said a similar thing at Pentecost: "Repent, and let *every one* of you be baptized" (Acts 2:38).

If repentance wasn't necessary for salvation, why then did Jesus command that *repentance* be preached to all nations (Luke 24:47)? With so many Scriptures speaking of the necessity of repentance for salvation, we dare not omit it from our gospel presentation …for the sake of the lost.

The Sinner's Prayer: To Pray or Not to Pray?

The question often arises about what a Christian should do if someone is repentant. Should we lead him in what's commonly called a "sinner's prayer" or simply instruct him to seek after God? Perhaps the answer comes by looking to the natural realm.

As long as there are no complications when a child is born, all the doctor needs to do is *guide the head*. The same applies spiritually. When someone is "born of God," all we need to do is guide the head —make sure that they *understand* what they are doing. Philip the evangelist did this with the Ethiopian eunuch. He asked him, "Do you understand what you are reading?" (Acts 8:30).

In the parable of the sower, the true convert (the "good ground" hearer) is he who hears "and understands" (Matthew 13:23). This understanding comes by the Law in the hand of the Spirit (Romans 7:7). If a sinner is ready for the Savior, it is because he has been drawn by the Holy Spirit (John 6:44). This is why we must be careful to allow the Holy Spirit to do His work and not rush in where angels fear to tread. Praying a "sinner's prayer" with someone who isn't genuinely repentant may leave you with a spiritual stillborn on your hands. Therefore, rather than lead him in a prayer of repentance, it is wise to encourage him to pray himself.

When Nathan confronted David about his sin, he didn't lead the king in a prayer of repentance. If a man committed adultery, and his wife is willing to take him back, should you have to write out an apology for him to read to her? No. Sorrow for his betrayal of her trust should spill from his lips. She doesn't want eloquent words, but simply sorrow of heart.

379 Seek and Save the Lost

The same applies with a repentant heart. Words aren't as important as the presence of "godly sorrow," which produces repentance leading to salvation (see 2 Corinthians 7:10). The sinner should be told to repent—to confess and forsake his sins. He could do this as a whispered prayer, then you could pray for him. If he's not sure what to say, perhaps David's prayer of repentance (Psalm 51) could be used as a model, but his own words are more desirable.

Resources

If you have not yet placed your trust in Jesus Christ and would like additional information, please feel free to visit LivingWaters.com and check out our resources. The following items may be especially helpful to you:

How to Know God Exists: Scientific Proof of God. Clear evidences for His existence will convince you that belief in God is reasonable and rational—a matter of fact and not faith.

Made In Heaven. Discover how the most innovative ideas of modern human ingenuity are actually features borrowed from the amazing work of God in creation.

Scientific Facts in the Bible. Most people don't know that the Bible contains a wealth of incredible scientific, medical and prophetic facts. The implications are mind-boggling.

See our YouTube channel (youtube.com/livingwaters) to watch free movies such as "The Atheist Delusion," "Evolution vs. God," "Crazy Bible," as well as thousands of other fascinating videos.

For Christians

Please visit our website where you can sign up for our free weekly e-mail update. To learn how to share your faith the way Jesus did, don't miss these helpful resources:

- "Hell's Best Kept Secret" and "True & False Conversion" (listen to these vital messages free at LivingWaters.com)

- *God Has a Wonderful Plan for Your Life: The Myth of the Modern Message* (our most important book)

- "The Way of the Master" Basic & Intermediate Training Courses (DVD)

- "Tough Questions" Apologetics Study (DVD)

- What *Did* Jesus Do?

- *How to Bring Your Children to Christ . . . & Keep Them There*

- *The Way of the Master for Kids*

- *Out of the Comfort Zone*

- *The Word on the Street: How to Share the Gospel in the Open Air*

You can also gain further insights by watching the weekly TV program *Way of the Master* (WayoftheMaster.com), as well as countless videos on our LivingWaters YouTube channel, with over 200,000,000 views.

For more resources, visit **LivingWaters.com**, call 800-437-1893, or write to: Living Waters Publications, P.O. Box 1172, Bellflower, CA 90707.

THE EVIDENCE
STUDY BIBLE

"An invaluable tool for becoming a more effective witness."
—FRANKLIN GRAHAM

The Evidence Study Bible arms you not just with apologetic information to refute the arguments of skeptics, but with practical evangelism training on how to lead them to Christ.

- Discover answers to over 200 questions such as: Why is there suffering? Where did Cain get his wife? How could a loving God send people to hell? What about those who never hear of Jesus?

- In addition to thousands of verse-related comments, over 130 informative articles will help you better comprehend and communicate the Christian faith.

- Over two dozen articles on evolution will thoroughly prepare you to refute the theory.

- Dozens of articles on other religions will help you understand and address the beliefs of Mormons, Hindus, Muslims, Jehovah's Witnesses, cults, etc.

The Evidence Study Bible provides powerful and compelling evidence that will enrich your trust in God and His Word, deepen your love for the truth, and enable you to reach those you care about with the message of eternal life.

School of Biblical Evangelism

Do you want to deepen your passion for the lost, for the cross, and for God? Then look no further. Join more than 20,000 students from around the world in the School of Biblical Evangelism, to learn how to witness and defend the faith.

With 101 lessons on subjects ranging from basic Christian doctrines to knowing our enemy, from false conversions to proving the deity of Jesus, you will be well-equipped to answer questions as you witness to anyone. This study course will help you to prove the authenticity of the Bible, provide ample evidence for creation, refute the claims of evolution, understand the beliefs of those in cults and other religions, and know how to reach both friends and strangers with the gospel.

"A phenomenal course."
—JIM CULVER

"Awesome... This course should be required in every theological seminary."
—SPENCER S. HANLEY

"As a graduate of every other evangelism course I can find, yours by far has been the best."
—BILL LAWSON

"I have never seen anything as powerful as the teaching in the School of Biblical Evangelism."
—JAMES W. SMITH

Join online at **BiblicalEvangelism.com**
or, to obtain the entire course in book form,
call **800-437-1893** or visit fine bookstores everywhere